TREE OF LIFE, VOLUME ONE

LEVEL 1
SPIRITUAL FOUNDATIONS
BASIC RELIGIONS – PART 1 AND PART 2

HOLY ORDER OF MANS

Published by Holy Order of MANS
Corte Madera, California

Cover and interior layout and design by Carolyn Oakley,
Luminous Moon Design + Press, Boulder, Colorado

First Edition
First Printing: February 2026

ISBN-13: 979-8-9889669-9-9

Religion: Spirituality — Religion: Philosophy — Religion: Mysticism
— Religion: Religion & Science — Body, Mind & Spirit: Alchemy,
Mysticism or Spiritualism — Body, Mind & Spirit: Mindfulness &
Meditation

Printed and bound in the United States of America

OTHER PUBLICATIONS BY
HOLY ORDER OF MANS

The Golden Force

Keystone of the Tarot with Meditations

Jewels of the Wise: Self-Mastery Through the Tarot

Tarot 22 Keys – The Major Arcana (tarot card coloring set)

Stars of Heaven: Mystical Astrology

The Discovery

FORTHCOMING

Tree of Life, Volume Two

History of the White Brotherhood and Its Teachings

La Fuerza Dorada (The Golden Force, Spanish edition)

El Árbol de la Vida, Volumen Uno
(Tree of Life, Volume One, Spanish edition)

La Clave del Tarot con Meditaciones
(Keystone of the Tarot with Meditations, Spanish edition)

Estrellas del Cielo: Astrología Mística
(Stars of Heaven: Mystical Astrology, Spanish edition)

DEDICATION

*To those who pursue their own destiny and wish to achieve
the ultimate human experience—Christ Consciousness.*

Tree of Life, Volume One

ACKNOWLEDGMENTS

Keeping this book available to readers since it was originally published by the Holy Order of MANS in the 1960's has been successful due in great part to the unfailing perseverance of Rt. Rev. Helen Blighton, wife of Dr. Earl W. Blighton, Founder of the Holy Order of MANS. By the late 1980's the Holy Order of MANS changed its name and structure. Special thanks to Rev. Mark and Rev. Mary Anderson of the Science of Man, which created a website www.ScienceOfMan.org in the 1990's, where some of the Order books were made available. Special thanks to the hundreds of Order members who made it a point to keep copies over the years of all of the literature of the Order, which included this book. Special thanks to those who continue to do the Work of the Order. Thanks to Rt. Rev. Mary Ray for creating the website www.HolyOrderOfMANS.org.

In 2012 Rt. Rev. Marguerite Whitney, with Rt. Rev. Michael Maciel, initiated the resurrection of the Holy Order of MANS for the 21st century. The website www.HolyOrderOfMANS.org was updated, and both a Holy Order of MANS YouTube Channel and the website www.HolyOrderOfMANS.com were added. The Order could now publish its books. With sincere and heartfelt appreciation we wish to thank Carolyn Oakley of Luminous Moon Design for her technical and artistic skills on creating the Order websites and help with publishing our books.

Tree of Life, Volume One

CONTENTS

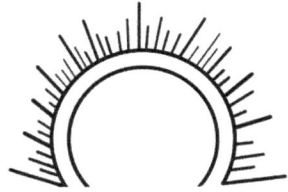

The Holy Order of MANS is an organization dedicated to a more thorough understanding of the universal laws of the Creator so that all might better manifest God's Creation and thus promote Peace and Harmony among people everywhere. Our purpose is to teach the Ancient Christian wisdom to this new generation as it was taught in the past.

Our organization is called the Holy Order of MANS because the universal laws of creation, the law of prayer, and other principles can be taught and, in your everyday life, you can become the master of your fate through conscious application of these principles.

We use the term "man" to include both men and women.

Tree of Life, Volume One

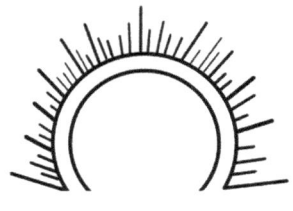

Introduction

Holy Order of MANS Tree of Life lessons were originally created and distributed to the Order's Seminary students. They were the Order's core curriculum, giving students the foundation and basic understanding they would need for their further training, which included literature, lectures, and ministerial practicum. The Tree of Life lessons are now being published for the first time in two volumes.

Volume One contains Level 1 – Spiritual Foundations, Lessons 1 through 6. Each of the six Lessons has three subsections. Level 1 also includes Lesson 7: Basic Religions – Part 1 and Part 2.

Volume Two continues Lesson 7: Basic Religions – Part 3 and Part 4. Next is the topic between Level 1 and Level 2 called The Element Fire. Level 2 – Universal Tools of Man, Lessons 1 through 7 completes the volume.

A diagram of the Tree of Life Study Plan follows on page xv.

When you study these Tree of Life lessons, keep in mind that when we use a word, we expect that you are going to take its literal meaning as defined by any standard dictionary. Please do not try to attach some hidden meaning to it. Forget all the metaphysical meanings, religious interpretations, and allegories that you may have studied. If we express a Truth allegorically, we will indicate it as such.

We do not teach a dogma that we say you must believe, nor do we impose rules that you must follow. The only rules we use are nature's own set of scientific laws, which we have nothing to do with. This is the way the Great Creator made this Universe, and we cannot change the rules. For example, when we use the term "Holy Bible," we are not inferring or implying by this name, or term, that this is the only book there is that has truth in it. There have been many Avatars that have come to Earth and have helped to raise the consciousness of Humanity. Truth is, and always will be. And that Truth is within each person.

There is nothing that we can teach you—we can only help you to remember who you are. Most beings need only to have their thinking stimulated in order for them to bring back to their conscious mind the facts contained within themselves, for they have lived many lives.

We do not separate God, the Supreme Being, or the Creator from Matter. Otherwise, God could not answer our material needs. There is a way in which these results are obtained. In order to work in harmony with the laws of creation and get good results, it is first necessary to develop in our consciousness an idea of the nature of the God who created this creation. For who can love so great a being— our Creator—if we do not have some idea of Its way of working and Its nature. The first thing we must begin to realize is that Spirit, Soul, and Consciousness all demonstrate and manifest through matter.

Tree of Life Study Plan
Holy Order of MANS

Tree of Life – Volume 1	Tree of Life – Volume 2		
Level 1 – Spiritual Foundations	Level 1 – Spiritual Foundations, continued	Topic Between Level 1 and Level 2	Level 2 – Universal Tools of Man
Lesson 1 Creator Mediator Creation			Lesson 1 Symbolism
Lesson 2 Prayer Meditation Blessing			Lesson 2 Communication
Lesson 3 Light Life Love			Lesson 3 Power
Lesson 4 Spiritual Body Soul Flesh Body			Lesson 4 Universal Vehicle
Lesson 5 The Word Mind Faith			Lesson 5 The Law
Lesson 6 Awakening Return Feast			Lesson 6 Epigenesis
Lesson 7 Basic Religions Part 1 Part 2	Lesson 7 Basic Religions Part 3 Part 4		Lesson 7 The Way
		The Element Fire	

Level 1
Spiritual Foundations

Himmel/Unsplash

Lesson 1: Creator • Mediator • Creation

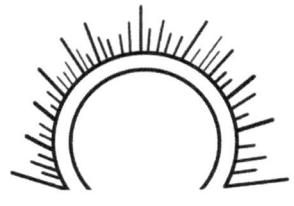

CREATOR ONE

REMEMBER — HOW TO STUDY

In studying our work in this New Age school, when we use a word we expect that you are going to take the literal meaning as defined by Webster or any standard dictionary.

DO NOT try to attach some hidden meaning to the word or words. Forget all the metaphysical meanings, religious interpretations, or any of the allegories which you might have studied. If we should wish to express a Truth in allegory then we will say so.

Remember that we do not teach a dogma or set of rules that we say you must follow. The only rules we use are nature's own set of scientific laws which we have nothing to do with. This is the way the Great Creator made this Universe and we cannot change the rules.

For example, when we use the term "Holy Bible" we are not inferring or implying by this name or term that this is the only book there is that has truth in it.

There have been many Avatars who have come to Earth and have helped to raise the consciousness of Man. TRUTH is and always will be, and that Truth is all within Man himself.

NOTHING NEW

There is nothing that we can teach you. We can only help you to remember. Most beings need only to have their thinking stimulated in order for them to bring back to their conscious mind the facts for they have lived many lives.

GOD

We do not separate God from Matter This must be true or else God could not answer our material needs There is a way in which these results must be obtained. They are received, for the WORD must be fulfilled.

In order to work in harmony with the laws of creation to get good results, it is first necessary to develop within our consciousness an idea of the nature of the God who created these laws. For who can love so great a being as our Creator if we do not have some idea of His way of working and His nature?

First we must bear in mind that Spirit, Soul, and Consciousness all demonstrate and manifest through matter.

PREPARE FOR THE NEW EARTH

MATTER

Some people try to turn their back on matter by saying that matter is merely an illusion. That is not true. It is the way they use the word matter.

It is quite evident that it would be poor judgment to disregard the substance of the world or the plane on which you are operating and functioning at this time. This would only be a half-reality.

The second thing to remember is that the material world did not exist. God created it. Mankind has no right to ignore God's creation but instead must become master of it. For just as Jesus did, he too will become Lord Of Earth. Again, man did not create matter, God did.

For many centuries man has had his consciousness of the unseen dulled by the seen. He turned his whole consciousness to what he could see with the physical eyes alone and disregarded the Creator.

CLEANING OF MIND

Man was a very unsanitary, evil and negative acting person. As the shedder of much blood he was not Godly in idea or mind. He killed not only for meat but in wars and by murder. Now man is improving. He is becoming cleaner, at least outwardly.

ADJUST OR PASS

Man is learning that it does not pay to go against basic natural laws. He is getting rid of the dirt and negative part of his nature slowly but surely. The overall level of man's consciousness is raising and will now raise rapidly in this New Age. Those who refuse to adjust will not stay long but will pass beyond.

When the name "GOD" is used it is always hard to understand as to whether the Absolute is meant, or the One existence, or the Supreme Being who is the Great Architect of the Universe, or is it the God that is the Architect of our solar system?

OUR SOLAR GOD

So let it be understood that the word "GOD" means the God of **this** solar system. For honestly, I have been told that if we can get across to man the understanding of this solar system then we have done a really good job and it will be a pretty swell place to live in.

HOLY TRINITY

The division of the GODHEAD into the Father, the Son (Sun), and the Holy Spirit is confusing. Although these three beings designated by these names are immeasurable above the average man and worthy of all reverence and worship, God is capable of rendering to man his highest conception of Divinity. In addition it is factually true that they are each different from one another.

They are all present in our world and are nearer to us than our hands and feet.

WHERE IS GOD

It is a literal truth when we say, "In Him, we live and move and have our being," for none of us could exist outside of these Great Intelligences. They pervade and sustain our world with all Life.

This will be shown from a scientific and material side later in the studies of the Law and Prayer.

This understanding of GOD is very essential in order to work with the forces of nature.

But if you don't grasp all at once the understanding of these realizations of the real GOD and this solar system, be content at present to know that there is a Great Creator or creative SENTIENT POWER that sustains us and it pervades all space and time.

EVIL

In the words of Plato, the first "expression of idea" is that God and Nature, which manifest in all things seen and unseen, are working together CONSTRUCTIVELY for good. That good is the only resultant that is indestructible. Plato says that Evil is but our own interpretation of the work, or processes of nature, that does not appear constructive.

The keynote on this subject is "BEING IS ESSENTIALLY BENEVOLENT."

SOUL

Plato accepted the Soul of Man and the Soul of the World. He called this Kosmos. The reasoning of Man, known as the tool of the Mind of Man, was composed of the same substance.

This realization also gives Cosmic Divinity, the Universal Power and Intelligence, as the Soul of God.

MIND OF GOD

Think of the Solar System as the space and expanse of the Mind of God. Within that boundary exists the twelve planets of this system and that this entire space is filled with the ARCHITECT of this Solar System.

MYSTERIES

The understanding of the Trinity is like all great mysteries of the ancients and their teachings. It is so simple and yet a reality. At that time they felt that some would misuse their teachings. This is the reason why they were called Mysteries.

Today in this New Age they are still called Mysteries because the mass of the people have been taught to think in a complicated way in anything they cannot feel, see, or touch.

Let us remember that GOD and the other Great Beings are not far away in past ages of space or time.

CHRIST

The SUN is the visible manifestation of the ARCHITECT of this solar system.

The supreme beauty and good of Mankind is the Imitation of God. It finds its counterpart in Christianity as the "Imitation of Christ," follow the example of Jesus.

FIRST THINGS FIRST

In learning to do the thing that every Man/Woman must do in order to be a Man/Woman of God begin with the First Commandment: "I AM THE LORD THY GOD, AND THOU SHALT HAVE NO OTHER GODS BEFORE ME." The truth behind this is that the Creator is the All that is in the substance of "Being." It is the One Mind and a Self-less Creator.

EARTH

The Creator is Self-less because alone He senses not, not in the dense world or psychic world.

Only through the emotions and senses of His Creative Man can GOD attain the joy and sorrows of dense matter. You might ask, "Why would GOD want to experience these sensations after experiencing the bliss in the plane, or realm, of higher vibration which is so much greater?"

Why is Man, then, concerned about Life if he is only a channel for GOD's experiences?

KNOW THE SELF

In the old school of Delphi, there was an immortal bit of wisdom given. It was, "MAN, KNOW THYSELF."

Another statement which comes out of the mist of antiquity is, "AS ABOVE, SO BELOW."

If you will take these two statements, and sit quietly in thoughtful meditation, or just sit and think, you will learn much.

LIFE

Again remembering the above statements, you find the object of LIFE on the spiritual plane above (in vibration) in all lives is a spiritual Man in a spiritual world of Reality. This is with the objective of experiencing joy and giving continuous joy by and through GOD, the Creator.

The Bible says in Rev. 4:11, "Thou hast created all things, and for thy pleasure they are and were created." Phil. 4:4, "Rejoice in the Lord always and again say rejoice."

HELL

The world we live in, unfortunately, appears so distrustfully reactive. The only hell man shall ever know is his own.

Therefore, our joy should start in this dense world by helping to relieve the apparent disorder of those around us.

Remember in Luke 11:52, "Woe unto you, conventionalist, for you took away the sacred science; you did not go in and those who were about to go in you prevented."

This is the real science of Mankind you are about to study.

PEACE and **FULLNESS of LIFE** abide with **YOU**.

I thank the Father
For this day,

I thank the Father
For this way,

I thank the Father
For a world so joyful,

So tonight with moon
So bright
We rest in pure delight.

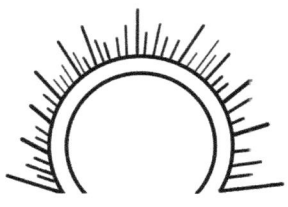

CREATOR TWO

We have called these studies a science because it relates to the use of the tools God gave man and how to use the force and power of God and its various manifestations.

There is an interesting reaction to the above statement which has been made many times. That reaction is that they feel that this attitude toward God is cold and unfeeling. But in reality that is not what they are saying at all.

What they are saying is that you are making this God a real dynamic force and power. If I do not get my prayers answered then I must look to myself to see what is wrong with my thinking and I can't blame God for it. In other words there is no room for excuses, no alibis. That is right.

When there is Law and Order there is science, an overall pattern, and things in the act of being created.

For example, on the earth plane there is an ebb and flow of all things. "As above, so below." It is true in the microcosm of the human heart as well as it is true in the macrocosm of God, the whole, the One Mind.

Our heart's diastole and systole, commonly called heartbeats, is in harmony with the blood's ebb and flow, a rhythmic pattern. It is also in the lungs in inspiration and expiration and in the psychic body's throb with electronic manifestation of spirit energy.

The ocean tides come in and go out, day succeeds night, seasons arrive and pass, the ages of time incline and decline, constituting eons of time.

So vast is this latter conception that we are careless about retaining it within the consciousness of our mind and tend to dismiss it from consideration. This is with the same attitude we carry toward other abstractions such as the vagueness of a poetic statement as belonging to the whole of Creation or such as the life of the gods as of no comparable relation to this mundane life here.

Involution and evolution forever succeed each other and may be known in the wide horizontal view as the heartbeat or the ebb and flow of the manifestations of God.

Time itself is not existent in God's world. Time in the plan of earth's limitable subsistence is but the tick-tock with the existence of GOD.

Remember God geometrizes, for geometry is but the Numeric of form. Another has said when God created the world His first thoughts were expressed in numbers.

Thales, one of the ancient Sages, in talking of God says, "The most ancient of all things is God, for He is not begotten; the fairest is the world, for it is His work."

"The world is animated, and that God is the Soul thereof, diffused through each part, whose divine moving virtue penetrates through the element of water."

Thales, on being demanded what God was, answered, "That which hath neither beginning nor end."

Socrates said, "Philosophy is the way to true happiness, the offices whereof are two: to contemplate God, and to abstract the soul from corporeal sense."

It is not that we cannot picture God for you the same as the ancients but realize that these quotes were made five and six hundred years before the Master Jesus was here. Somehow people often feel that this business of getting acquainted with God is a new deal.

In a most abstract sense it is a new deal for the conditions electrically, mentally, and from all sides are different.

The point however is that we must all be philosophers to some degree if we are going to survive the radical changes taking place.

In Chicago, June 13, 1963 (United Press International) an article was headed, "A Scientist Looks at God and Atomic-Age." In the article he goes on to say, "A nuclear scientist said this week science seems to be on the verge of discovering God on every frontier, not as an ideal, but as the most fundamental fact of nature."

Francis B. Parzel, senior scientific advisor of the Armor Research Foundation, addressing the City Club of Chicago says in appraising the nuclear threat, "readjustment to the nuclear age hinges on what we put first, to abide by universal moral and logical rules for the sake of humanity as a whole, or merely to have our own way." The best way I know to tell the difference is to ask the question, "Do you really believe in God or not, and to what extent do we regard the existence of God as an issue in the cold war?"

Again it is a case of whether you really want the peace taught by the Master Jesus or must your ego be fed?

The first step to understanding the Great Creative Power, GOD, is to realize "IT". Energy is Power. Energy is that which the Spirit motivates. Energy is the Life Force after it has taken on the characteristics of the Christ and His Principles. You are using energy every moment of your Life. It is Light, it is God in action.

You could not live without energy. It is manifest on every plane and in all the multi-waves. "IT IS ALL THERE IS."

Be consciously aware of this mighty force and consciously try to work with It. The greatest of all Mysteries is that of God's consciousness in Mankind.

USE THE FOLLOWING AND REPEAT THEM OVER AND OVER AGAIN.

Take one and use it as the Day's Thought. Carry it on a card. Read it until you can repeat it from memory.

MONDAY:
I cease to think of God as external. "IT" is within me.

TUESDAY:
It is "I", Man/Woman, who is IN the Universe, and not on it, or merely of it.

WEDNESDAY:
The consciousness of God is Life, but it is more. It is love and it is power unlimited.

THURSDAY:
The greatest attribute is Love. Love is creative and protective.

FRIDAY:
Love is inspiring and illuminating, therefore it gives Life and Light.

SATURDAY:
These are existent actions. If man will consider himself as the Light of the Life in the Love of God within him.

This is a prayer or poem which is a starting point of understanding.

THANK YOU!

I thank the Father
for this Way.

I thank the Father
for this day.

I thank the Father
for a world so joyful,

So tonight with Moon
so bright,

We rest in pure delight
In the shadow of God's
night.

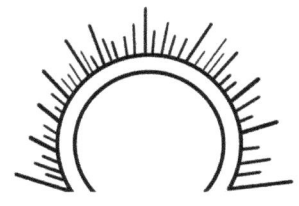

LESSON 1

CREATOR THREE

Let us first realize the greatest in line of importance of all facts. When we deal with Life we are dealing with the Power of God flowing through His Son. I could write all day, and if you would, you could read all year on the subject of this dynamic force. It is real, is everywhere, is all that is, and is all we can hope to be.

In the religious teachings of most organizations little is said about God. A great deal is said about what GOD said in the Holy Bible and the Jewish Book of the Law. Then there is the Prayer in the Siddur to God.

In other Faiths of Eastern religions GOD is called Allah. The Christian church has sent many missionaries in an effort to convert those in Asia and the East. The interesting thing here is that the people of the East are very concerned about GOD even though they call him by another name. They will sit for hours in meditation in an attempt to gain greater wisdom.

For you GOD may manifest as sunlight, the song of the birds, or as the new-born baby in its mother's arms. But it is one and the same GOD.

In this age we must learn to feel GOD'S presence and the presence of the GOD Force moving through us. Know that it is right here and not in some far-off distant heaven.

The ancients considered this as of the first importance. If you do not feel the presence of the teacher how can you communicate?

As yet few people in the New Age really understand today what the ancient Greek philosopher Plotinus tried to give to the world. Nor did many realize it in that day, but now the sands of time of that age have run out and this is the new age. Today the thinking of the "mass mind" is still trying to blot out the light of wisdom that Plotinus gave to the world, the same as the words of Jesus.

Plotinus says there exists nothing in this universe or this Solar System but God. We know the ego will not like this, but whether it does or not, does not change the fact. If you speak of the subject of God then you are always thought to be speaking of some external and personal God. This is absurd because there is no place in nature for such a God.

To Plotinus nothing has any real existence but God. This is when we use the word "real" on the level of God-existence. That is all the things, forces, energies, and laws in this universe are creations which are created by the internal activity of God, of His consciousness. These creative phenomena are best explained as follows. No man can see his own face without the use of a mirror of some kind.

Thus likewise God, when starting a cycle of activity, cannot Himself see without some substance to reflect in.

There is no other substance except that which belongs to the God consciousness to serve as a mirror, thus it steps out of itself, out of its own center for self-examination and looks within. Thus an intellectual is created by GOD perceiving the images existing within its own substance. So the activity is the periphery toward the center, its radiant field, has created the Universal Mind. This is a demonstration of "As above, so below". For this is the way man prays, by direction of his own thoughts to his own center, the center of his consciousness the Heart.

In the Holy Bible in Ezekiel 18:4, "Behold, all souls are mine, the soul of the father as well as the soul of the son is mine, the soul that sins shall die."

External objects present us only with appearances of these. Therefore, we may say we possess opinion rather than knowledge. We are interested in appearances only because they are reflections of the patterns in the unseen world. Our questions lie with the ideals in the Mind of God that exists behind appearances.

Are they without us and is the reason, like sensation, occupied with objects external to itself? What assurance is there that our perception is infallible? The object perceived would be something different from the mind perceiving it.

We should have then an image instead of the true picture in the Mind of the Father. It would be out of all proportions with Nature to believe for a moment that our mind was unable to perceive ideal truth exactly as it is. We do not have a certainty of God Knowledge concerning the world of intelligence. It follows, therefore, that this region of truth is not to be investigated as a thing external to us, thus only imperfectly known. This region of truth is within us. Here the objects we contemplate and that which contemplates are identical, both are thought. Plus, subject cannot surely know an object different from itself.

The world of ideas lies within our intelligence. Truth, therefore, is not the agreement of our apprehension of an external object with the object itself. It is the agreement of mind with itself. Consciousness, therefore, is the sole basis of certainty.

The mind is its own witness. Reason sees in itself that which is above itself as its source and again that which is below itself once more.

Therefore, it is a fact that God does exist. We only know It because we can only know what God knows in His mind. Our mind is only an individualized part of God's mind.

THUS GOD IS A MATERIAL FACT IN THE REALM OF HIS LEVEL OF CONSCIOUSNESS.

THIS WEEK'S MEDITATIONS

MONDAY:

In God's Mind do we (God and I) create all things in my life.

TUESDAY:

In God I rest.

WEDNESDAY:

With God all things are possible.

THURSDAY:

In God I rest.

FRIDAY:

This is the way: I accept my supply and good this day from God.

SATURDAY:

I love, through action, my fellow man.

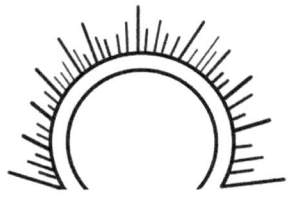

LESSON 1

MEDIATOR ONE

A mediator is a go-between, one who interposes between two parties in order to harmonize or reconcile them. The great Christ is the Mediator of this solar system. He diffuses unto all of creation the Light, Life and the Charity of the Father.

Here on the Earth the Lord Jesus Christ is the Mediator between us and the Great Christ, for Jesus says, "Only through Me shall you see the Face of the Father." Through Jesus's consciousness and His mantle men can reach the great reality of themselves and their Father.

The term go-between is a very realistic term. It points out the realness of our Lord Jesus and His great function for man who has lost all consciousness of life and of the Great Creator of life.

Mankind struggles along in life straining with those things of the earth, striving to have two cars, two houses, to have a good-paying job, to have a nice-looking partner, and all other worldly goods.

The whole of a man's existence today is wrapped up within himself. He can no longer reach out from himself to see the world as it truly is. For even as he walks down the street, he sees the buildings and those passing by through his own thoughts and with all of his bias and narrow-mindedness. He sees but not even a fourth of the material world.

The use of a go-between here is one who has reached and sees past the things of the world, the concepts and ideas of man, and reaches into the greatness of the Creator without opinion and without desire. Thus he links the two together, being on earth but giving out the Truth and the Light and the Reality of the One World.

Jesus stated in the New Testament, "For, lo, I will be with you unto the end of the Age." He is ever-present and always at hand, unifying man and the Creator. He is a channel of the Great Light and Wisdom of the Father for the earth.

In prayer when one reaches his mind and his Soul upward towards the Creator he travels through this Great Master, for Jesus has given Himself as a channel for the Word.

Man can no longer stand the Light or the Truth of God so there has been placed for him a Mediator who brings things down to the level man can understand and cope with.

By man's act of harmonizing himself with this Mediator he then becomes in harmony with the One for whom the Mediator mediates for.

Jesus says, "I am the Way, the Truth, and the Light." Thus, He took on the greatness of God while here on earth so that man could see it. After the ascension, His spiritual body diffused around the Earth and thus became the mystical body of Christ of which all men who receive the Light of Christ become living, moving, active cells within this body. The ruler of this body is the God head.

To get in tune with the Mediator, one must follow implicitly all of these Commandments, which bring forth out of the depths of man the great love for his Creator.

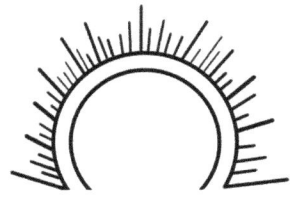

MEDIATOR TWO

In the previous lesson we learned of the Creative force and the power of the spoken word. This gives to man a choice and control of his life which we will learn of in the lessons on the Law as taught by Jesus in the Second Level Lessons.

In the lesson on the Creator, we are actually covering the ACTION brought about by the God Force. This lesson is the covering of the "What Happens" in the dense material which we handle every day.

By observation of denser matter and the condition the World is in today you might have guessed by this time that the Creative power has been abused.

This having happened necessitates the presence of a Mediator, or Medium. What is a Mediator? It is a person who is a go-between or channel.

In order to clarify this word let us see what Webster says, "something intermediate; a middle state or degree; an intervening thing through which a force acts or an effect is produced; any means, agency, or instrumentality."

Our first scripture reference is First Timothy, Chapter 2, verses 3, 4, & 5:

Verse 3: This is good and it is acceptable in the sight of God our Savior.
Verse 4: Who desire all men to be saved and to come to the Truth.
Verse 5: For there is one God and there is one mediator between
God and Men, the man Christ Jesus.

The situation in the world as it stands today is that all planes of consciousness need an awakening.

The Vital Force which is Divine and should be manifesting itself through man is absent. Sin is transgression of the Law. It is also ignorance of the Law.

THE LAW IS SPIRITUAL

When man who is also spirit violates the Law the spiritual state of Mind is disturbed. Man's denial of truth and acceptance of "only the apparent" has caused the Adam state of Mind to manifest and then death, which is a chaotic condition. A false state of consciousness swoops down over the creation and lulls it to sleep, known in very severe states as death.

The divine Son of God must then become the Herald, the Messenger called the Mediator. The Herald shall declare, "Arise and Shine for the Glory of the Lord is risen upon the Earth."

The Mediator seeks and saves that which is lost. He is the divine Humanist. Paul said that the Mediator is between God and Man. He is the man Christ Jesus. Christos translated is to be interpreted "the anointed Savior."

Once we are fully aware of our Creatorship we begin to Mediate between Light and darkness, between the real and the apparent. This is not saying that the dense world around us is not to be mastered and worked with but it does say the Law is changeless and eternal. Also, the cause of what is apparent is the Law working through the Mind and the pronounced Word by man given by the Creator.

Paul says in First Timothy 1, verse 8, "Now we know that the Law is good, if anyone uses it lawfully..." Understand this that the Law is not laid down for the just but for the Lawless and disobedient. The Children of Earth today are disobedient. That is why all have sinned and fallen short of the Glory of God

The Mediator, called the Son of righteousness with healing in his wings, brings into manifestation the Law. The infallible Law, therefore, changes the atmosphere from a negative cycle to a positive cycle, transforming Heaven out of Hell. Paul says, "be ye transformed by renewing of your Mind." We must, therefore, come to the Consciousness that the Mediator uses Mind in operation of the Law.

This School teaches that Mind is the Father, that the Body is the Son, and Spirit is the Holy Ghost. Therefore, the Godhead itself manifesting physically becomes the Mediator.

Jesus says, "I and the Father are one" and "I go to prepare a place for you, and I will come to get you, that where I am you may be also."

Though the Power operates through the Son of God, man's physical body, it is still another form of Mind. For Mind is the primal will for good, the operator of the Law.

Salvation is the cleaning and the perfecting of your individuality through Christ. It is the anointing.

We are the congregation of the Earth gathered in the outer court of the Temple of Life and the divine Man is the Master. He who has become enlightened and perfected is the High Priest after the order of Melchizedek.

Read Hebrews Chapter 7. While reading, keep in mind the following that you may understand better:

1. Know that a real order of Melchizedek does exist and that in this chapter is described many things about it.
2. Our bodies are the temple.
3. Our will and personality the Lamb of God for sinners slain.
4. Our hearts the Altar.
5. The Law operating through us is the High Priest.

By enlightenment of Mind, strengthening of will, singleness of purpose can we save and unite the World, the entire cosmos. This is through Jesus Christ the Way Shower, the first among many brethren.

Christ must and is returning. The return of Christ will be complete. This is the return of Law and order, peace, joy, justice, love, and compassion.

The divine Self will reconcile us to the infinite Law of Cosmic Creation which up to this time has been accursed and cut off.

The key that makes you one with the Mediator is the manifestation of the Christ Mind in you. The Christ Mind is the anointed Mind, the perfected Mind. It is the mind of the Father through the son (flesh). That is why Paul said, "Let this Mind be in you which was also in Christ Jesus," who walked not after the flesh but after the spirit.

In conclusion, Life Science teaches us that to be Lawlessly Minded is death. To be Spiritually Minded is Life.

In Adam we die. But by Christ we are made alive.

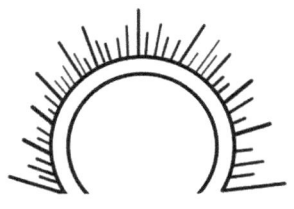

LESSON 1

CREATION ONE

THE ORIGIN OF THIS SOLAR SYSTEM AND ITS CREATION

Many times during a month I am asked the same question, "How was our Solar System created?"

To begin with we should quote the first chapter of "The Gospel According to John" verse one, "In the beginning was the word, and the Word was with God, and the Word was God. He was in the beginning with God; all things were made through him, and without him was not anything made that was made."

Man is trying to understand God both with the Bible and the Great Philosophies and now his great striving is Science. But like all of his strivings he looks first to what he sees in the material world and material experiences. He bases his Mathematics on this also.

Therefore, all of his theories or premises are all in accordance with his level of Consciousness which determines his concepts.

Like everything created the understanding of it grows with its use and its existence in the Minds of people. So it is with theorem, especially those that leave out God and the Great Creative Energy of the Father's Mind. These ideas become incompatible with observed results, so they are abandoned.

The state and level of our understanding of the origin of this Solar System will not bring us any closer to the original truth than our general understanding of nature as it truly is.

Until we know what we are and until we know our SELF, we cannot conceive from whence we came or for that matter, from whence the world came.

Any thoughts of things in this category of speculation are only to be regarded as unproved theories.

This does not mean that at some time even a better understanding than is given here will be obtained. This is not a complete theory but the basic parts so that you can put them together and understand.

We will avoid in this course considering the origin of the Universe. By understanding its nature then its origin can come to light within YOU, insofar as the substance and its nature are clear in your mind.

COSMOLOGY

At this stage of development we will explain this question of our Universe in the following way.

Let it be first understood that there are not destructive acts in the Mind of God.

We know that this Solar System is continually building itself up to complete the original WORD of the Father.

It is evolving order out of Chaos. There is no such thing as immaterial substance and, therefore, non-existence will never come.

There is only the transformation of energy from one form to another: some into denser forms, some into less dense forms, some seeable, and some unseeable with the human eye until the Eye is more highly developed.

We know all is a fundamental part of the same being, "The Father."

One of the classic differences between scientific investigation of this subject is that one sees cosmic radiation and secondary radiation of lower frequency being the resultant of disintegration of substances.

Whereas the other regards cosmic radiation as a byproduct of the creation of matter in outer space.

The fact of the matter is that cosmic rays are not cosmic creations in outer space but are created in our own atmosphere by the ultra-violet seeping in and there uniting with nitrogen and two other elements which produce what man calls cosmic rays.

In fact, it is both the sun's rays and the forces in our atmosphere which create cosmic rays and they will not injure those that have started to accept the Christ Light into their bodies.

One of the elements in our Solar Concept of creation is Time.

Time is a point in RELATIVITY, both in relation to cyclic motion and the state of density. When this takes place in one state of frequency we have a dimension of time related to that particular time.

Nevertheless, when you are in any world or plane of vibration and you wish to relate one plane to another you will have time equivalents of (+) or (-) to some relative interims.

Events are coincident of vibrations and depend upon vibrations and their positions.

Time is being seen as the transient flowing framework of matters, events and living substance.

Think of time as it is possible to regard matter as nothing more than such a series of events with an interval of recurrence shorter than the minimum interval of sensual perception.

One of the second most important factors to think of in creative analysis is that of space.

We are not going to tell you all of the controversies. We are going to state simply that there is no such thing as space in this solar system. What they are calling space lies in concentric layers around the Sun in this Solar System.

Linear three-dimensional space is a measurement for a building, a road or some small object.

Light radiates from its source and is globular.

The measurement of the speed of light is another test made under minor conditions. In other words, light's speed of 186,324 miles per second is very much out of line. Einstein's work was relative to other straight-line paths.

Another way to say this is that time is the result of periodic alternations or vibrations.

A solar day is a primary period, the period of light and darkness of which the Bible speaks.

A solar sun cycle is a second factor as it swings North or South of the equator.

A third factor is the Earth's cycle around the sun.

All other measurements are subdivisions of these factors such as seconds-numbers-hours, frequency of light, sound waves, the motion of the planets and moon, life, and transition.

Time does not exist except as a relative standard of vibration frequency measurement.

These definitions of time should help you to get a new concept of the origin of this Solar System.

The origin means the first vibration, the Word spoken by the Creator.

The process of Creation means the evolution of harmonious secondary vibrations from the primal one.

The continually sounding Word of GOD, the formed, is the source of the great Harmony.

The fundamental universal vibration is the one known as the constant, which is a vibration of 3.29×10^{15} cycles per second or 2.843052×10^{20} cycles per mean solar day.

It corresponds to a calculated wavelength of 911.27×10^{8} centimeters of 911.27 angstrom units.

This is the fundamental frequency, or internal frequency, of both the positive and negative electrons which are the primary unit of matter.

One of the laws of vibrating bodies is that a vibrating body sets up harmonic vibrations at intervals of one octave or at a point of successive doublings +1/2 of the fundamental frequency.

In a musical sense, these harmonic notes are the closest possible to the fundamental vibration.

It is found that the intervals numbers squared show up more frequently than the one between and that octaves 4, 9, 16, 25, etc. both above and below the fundamental octave 1 show up more than prime numbers.

In limited vibrations, such as string or reed instruments, the frequency is above that octave 1 or bound vibration.

A cell is a persisting condition of electrical tension in free vibration within the body of a larger cell.

These cells are a lower frequency of vibration than the octave 1.

The harmonic cellular intervals are 1/2, 1/3, 1/4, 1/5, etc. of the fundamental frequency, while those of a bound vibration are 2, 3, 4, 5, etc. lines of the fundamental frequency.

The heterodyne or beat vibration exists when two different frequencies exist together and create a beat pulsation which is set up compositely equal to the difference between the two primary frequencies.

The following is expressive of the condition:
F = induced beat frequency
f = the higher or primary frequency
f1/2 = lower or secondary frequency
P = primary period or reciprocal of the primary frequency
s = the secondary period
p = the beat period or 1/F

The production of vibration of all possible frequencies from one fundamental vibration is accounted for by extensions of these two Laws.

F = the fundamental vibration of 1 or unity with this —

The harmonic frequencies are 2, 3, 4, 5, 6, 7, 8, 9, and 1/2, 1/3, 1/4, 1/5, 1/6, 1/7, 1/8, 1/9, etc. units with octaves 4, 9, 16, 25 with 1/4, 1/9, 1/16, 1/25 etc. accentuated.

Each octave is subdivided into notes.

They are beat frequencies = product of second law

For instance, F = 1 - 1/3 = 2/3 or the induced beat frequency is 2/3 of the fundamental frequency.

This shows that the induced beat frequency is 1/16 of an octave above the 1/2 harmonic or 5/6 of an octave below 1.

The combinations between the fundamental and various harmonic frequencies induce corresponding beat frequencies which are not harmonics.

Combinations of these make possible the forming of many notes in each octave.

The intensity or importance of the note and degree of harmony depends largely upon the emphasis of the squares of each harmonic interval.

The third point is that each of these combinations of simpler units or cells, brought together produce a new unit. This results in a new fundamental frequency for the individual, higher than that of the part thereof, with the vibration largely absorbed internally by its parts.

When positive photons, neutral neutrons, and negative electrons unite to form an atom, the fundamental and characteristic frequency of the atom is higher than the 3.29×10^{15} cycles per second or the Rydberg constant.

Every composite form has a higher fundamental than its composite parts.

The larger organized combination of molecules or cells, and Man himself, has a higher fundamental frequency.

The universe, or World cell, has the highest fundamental of all.

It is possible to calculate the fundamental characteristic, or Rydberg factor, of frequency of the World cell and of Man.

Vibration has three characteristics: frequency, position and amplitude.

The study of vibration always resolves itself to the study of numbers.

Integers assume a cosmic importance which has been acknowledged.

The unit represents the vibration of unit frequency, of unit period, and the multiples 2, 3, and 4 as well as basic divisions of 1/2, 1/3, 1/4 etc. become correspondingly important.

When stretched string vibrates, the unit frequency corresponds to the length of the string; the first harmonic, with a node at the midpoint, has a frequency of 2; the second harmonic, with the string divided into thirds by two nodes, has a frequency 3 octaves above the fundamental, etc.

The periods are the reciprocals of the frequencies.

The divisions into 1/2 and 1/3 forms a basic contrast in the nature of things. These are the simplest divisions into halves or multiples of 2 and are fundamentally the expression of octave intervals, or harmonic notes, and they are regarded as identical in a musical way.

The division into thirds is the expression that the fundamental harmony knows.

The division into halves and especially squares, fourths, forms an energizing and often disagreeable beat frequency.

The divisions into thirds form basic harmonies of musical sounds, of primary and secondary colors, and of planetary configurations.

The higher primary numbers are less important, and their effects are not seen.

- Five is the next in importance, then 7.
- Six is a combination of 3 and 2.
- Eight is all twos.
- Nine is all threes.

- Twelve is of particular importance, being the product of the harmonious three and discordant four, and so contains both elements.

The common tendency to count by twelves or its multiples, such as 1 dozen, 12" = 1', 360 degrees in the circle, which is divisible by 12, 12 signs of the zodiac—they are expressions of importance.

The spectrum lines in both x-ray and the optical spectral range are the beat frequencies found by the combination of equivalent vibrations of positive and negative electrons and are the product of the component frequencies.

The solar day, being the natural unit of time, implies that it is a natural frequency measurement.

The following formula is used on that basis, where F is the number of vibrations per mean solar day:

$$F = \frac{2590.790 \times 10^{20}}{\text{wavelength in Angstrom Units}}$$

The note n, given the octave and decimal fraction of an octave of any vibration, is really found from:

$$n = \frac{\text{logarithm of F}}{0.3010300}$$

These relations make it possible to correlate musical tones, colors and all things in God's creation: even the heartbeat, the breath, life periods, and the movements of the heavenly bodies.

Things of a psychic and cosmic radiation are correlated.

For example:

> If the constant v represents the number of solar days in a year divided by 1000 or 0.3652422.
>
> $F = 105^v$ by this it is found that the value of v for the fundamental Rydberg constant R is exactly 56 or 8 x 7 and for the critical frequency at which radiation begins to escape from the earth surface, between TV and short-wave radio, is 35 or 5 x 7.

The value of Y for the day is 0 by definition the U constant or 0.3662422 the number of sidereal days in a year divided by 1000 is used instead of v.

The value of Y for the Sun = -7
>   Jupiter = -10
>   Mars = -8
>   Saturn = -11
>   Asteroids = -9
>   Uranus = -12
>   Neptune = -13
>   Pluto = -13.5

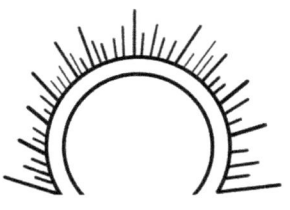

CREATION TWO

In accordance with the usual stages of growth and manifestation, it is necessary that man understand the more realistic approach in that philosophy. Otherwise the teachings in the New Testament are not merely words of guidance, but also within them are held some of the secrets of creation.

In the creation of Man there are three orderly stages:

1. Formation
2. Growth
3. Perfection

The scriptures are in harmony and truth. We say harmony because certain scriptures are related to one part of creation and others are related to other things in creation. We say that the hand of God has guided man to tell the truth throughout all the ages.

Let us now refer to the scripture references on Formation.

FORMATION

Genesis 1:26 – "And God said, Let us make man in our image, after our likeness; and let them have dominion over the fish of the sea, and over the fowl of the air, and over the cattle, and over all the earth, and over every creeping thing that creepeth upon the earth."

"Let us make man in our image." This shows that man was made with all the ability of God and the nature of God. This also shows that man was set in the position of a god over the animal kingdom, or over all the earth. Therefore, man may look around him and see the earth for which he is responsible.

MATERIAL USED

Now, let us see what man was made of.

Genesis 2:7 – "And the Lord God formed man of the dust of the ground and breathed into his nostrils the breath of life; and man became a living being."

Note that the Lord God formed man of dust from the ground. The term "formed" shows that something else was used which confirms many scientific findings. Of these things we will speak later on the vehicle in LEVEL II of the lessons.

GROWTH

Now for the second stage of creation.

Colossians 2:19 – "And not holding fast to the Head, for which the whole body nourished and knit together through its joints and ligaments grows with a growth that is from God."

In other words, your body is what your mind determines. The body grows by the power of God.

Mankind is the physical aspect of the Creator. It is the being through whom the spoken word of creativity is manifest. It is God's vehicle of expression.

These lessons will teach you to move, live, and have your being in the Creative Word. This is the supporting evidence of the saying the Law works whether you know it or not. For you are using it every day if you are living and breathing.

The secret of this lesson is found in Genesis 1:12, where it is stated, "and God saw that it was good." We must be able to see that there is nothing but good in manifestation around us and especially in our world, our personal universe, our atmosphere.

I wish to emphasize at this time that I do speak and not affirm the "Word." Speaking the Word of power is as different as night is from day. Speaking the Word of power makes you the Creator, not an empty boat in a storm-tossed sea.

The scripture declares in Colossians 1:15-16, "(He) is the image of the invisible God, the firstborn of all creation. For in Him all things were created, in heaven and on earth, visible and invisible, whether thrones, or dominions, principalities, or authorities. All things were created through Him, and for Him." Though Paul was speaking of Jesus he also reveals to us the secret of this. It is applicable to us.

For Jesus said, "...of these things I do so shall ye do also, and greater than these." Therefore, Jesus associated himself with the person on the street, to you and me. For we are also partakers of that divine nature. As creators we can recognize nothing else but that divine nature of the God creation. There is simply nothing else to recognize.

Paul declares, "For in Him, all the fullness of God was placed to dwell." Since it refers to Jesus it naturally refers to the Son of God. As Jesus is our elder Brother we are joint heirs with Christ. Therefore, we also are sons of God.

THIS IS A LAW—AN IMMUTABLE FACT

It is indivisible and eternal in the heavens of all this solar system.

Using this knowledge and the power contained within it we open a door which no man can shut. In case of necessity, we can shut a door which no man can open.

John declares in Chapter 1, Verse 1, "In the beginning was the Word, and the Word was God." Compare this with the writings of Moses in Genesis 1:1 where he tells us that in the beginning GOD Created.

Jesus showed us the power of the spoken Word through many healings, producing food which fed five thousand, and many other events. All of these were done by speaking the WORD OF POWER.

I will cite only one example. In John 11, Jesus said: "Lazarus, Come forth!" You know that Lazarus did come forth and was healed—RIGHT THEN.

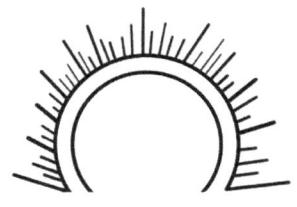

LESSON 1
CREATION THREE

CREATION AND ANGELS

Occult teachings give a dual explanation concerning the emanation and constitution of the Universe. They state that in Nature there exists a Directive Intelligence plus a Sustaining Life and a Creative Will. Secondly, they inform us concerning the existence, nature, and function of certain individual embodiments of these three powers in Nature. In Egypt and Greece they are called "gods," in the East "devas," and in the West "Angelic Hosts."

Occult Philosophy agrees with modern science that the universe consists not of matter but of energy. The universe of force is the Kingdom of the gods. For these Beings are fundamentally directors of universal forces and power agents of the Logos, His engineers in the great and continuous creative process.

Creative energy is perpetually being poured out. On the way from its source to a material manifestation as physical substance and form, it passes through the bodies and auras of the gods. In this process it is transformed, or "stepped down," from its primordial potency. Thus the creative gods are also the "transformers" of power.

The super-physical worlds which are the abodes of the gods consist of matter of increasing tenuity of substance ranging from the density of the finest ether up to the rarest and most spiritual condition.

Highest among the objective "gods," or those aspects of God fully manifested, are the seven solar Archangels, the Seven Mighty Spirits, which include the well-known Michael, Gabriel, and Raphael.

The ministry of angels has been an accepted teaching of many faiths and a living reality to a great number of people. Occult research supports this doctrine, revealing that during such ministrations, certain Orders of Angels at once appear as the natural agents of those forces being used.

Their function is to converse and direct the forces generated by ceremonial action, prayer and adoration, and to serve as channels for the power and the blessing which descend in response. This ministration is far more effectively carried out when recognized by both ministrants and congregation.

Other aspects of the subject worth considering are what is the effect upon the evolving life in Nature of the church services, such as the Celebration of the Holy Eucharist, and the participation of the nature spirits and the Angelic Hosts in human worship?

While ceremonies intelligently performed are one of the most effective means of cooperation between angels and men, these are not required. For the human mind is, itself, a powerful broadcasting and receiving station. Given the power of a strong will with training in concentration and illumined by intuitive knowledge of the unity of life, the mind becomes an extremely potent instrument.

Whenever a human thought is strongly directed toward one particular Order of angels, the mental signal being dispatched is received by members of that Order. If the person sending the message has attained to a definite universality of consciousness, and his motive is in consequence entirely selfless, the angels will unfailingly respond. Man may then direct his thought power into his chosen field of work assured of angelic cooperation that he may enter therein.

Their active cooperation may involve such ministrations to others as spiritual healing, inspiration, protection, or helping to overcome a weakness of character. Collaboration may also be sought in order to gain the inspiration required in the performance of certain altruistic work.

Angels can be powerful allies in such ministrations, having the ability to open up the channels of inspiration between the higher consciousness and the brain, and to convey telepathically a train of illuminating ideas to minds which are receptive.

Continued practice of invoking the help of the angels has been found to produce a change in the human aura, the link thus formed being visible as an area of brilliant light vibrating at the higher frequencies which characterize the auras of angels.

When this "devic seal," as it is called, has been enlivened by ceremonial action or by thought and will alone, it "transmits" a signal on the wavelengths of the particular Order of Angels whose aid is being invoked. This call is then "picked up" by the corresponding angels in terms of vibratory frequency. Their attention being gained, they are at once ready to help.

Clairvoyance is useful in this process but not necessary. Regular practice based upon intuitive recognition of the truth of these ideas will quickly provide convincing evidence of the reality and effectiveness of cooperation between angels and men. This cooperation is constantly occurring in the realm of man's higher SELF, however unaware of this fact the lower self may be.

The Archangels, which in Christian terminology are called "Thrones," find it their special mission to inspire nations through their Higher Selves.

Under these conditions of angelic inspiration, the statesman becomes possessed of powers not previously suspected in him. As long as he selflessly serves his nation, this power will grow. But should selfish interests interpose, the angelic and other inspiration would be withdrawn and power soon decline.

Lesson 2: Prayer • Meditation • Blessing

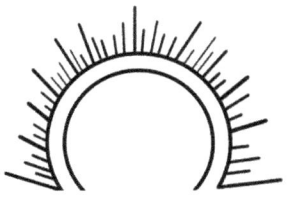

PRAYER ONE

Prayer is the scientific method of communication to our Creator. Scientific in that Jesus said, "Whatsoever ye ask in my name shall be given unto you." Anything that is scientific means you get results each and every time. The Law of Prayer works each and every time. This shows the eternalness of the giving of the Father. All you ask for is given to you.

The scientific method of prayer is: before you pray you know what you are going to pray for. You know in detail that which you want. Draw a mental picture of what you need, for there can be no confusion in your mind as to what you want.

Then you establish contact with the Father. When this contact is established, you can feel it. He is here, closer than your hands and feet.

Getting in contact with the Father is like contacting your friends. When their cell phone rings, the person on the receiving end of the call answers it. When the call is answered, you know contact has been made without his saying a word. As in the mechanics of the cell phone, the contact made between you and your friend, so your thought is the contact made between you and God.

When you have established this contact, then you ask for what you want or need. You ask in the name of our Lord Jesus Christ. As Jesus said, "Whatever ye ask in my name shall be given unto you." What you have asked for is then yours. Hang up the phone. It has already been given to you so you can go on about your business and forget about it. As the student says, "You let go and let God." Say thank you! Thank the Father for what He gives you. For it is His power and His force that has brought this into your life.

The Law of Prayer is shown in the symbol of the Triangle which gives you a picture of what it looks like graphically:

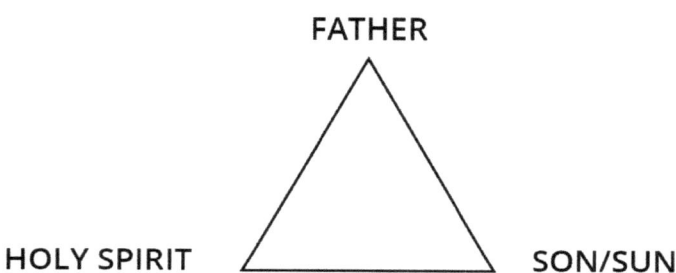

When you contacted the Father, you were at the uppermost part of this triangle marked the Father. When you asked for what you wanted, you moved your consciousness from the Father point of the triangle to the Son (Sun) point of the triangle. When you received that which you asked for, this is shown in the motion from the Son to the Holy Spirit, the third point of the triangle.

For many thousands of years the triangle has been used for this purpose so that man could see the action of this Great Being he is living within.

The Master Jesus manifested the second point of this triangle, the Son (Sun). St. John called this the Logos or the Word. The Son is the eternal Word of the Father. At this point of the Law, you use the Word as Jesus said, "The Father gave unto Me the Word so I give it unto you."

This triangle shows the action of God from the Father to the Son, then to the Holy Spirit. So in using the Law you must start with the Father by contacting Him. Like saying "hello" to your friend at the other end of the phone.

In the New Testament Jesus talked about the Pharisees and their prayers. They would stand on the street corners and make long and beautiful prayers so that those around them would hear them. They forgot to contact the Father. For if they had, their prayers would have been fulfilled.

The science behind the statement Jesus made, "Whatsoever ye ask in my name shall be given unto you," is that nature abhors a vacuum. Your asking creates a vacuum which shall be fulfilled. A vacuum is a space or something that is missing. The Word creates the physical vacuum, which is physically fulfilled.

The Law of Prayer, being scientific, is also extremely simple. For if man would use pure logic as the reasoning of a child, he would know his Creator and would have all of his prayers answered.

Prayer is a tool for all man. It is one of your tools of life whereby you can govern your life and control your personal universe. Accept into your life that which you desire and reject all negative things for your health.

Man is not a ship on a storm-tossed sea, being tossed to and fro at the slightest whim. He is a creator who designs his own destiny. For without the knowing and use of the Law of Prayer, it is an impossibility for man to be the creator he truly is.

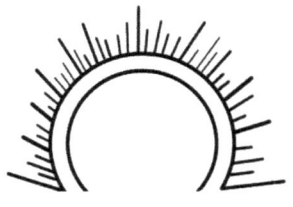

PRAYER TWO

Our prayer work is scientific. Our definition of prayer is the scientific lifting up of our hearts and minds to God our Creator. We pray in three forms: vocally, mentally and positively.

VOCAL PRAYER

We pray vocally because it is necessary to voice the Word. As we speak our words produce a certain rate of vibration which sets up a certain rhythm. It can be measured scientifically.

Our scripture text supporting this is taken both from the Gospel of St. Matthew, and the Gospel of St. Luke. Jesus says in St. Luke 11:2, "When ye pray, Say..." In Matthew 7:7, "Ask and it will be given unto you, seek and you will find..." In Matthew 6:9, "Pray then like this, Our Father which art in heaven..." This will show the importance of voiced prayer.

MENTAL PRAYER

We teach prayer mentally because Mind is the realm of the Father. It is the place of creation. Our prayer in order to be scientifically powerful should be creative.

Read Matthew 7, Luke 11, and John 17. In Matthew it says as stated before, "Ask". In Luke 11:9, he repeats again, and says, "Ask." And in John 17, Jesus says that the Father gave Him power over all flesh to give eternal life to all whom He had given Him and that He

(Jesus) has given this to man. These are the ones which are the body of the Church, the ones that accept God wholly and multiply His works. This is one of the most exalting chapters in the Bible to show man's divinity.

In the 20th verse Jesus goes on to say that He prayed not only for the Elect but also for those that became chosen through the acceptance of God, knowing that the Father was in them, as they were in the Father, thus becoming one with the Father. Here again this was a voiced prayer by Jesus.

SCIENTIFIC PRAYER

The use of Scientific Prayer brings into our life the manifestation of the Kingdom of God. In this School we understand that prayer is talking to God and Meditation is the process of receiving an answer.

Contemplation is the process of revelation of our prayer. Meditation is the formula through which it works. Contemplation is the laboratory where the science of prayer and meditation are analyzed and proven scientifically correct.

That which is not scientifically correct is not spiritually correct. That which is not scientifically or spiritually correct is not metaphysically correct. That which violates the basic metaphysical laws such as the Law of Cause and Effect, etc. also violates spiritual law.

The perfect prayer should contain praise and glory and worship to the Creator as is shown us in Matthew 6 (King James version) where Jesus says, "...For thine is the kingdom, and the power, and the glory..." The perfect prayer also contains thanksgiving to God for His many benefits.

The perfect prayer contains supplication to God for those things which we require, desire, wish, and want. The scriptures which back up these statements are of praise and worship:

Psalms 69:34, 9:2, 102:18, 104:35, 138:4, 95:6
Matthew 21:16, 2:2, 4:10
Luke 2:13, I Samuel 1:27, John 12:43, Acts 13:2
Deut. 10:21, Romans 12:1, Acts 3:8, Rev. 5:14

Read the scriptures above and, while reading, read three verses before and three verses after the quote. This is so that we may know the truth ourselves. Thus we become familiar with the Bible. Later in the lessons we will become closer to great men of other times and faiths.

THANKSGIVING

Psalms 50:14, 95:2, 106:1, 145:10
Matthew 15:36, 26:27
Revelation 11:17
Read the same as the first group.

SUPPLICATION

Psalms 28:2, 130:2
Zac. 12:10

GLORY

Psalms 104:31, 149:9
Matthew 6:13
Exodus 24:16, 35:18, 40:34, 16:7, 16:10

From your first observations of these studies you may have some questions. Do voice them. Let us say here that there will be more work on prayer from the scientific standpoint in the Second Level work in Communication. All of these scriptural references support our stand on Prayer.

Paul told Timothy "to study, to show himself approved a workman, not needing to be ashamed, but rightly dividing the word of truth." (R.V.)

This is good advice for the students of this School to follow. In fact it is good advice for any Christian. Search these scriptures and study them. You will find the power of prayer.

Remember Paul's advice, "prayer without ceasing!" It is a good example of conclusive supplicative prayer. It is the prayer that was prayed by Jesus (found in St. John 17).

PRAYER AND THE LAW

The Law is the most important facet of prayer. For the Law can become the nature of one's own Spirit and is the spiritual essence of this Law. King David said, "I delight in Thy Law, day and night." This is prayer without ceasing.

The first portion of the Law is discussed in this lesson from Biblical references. The ever-active part of the Law and its place in creation is discussed in the Light-Life-Love lessons. The remainder of the study of Law will be in that portion of our studies under the tools of man in the Second Level studies.

The portion of the Law which we will now study is covered primarily in Matthew 7:21, "Not everyone that saith unto me, Lord, Lord, shall enter into the kingdom of heaven; but he that doeth the will of my Father which is in heaven."

So the first portion of the Law of Prayer is the secret of using the Will power after you have praised and worshipped and glorified God, after you have thanked Him and made your supplications known to Him. Use your power to bring into spiritual or mental manifestation the pattern or word form of the thing or relationship you want to manifest. Then the Will of God will be manifest, "Because He wants to give you the Kingdom."

Setting Law of Prayer into action consists of demanding, affirming its presence, and doing. By this you move out on the physical plane as if you could already put it in your pocket, making yourself accessible to receiving it.

After you have done this you must go about acting as if you really know your prayer is already answered affirmatively. Therefore, you will be demonstrating to the unseen Creator your ability to use the power of prayer, to bring about the material manifestation of His unseen reality.

Matthew 7:7 says, "Ask, and it shall be given you; seek, and you shall find; knock, and it shall be opened unto you." Analyze this statement. Look at the changes it can bring in your life. Put it to the test! See the effect of the Law.

When the Law of asking is put into effect the result is that it will be given.

The Law says, "Knock!" When you have done this the result is that it will be opened.

The Law says, "Seek!" And when you have sought you will find. Because there is no such thing as a negative prayer.

There is not and cannot be a negative answer to prayer. Remember! You shall reap what you have sown.

The effect of a fervent, righteous prayer shall be: everyone who asks, receives; he who seeks, finds; and to him who knocks, it will be opened.

We are sure that after studying this lesson, you will find irony of the Word spoken by the Apostle James. "The effectual fervent prayer of a righteous man availeth much."

We shall conclude this lesson with another statement from the Apostle James: "Be doers of the Word and not hearers only, deceiving yourselves. For if anyone is a hearer of the Word and not a doer, he is like a man who observes a natural face in a mirror. For he observes himself and goes away and at once forgets what he is like. But he who looks into the perfect Law, the Law of Liberty, and perseveres being no hearer that forgets but a doer that acts, he shall be blessed in his living."

PRAYER FULFILLS THE LAW OF DOING.

PRAYER FROM THE BOOK: *THUS I HAVE HEARD*

The following prayer quoted from the *"Aquarian Age"* May-June 1924, is given here as an unfailing means of finding the Master in the heart. It should be meditated upon phrase by phrase with deepening realization until the full beauty and truth of the final words become matters of experience.

Bishop Leadbeater gave this prayer to his class in Melbourne, Australia, for a daily meditation. Every word was thought over for many months—then, thought out as to its connection with every other word. There is a deep occult significance in the combination of words, sentences, and ideas. There should be a pause after each phrase with deep meditation.

"O Gracious Lord, I enter Thy radiance, and approach Thy Presence, bearing with me the service done in Thy Name, and for Thee. I seek to become a more efficient server, and I open my heart and mind to the power of Thy Love, and Thy Joy, and Thy Peace.

"In Thy presence, Thy Peace enfolds me, and fills me with contentment, certainty, rest, stillness, Thy Peace which passeth understanding. I must, therefore, be a center of love, joy, and peace in the world.

"I place my hand in Thine with all love and trust and confidence, for Thou art indeed my Lord. From the unreal lead me to the Real, from darkness to Light, from death to Life Eternal. At Thy feet, and in the Light of Thy Holy Presence, I strive to realize what I am. I am not this body which belongs to the world of shadows; I am not the desire which affects it; I am not the thoughts which fill my mind; I am not the mind itself. I am the Divine Flame within my heart, eternal, immortal, ancient, without beginning, without end. More radiant than the sun in all His noonday glory, purer than the snow, untouched, unsullied by the hand of matter; more subtle than the ether is the Spirit within my heart. I and my Father are One.

"I worship Thee. I adore Thee; Thou my Life, my Breath, my Being, my All. I am in Thee and Thou art in me. Lead me, O Gracious Lord, through Thy illimitable Love to union with Thee, and the Heart of Eternal Love.

"In Thy Love I rest evermore." Amen.

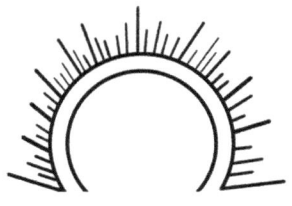

PRAYER THREE

It is foolish to pray to God to cure a disease while we continue to violate some natural law that has caused it. We cannot ask Him to suspend temporarily all His laws on earth and through an outstanding miracle cure us of disease while we are indifferent regarding our duties and obligations.

Mere words without deeds on our part are not sufficient. We must have faith in the perfection, magnificence, and immutability of God's laws and of God's power.

The mystic knows well that God will never revoke or even slightly modify any one of the fundamental laws existing in the universe. Hence he never asks God to set one of them aside. But the mystic may pray, will pray, and otherwise bring about a different form of manifestation of the Law consistent with the purpose and motive in back of the action of the Law.

The man who discovered that whenever lightning struck the lightning rod on the roof of his house the water in his well was purified because the rod had a slight connection with the water pipes. He produced Only a Change in the Manifestation of the fundamental law by putting the end of the lightning rod down into the well itself. The whole well full of water would be clarified by the action of the lightning.

The fundamental Law was in the fact that the lightning would go to the ground and there spend itself harmlessly. But he directed the

Law so that it would not only spend itself harmlessly but constructively in purifying the water. Did he change a fundamental law? Or did he direct the Law into a different manifestation by looking at the secondary principles involved and Directing Them?

When man found that water dropping over a cliff had power to destroy things beneath its weight, he invented the water wheel so that the law in the action of dropping water would manifest differently, constructively, instead of destructively. No law was changed but other laws were properly applied to the fundamental one.

This is the work that the mystic does. It is the work you must do in the attainment of mastership over the finite part of your existence.

Prayer is the lifting up of heart, emotional and unemotional, to the Creator in words. Words produce a rate of vibration, rhythm, measurable as it leaves the body.

Voice is a sound. The whole system vibrates creation: rhythm. The pulse of the body varies. We set it in motion and it does the work.

If we raise enough feeling, confirmation, and realization within ourselves, the prayer will get through the inner form, the spirit of the individual. Prayer should be creative and then prayer is working through Law. The power is flowing through us, humanity, whether pictured or imagined. Jesus set a new pattern.

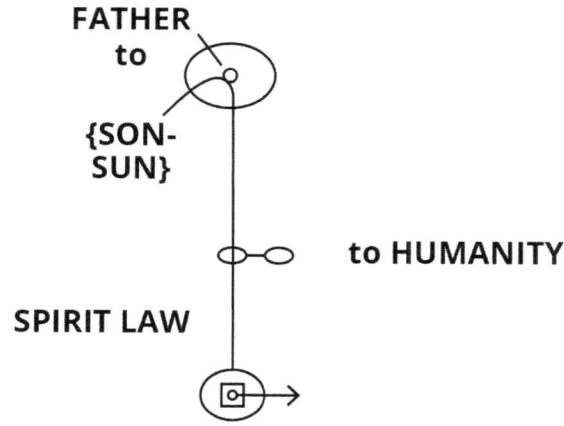

FROM PLEXUS INTO VOICE & PUT FORTH

Pray just once. Don't peek back over your shoulder at it. But you can reaffirm a prayer if needed.

Meditation is the vehicle or formula through which prayer works. If not scientifically correct the method is not spiritually correct. The Perfect Prayer Contains:

1. Praise, glory, and worship to the Creator (see Psalm 69:34; Matthew 6).
2. Thanksgiving for His many benefits.
3. Supplication for those things we require or want.

If we want a thing bad enough and voice it, the Law will open the door.

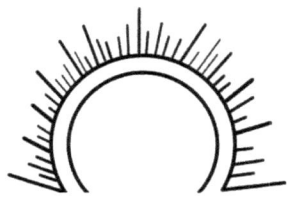

LESSON 2

PRAYER FOUR

PRAYER:

Blessed is the Light. Shower on me Thy Ray. For as I travel in the darkness of this world of mine, I beseech Thee to illuminate my path.

I petition Thee, O Christ, to lead me into Thy midst and that I may be filled with Light.

For unto my light I ask that my brothers may add their light under the Divine mystic Holy Order of the Golden Cross and with the help of the ancient Brothers and Masters. O Christ, may I be filled with Light so that I may find my way to God.

I, the mortal body, need this Divine strength that I may face in reality sins of the past.

That when I am ready to look upon the God of my Being and see the glory of all Creation I will then have the strength to turn my back on the world and accept the eternal divinity.

I hail the symbol of our Order knowing the use of and accepting the responsibility of the elements of Creation, the power of the Word and Law.

Thus I offer myself on the fire-cross of the Spirit of God surrounded by His Omnipotence with Life, Love and Light with the strength of the experience of my Soul.

Now that I pass through the crucifixion I now seek the resurrection through regeneration. Thus comes peace and freedom eternal.

I now realize:

1. Oh Mortal thou art the densest form and vehicle of God-Self.
2. Oh Mortal Body thou art transitory.
3. Thou canst deceive me no longer for thou art only what the real SELF makes of thee.
4. My Soul I am only what thou art. All else is a passing fancy like the image in the mirror.
5. Therefore, I command my outer Being to humble its ego, and cast aside the veil and permit me to express from within, for God is within and without. We are inseparable.

MEDITATE:

O Soul of me do reveal in retrospection as I am in the eyes of the Cosmic.

Let man sit alone and keep silence. Amen.

THE LORD'S PRAYER

(in Aramaic)

Abon dbashmaya	Our Father in Heaven,
Nith qadash shmakh;	Hallowed be Thy Name.
Tete malkuthakh; nehbe suya	Thy kingdom come; Thy will be
-nakh; aykana dbashmaya ap	done, as in heaven, so on earth.
Barah; holan lakhma dson	Give us the bread of our
qanan yomana	need this day.
Washboqlan Khobain	And forgive us our offenses,
Aykana dapkhnan shbaqan	as we have also forgiven
Ikhayabane	those who have offended us;
ola talan nisyuna	and bring us not to trial
ela passan min bisha;	but deliver us from the
mittul dilakhe malkotha	evil one. For Thine
okhaila otishbukhta	is the kingdom, and the power,
lalam almen.	and the glory forever and ever.
Amen.	Amen
(pronounced ameen)	

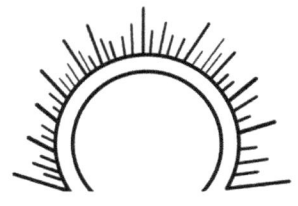

MEDITATION ONE

An excellent time for suggestions is late at night just before retiring. Here we have the very opposite condition from the morning. We now have fatigue, congestion of thoughts, and a myriad of flitting ideas trying to occupy our mental attention. Here we must willfully clear the brain and make ready for the wonderful mental state which comes with sleep.

During sleep, the brain is absolutely inactive if the sleep is complete and thorough in relaxation. Therefore, the mind, or the subconscious mind as some persons wish to call it, has greater opportunity to carry on its activities because it is not hampered by the incoming impressions from the brain.

If, therefore, just before going to sleep you willfully cast out all other thoughts and concentrate your brain and whole attention on some idea and fall asleep with this one idea occupying your consciousness, it will pass from your brain, or outer consciousness, to your subconscious mind.

But a formula must be used. Your thought must be in the form of a suggestion. It must be so visualized, pictured, and worded that it is not a mere, vague, abstract idea, but one that is reducible to a command, or law, or statement that is in the form of a decree.

For instance, if the idea that you wish to hold in your mind when you go to sleep is in regard to something you wish to do or accomplish the next day, you must visualize yourself doing the act. But your thought must not be a mere abstract. It must be a command, worded something like this, "Tomorrow I will do this or that." Or, "Tomorrow I will accomplish this or that."

In this way you are really commanding your subconscious mind to accept this statement as a decree. It will be received by the subconscious mind in that form during your sleep and it will become a law, a paramount law, an absolute law with the mind. It will be so established there by morning that it will be the first thing your brain contacts upon awakening. You will feel the effects of it all day as an inner command, an inner reminder of what you are to do.

Incidentally, the thought coming from within during the day will be an inspiration and will give you confidence to proceed to do the thing you wish to do.

So you have these two periods during the day, early in the morning and late at night, when you are most susceptible to the influence of suggestion.

Other times during the day when you are relaxed or in a meditative mood if you can get away long enough to look out of a window into space, or look at some green trees, or flowers, or into some dark corner of your home or office then go into what some call reflection, which the mystics call meditation, with but one thought occupying your mind. This is a thought arranged as we have said before. It should be arranged at night when you go to sleep. Then you will find that this thought in the form of a suggestion or command will slip over from your brain into your subconscious while you are lost in this spell of meditation and reflection.

The more completely you forget your environment and forget where you are for two or three minutes and have nothing but the one thought inhabiting your whole consciousness, the more completely and the more commandingly will the idea and suggestion pass on to the subconscious mind.

We suggest to you to try this matter of suggestion during the coming week in connection with your daily affairs and learn the first principles of self-mastery and self-mastership as it relates to your very intimate personal affairs.

Much has been said in recent years about the influence of mind over matter. In many of the modern philosophical writings we find innumerable new metaphysical terms such as Infinite Mind, Divine Mind, Mortal Mind, and so forth.

All such terms including the ones we use are the invention of man. Names for things are merely ideographs invented to represent an idea much like the strange hieroglyphics which the Egyptians cut into stones to represent the ideas they wished to express.

Different names for the same thing and different ideographs for the same idea cannot affect the nature of the thing or the idea. Whether you call an affirmation a command or whether you call it a plea or prayer makes little difference in the operation of the Divine Law.

Many persons will find it more convenient to think of the inner subjective mind and consciousness of man as the Divine, Immortal Mind, which it is really. They will likewise want to think of the objective outer mind as the mortal, transient mind of man, which it really is.

In the foregoing testing of the law, it is not a question of the mortal mind dictating to the Divine Mind while asking the Divine Mind to do that which the mortal mind cannot do.

This is the fundamental principle of metaphysical consecration to the Divine Mind and you will find the principle one that is easily demonstrable and very practical in its results.

The idea back of all this is to make you the master of your environment, master of your fate as others would call it, and the master of your affairs. So practice this at least for one week and note the results.

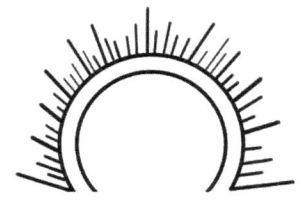

MEDITATION TWO

Meditation is the second stage of Scientific enlightenment. It follows after Scientific prayer and is not to be considered lightly. But it is to be observed with all diligence.

Meditation should be silent because you cannot pray through meditation if you have a noisy mind. This is why we recommend concentration first because through concentration you can gain control of the most unruly mind.

The force and power of concentration is brought about and brought into focus as Scientific understanding.

Contemplation is brought to focus in Scientific Illumination.

The psalmist in Psalm Chapter 119, Verse 15, "I will meditate on Thy precepts, and fix my eyes on Thy ways."

The Laws of God and nature are so evasive, in order that we may become spiritual they must be meditated upon.

The precepts of God must be studied, and our eye must become single and observe the works of God.

Meditation is the silent weighing the answers one gets to questions or the silent waiting for the answers.

When we meditate, we must block the mind of stagnant thought for the mind of the average person has many scattered thoughts per few seconds. But the mind must not be blank.

The thought process should flow freshly, and he who does the meditation should bless, and praise, each thought as it enters into his consciousness.

The 119th Psalm, verse 16, "I will delight in Thy statutes; I will not forget Thy words." Here the aspirant, the spiritual student tells the Creator that he will be happy and elated in the statutes of God. That he will rejoice over the responsibility and obligation which they impose upon him.

Next he makes his spontaneous scientific decree and solemn vow, "I will not forget thy word."

In the Psalm 119, Verse 34, "Give me understanding, that I may keep Thy Law." Meditation brings along with it the spiritual and Scientific power of understanding. The results of meditation are shown to us in the verses 44 and 45 of the 119th Psalm, "I will keep Thy law continually for ever and ever, and I shall walk at liberty, for I have sought Thy precepts."

Again we say he who meditates properly will automatically keep the Law and walk in Liberty.

Because in meditation the person has sought after the precepts of God. In Psalm Chapter 119, Verse 45, "and I will walk in liberty for I have sought Thy precepts."

Meditation shall teach you good judgment, it will help you achieve the Christ Mind, it will cause you to keep away from transgression and shame, and it will heal your entire cosmic structure.

He who cannot concentrate is not well balanced. He needs to obtain equilibrium which is the password unto the Kingdom of God.

Fatherhood cannot be obtained without it.

David said, "I will meditate upon your Laws by day and night." He also said in Verse 97, Psalm 119, "Oh, how I love Thy Law! It is my meditation all the day." In Verse 99, he makes mention that the Creator's testimonies are also his meditations.

By meditation on His precepts, testimonies, and His Law we get divine understanding. Through divine understanding we get divine illumination. Through divine illumination we arrive at the point of finding the SELF. Finding the SELF is the quest of this course of study.

1. Start with concentration. Pick an object in the room and look at it for 10 minutes under full light. Do this every day for four days. The next week for three days, the third week for one day, preferably Wednesday of the week.
2. Then we start on the fourth week with a darkened room and concentrate on the same object under the light of three candles. Do this for five minutes each day for four days, the first week. The second week, each day for three days. The third week, each day for two days. The fourth week on Wednesday.
3. The final exercise should be done in a completely darkened room and start visualizing the same object for 15 minutes each day for 7 days.
4. Then do this in the light and then the dark alternately: 10 minutes in light and 10 minutes in dark, once a day for 7 days.

This shall establish the power of concentration. Meditation is then a retroactive function from concentration, it will just carry you through.

Contemplation is merely a workable way of retrospection, a review of what we have learned in meditation.

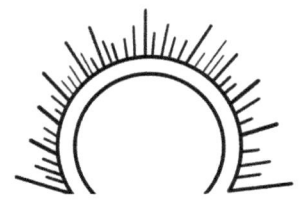

MEDITATION THREE

AN EVERYDAY APPROACH

This is a way in which to step up your day and your way so that you may obtain the consciousness of meditation.

Step 1: Keep in mind upon going to sleep that you are going to rise and meditate before breakfast. Thus, you will be wide awake and will obtain better results. This is also a good time to pray for something for the mind is yet uncluttered.

Step 2: Get yourself in the habit of thinking of the Father first and then call on the Master Jesus so that your consciousness may be immediately lifted.

Step 3: Try to use the same place whenever meditating, about the same time and don't allow other things to interfere if possible.

Step 4: Body, soul and mind are to be trained simultaneously to gain the necessary spiritual poise.

Step 5: Don't think of hastening spiritual development.

Step 6: Consider it a sacred duty to practice the exercise of meditation daily.

Step 7: Be kind, generous and tolerant of others but be very exacting with yourself and your spiritual exercises.

Step 8:   Do not criticize or condemn others. Keep your own doorstep clean.

Step 9:   Don't talk about your spiritual development except to your teacher if you have a true teacher or Priest.

Step 10: Spend as much time as possible without shirking your daily duties. Man is a subject to habit. Once you are accustomed and feel the benefits of the cosmic contained in meditation you will not be without it.

When starting meditation pick a Spiritual subject unless you have a mundane problem. After getting into a Spiritual attitude and forgetting all around you set up your subject and then clear your mind. Do not blank it. Let it stay alive but do not think.

The thoughts that enter should be strictly related to your subject and should not be foreign to it. However, this will not work if you have not learned concentration and mastered it.

Do not try to repeat this immediately unless you are successful the first time. Then you may meditate on other subjects.

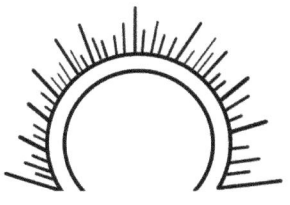

BLESSING ONE

A blessing is the movement of power, force, energy and life. It may be given in two ways: either by the laying on of hands or by prayer. When giving a blessing, you find out what the person needs. You make a mental image of that need.

If you are with a person, lay your hands on him and you draw the power, force, energy and life down within him filling that form or image. Then the blessing has been accomplished.

When you are blessing someone who is not present with you, you see the particular need of the person and you make a mental image of that need and you fill that need within that person with power, force and energy and then you know that need has been fulfilled. Drawing the power, force and energy within that pattern gives life to that pattern so it will manifest.

There are many different types of blessings which fulfill the needs of man outwardly or inwardly, such as a blessing of strength. When giving a blessing of strength you see the person strong, you draw power, force, energy and life to that person. Your thinking of seeing him strong is what determines that blessing. Through your thoughts you set up the pattern which is to be filled. The pattern was you seeing that person strong. Then your consciously drawing the power, force, energy and life to him is the fulfilling of the pattern. It will then manifest.

There are many people in the religious field who make a statement which is well known, "May the Lord bless you." The reality for this to take place when you say, "May the Lord bless you" happens when you see it being done. Then it is done.

Giving a blessing isn't some religious jargon. It isn't just words. It is real, things take place. The real spiritual world is a world of movement, a world of action, real action, real movement. For when Jesus laid his hands on a person and said, "Be thou blessed," they were really blessed in the highest sense, and He gave all of God's children this function.

For you to give blessings, you must **KNOW**.

The power of God is seen by seeing this world. This world we live in is real. It came about by God seeing this world and filling its form with power, force, energy and life. Then this world came into existence and His pattern and way of doing things is the way and pattern for man to do things.

If you know God is real then you can give a real blessing. If God is a mental concept or some nice idea to you please tear up your shingle and go home for you are doing nobody any good.

Every man should be a servant of God. For either you are serving God or you are serving you, yourself, and your petty little desires which are called Beelzebub in the Bible.

A priest is one whose whole life, inwardly and outwardly, is a conscious movement of service to God. His whole life is giving blessings to his fellow man and thereby bringing him closer to our Creator.

Three monkeys sat in a coconut tree
Discussing things as they're said to be.
One monk said, now listen you two,
There's rumors about that just can't be true.
That man descended from our noble race,
Why the very idea is a disgrace.

No monk ever deserted his wife,
Starved her babies and ruined her life,

And you've never known a mother monk,
To leave her babies with others to bunk,
Or pass them along from one to another,
'Til they scarcely know who's their mother.

And another thing you'll never see,
Monks build a fence around a coconut tree,
Forbidding all other monks a taste,
Even while coconuts go to waste,
Why if I'd build a fence around this tree
Starvation would force you to steal from me.

Here's another thing a monk won't do,
Go out at night and get on a stew,
Use a gun, or a club, or a knife,
To take some other monkey's life,
Yes, man descended, that we clearly see,
But, my brothers, not from our family tree.

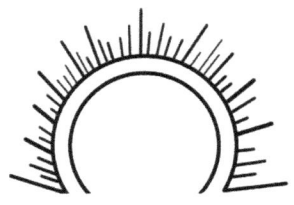

BLESSING TWO

In the scriptures it is recorded in 2 Samuel, Chapter 7, verse 29, "Now, therefore, may it please thee to bless the house of thy servant, that it may continue forever before thee; for thou, O Lord God, hast spoken and with Thy blessing shall the house of Thy servant be blessed forever."

A blessing is an invested power and privilege given to the Creation by its Creator. With this power and privilege comes the obligation to carry out the pattern and plan of the Creator.

To be blessed is to be joined together with the Creator as if He were a husband, and you the student, a wife.

The blessing is metaphysical and spiritual wedlock. "Works is the way." Monks, Nuns, and Priests receive this blessing at their ordination or establishment in a particular church. They are blessed into service.

The divine Master requires our whole being in service for His honor and Glory. Before the blessing is obtained many conditions are required of the candidate.

These blessings are especially for the following:

1. Poverty
2. Obedience
3. Chastity
4. Humility

The Way of Light is obtained in the blessings by starting with the Humility vow. When this vow is realized it will bring about a greater desire and acceptance of the vow of Chastity. The realization of the aspect and power of Humility will bring you to the level of Chastity.

The vow of Chastity is not a condition in which a person is not married. But it is a much deeper state of Mind and Soul than just not having sexual intercourse.

The fact of the matter is that many people who consider that they are married are not married. Legally yes, according to man's law, they are and believe they are married.

Chastity starts with the desires of the person in respect to their thinking, of their relations to the Creator, and the desire to know GOD or SELF. It is also to have a close feeling with the Creator, the all-encompassing one, the Elohim.

The desiring to know GOD above all other things, the realization of the marriage to the GOD of all creation, makes you chaste of all base self-desire. This should come at the time of the blessing.

A person, man or woman, may be married and be conditioned to conform to the Law of Chastity, or should we say vow of Chastity, "if" they both have given the other their freedom to seek Self, "if" each is considerate of the other's physical need. This is because the physical sexual act can, when performed in the rightful way, be a balancing of forces and giving.

It is true that it is for the purpose of bearing children but it is also a fact that a state of Unity exists in the Godly marriage. Just being unmarried is not Chastity. Many people, men and women, look at the opposite sex and go through all the desires and emotions of sexual relations without ever knowing the other individual. Actually the going through the physical sex act is a very minor part of intercourse.

More will be given on this subject. In the Science lessons, Marriage will be gone into so that a real understanding can be had.

Now if a person wishes to discipline himself for development and attainment then abstaining will do it fine. If single you also abstain from looking on another with desire.

Let it be understood here that we as disseminators of basic Creative Law do not and are not accepting or advocating promiscuity in any form. For this carries with it a Karmic indebtedness.

When Chastity has matured into full growth of consciousness it of itself shall create the desire to accept obedience, not to a person, place, or thing but to your own inner being.

There are periods during which it is advisable to be obedient to the Teacher you have accepted for your own Spiritual advancement.

But obedience to the Creator within, the Higher SELF, is as found in second Chronicles, chapter 7, verse 14: "If my people, who are called by my name, humble themselves and pray and seek my face, and turn from their wicked ways, then I will hear from heaven and will forgive their sin, and heal their land."

Healing is a blessing in this instance. The healing may transfer the power of the blessing to their land.

Humility, Chastity, and Obedience create the virtues of Poverty. Poverty is also humility. We are speaking of paving the way to the power of the Spirit, not necessarily of worldly goods.

But really He says, search first for the "Kingdom of Heaven" and that these things will be added to you.

When we have achieved spiritual poverty, then Jesus the Divine Son will bless us in His Father's name, and so will come to you the Words of Jesus, "Blessed are the poor in Spirit, for they shall see God."

When we say that Humility is poverty we are realizing the Divine Truth that those that are humble are truly poor in spirit. For humility and poverty say of themselves, "we are in each other as the Father is in the Son." Thus we can better understand that verse in Revelation which says, "I am the Alpha and Omega, the beginning and the End." Also the scripture which says, "that which shall be last shall be first."

In order to have a better understanding of our lesson on blessing read the 5th, 6th, and 7th Chapter of the Gospel of St. Matthew, the Sermon on the Mount, which teaches you the power of blessings.

The scriptures declare unto us in the first Psalm, "Blessed is he who walketh not in the path of the ungodly, nor standeth in the way of sinners, nor is seated in the council of the scornful." For he shall be as a tree planted by the water, he shall not be moved.

MASTERSHIP

When these requirements are met and the Blessing is obtained, the Disciple becomes the Master and his faith shall not waver. He then becomes the Tree of Life and the Lamb of God.

The blessed Master, or shall we say the blessed disciple who becomes Master, can then present himself faultless before God's glory with exceeding joy.

He will not stumble nor falter but have great victory. The blessing cannot be obtained before the transformation of Mind and brain can be made possible.

The 12th Chapter of Romans and the 2nd and 4th Chapter of Philippians, also the 4th, 5th and 6th Chapter of Ephesians can come to pass.

Let Us Prepare For The Great Blessing.

The above is accomplished only by setting our affections on things Eternal. The Key is found in the Gospel of St. Matthew Chapter 6, wherein Jesus says, "Do not lay-up treasure on Earth, where moths, rusts, etc." Verses 19-24. Following this Key, we shall open up the Blessing. For Jesus says, "Where your treasure is, there will your heart be also." God will bless us if we will comply to His Law and Order.

Remember this one saying, it should be in front of you at all times: "If Your Eye Be Single, Your Whole Body Will Be Full Of Light."

Lesson 3: Light • Life • Love

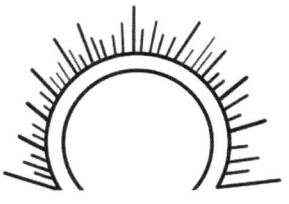

LIGHT ONE

Many people have written reams and reams of words about this subject. Yet they have failed to even begin to delve into it.

Man has based all of his work in studying the workings of the mind from a purely selfish way. Meaning that he has had the nerve to think that the mind within him is his personal possession. However, we of this age know better.

In studying the mind, we are studying the working out of the creative forces and energies of the universe existent in man. This is what man has for generations called God. The empirical mind out of which all things come and to which all things return.

To try and study the entire workings of this mind, would, to say the least, take a lifetime and then you would only learn how much you in reality don't know.

In this lesson we will endeavor to study how man uses or misuses this mind in relationship to himself. This, of course, opens the first point of conjecture. Man, who are you? Where do you come from? And what is your function in this plane of manifestation?

The first thing to take into consideration is that until you've seen the Self or the God Being within you, you don't know your Self.

Man has for over millions of years lived in this plane. Although the earliest forms of man were not as functional as this particular form is. But then it was not as necessary as it is now. For in the beginning man lived very simply. He used the earth to its fullest by living off the plants and animals put there for that purpose. He was very joyous and lived a long lifetime in peace. There was at this time no dis-ease. For man in the simplicity of his own nature did not then nor does he now need to think. He needs only to listen and follow the guidance of the inner man.

But man is the problem child of the universe. He was given the power to create and to think. For in reality, your every thought is a creation in its own right. Man, once he began to think, found out that he could no longer live in peace with those around him for he began to think himself better than his neighbor. This was then against his own nature.

Because, in the beginning, he did live in peace within his own being and with the Creator. There is an easy way to say this in saying that he knew God and lived in complete faith and his every need would be filled. This man can and should use this knowing today in this time of turmoil and havoc. For it is logical to assume that if man's thinking caused all this dis-ease in the world, it should be simple enough to clean it up by having man stop thinking.

This is proven scientifically by men who have for prolonged periods of time studied man when he is resting comfortably. The metabolism of the body smooths out and a calm and peaceful air falls upon the room. Now, mind you, I did not say asleep but in a state of relaxation. In the finding of one's own inner being, this is of primary importance. The ability to sit in a state of refined relaxation or rest. This allows the functions of the body to slow down. In doing this you will find, if you are interested in trying it, that you will stop the process of thinking.

When you have really stopped the thinking process, look within. You've given up enough to let the Light shine in. Then you can answer the age-old question of, "Who am I?"

Man is a cell in the Mind of God. That means that man has the opportunity and the access to all the intelligence in the Mind from which he was created.

You see by the grace of God all things of this or any other plane to which you wish to look to. In order to accomplish this you must first find the inner man. This is accomplished by seeking the Light. By this, I don't mean the light of understanding, or other various things that man in his own hypocrisy has called this Light. I mean just what is stated here, Light!! It is very simple, before you can see something you must first have Light. This is the presence made manifest in your own being of the power of God. Then, by consciously using this Light or power (whichever you prefer) you can see the Self. That part of God that dwells within you.

Science calls this a pipe dream and refuses to acknowledge this as true. But they agree that when a man is still there is an increase of light around the body. They know that there is a field of electrical impulse around the body.

Schools of enlightenment have known and taught for years that an aura exists around the human body. This, in reality, is Light.

You can by using your brain control this flow of energy and Light so that rather than it being continually cast out it is turned in. But only by the silencing of the mind because that way you have created a vacuum which this Light can fill. There is a law existent in the universe that is stated like this: Nature abhors a vacuum, thus it is filled.

To assure that you fill this vacuum with the pure Light of Christ, it is necessary to cleanse the field of energy around the body of the dark and/or evil thoughts which emanate from within you. To accomplish this it takes one who can see the field and know what it is within you that needs to come out in order that this can take place.

For, as was stated in the beginning of this lesson, man came from the mind of the Creator. Therefore, man in his essence is but a part of this mind made manifest. This being so he is but a thought pattern in that mind. When man will use that energy he is endowed with to cleanse this pattern of all impurity that was acquired by his not controlling what filled that pattern, he will be in a constant state of illumination.

To attain this state of being it is necessary to renounce the thinking or not thinking of those around you and to take conscious control of your atmosphere. To keep out thoughts that are not in accordance with the workings of your being.

We advise that a man not try this on his own for the simple reason that he does not know himself yet. Nor does he know what his function is yet with regard to creation. This is not made known to him until he has begun to work with God in peace and in understanding of the world around him by becoming that Self.

Therefore, it is advisable for a man to take a Master Teacher. This means one who does know and has absolute control of his being and of the world around him. These beings are more of God than of flesh for they are in continual communion with the inner man and with the forces of the universe. This is not to say that they are not in a flesh body, for some of them are. It is possible to receive instruction from the higher mind or rather from a higher plane of existence, through continual prayer and a conscientious striving to know. Though often they will merely guide you to a teacher on this plane for they have their function on that plane to attend to also.

Man's first duty is to find this teacher and then to be obedient to whatever this teacher asks him to do, bearing in mind at all times if he knew he would not be seeking a teacher to guide him to his Illumination. For all the things that you are asked to do are not always something that one considers pertaining to his illumination at all. But then the teacher will merely smile and say to you, "Just who the hell are you to tell me what is best for you." Remember, he does not need you as much as you need him. In fact most of the time these beings could find other means of service to be doing.

Now that we have taken the first step in starting our road toward the Illumination, we are ready to take another step. Once you have cleansed your mind of thinking what the other guy is thinking, you must cleanse the body of the results of all that thinking. This is accomplished by eating a well-balanced diet and by the continuance of sound thinking.

The most valuable thing in this cleansing process is to keep the mind only on that which you are doing. Therefore, you must be doing something. Work! Working on jobs of almost anything that will tear your mind off what you are learning and thereby letting them manifest in your being to replace that which you were thinking that caused you to need this teacher.

Once you have done this you are then ready to begin the process of looking within for the Light. During all the preceding time you have been learning to relax. Now you must learn to meditate. Most teachers will tell you to meditate when you first go into training. But if you're honest with yourself now you will know that you are merely relaxing and often fall asleep instead of meditating.

After a while of actual meditating you will feel the influx of power that comes each time. What you are actually doing is letting go of your thinking entirely thereby making yourself accessible to be filled with the Light and the Peace of God.

When you feel that power within you and you cannot find a way to get away from it as most people try to do and then finally just let go you will see that Light. Then you will begin to know where you come from. As you begin to work with the power of you, that is the inner you, you will know why you are here and what your function is.

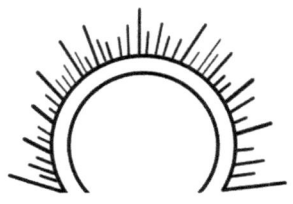

LIGHT TWO

As we begin to have a deeper conception of God, the musty veil of darkness is drawn to one side and destroyed by the divine light and illumination of Christ.

The Christ Light is the LIGHT which illumines every man, bringing into focus the desires, thoughts, and ideas of the Creator.

Appropriate work calls forth this phenomenon, the true Light which enlightens every man coming into the world. Christ also states that this Light is the Light of man.

Scientifically speaking, light is a form of radiant energy that acts upon the retina of the eye. This energy is transmitted at a velocity of about 186,000 miles per second, by wave-like motion, or vibratory motion. This is its relative speed in its travel through our earth's atmosphere.

This Light is mainly from the Sun of God, that which causes things to grow. Light moves at a very high rate of vibration.

The presence of Lights within the body and around it is a state which is congruent to divinity and activates illumination or a Christ state. It activates spiritual sight. It causes us to know and see and understand the things of God.

Jesus said, "You are the Light of the world." (Matthew 5:14) A city cannot be hid. Jesus is telling us that our spirituality is the very life of nature, that the Light power of our magnetic structure demonstrates the force and power of God to all the Universe.

Being the Light of the world, we must demonstrate the Christ to all beings. This is truly the Light which enlightens every man coming into the world.

Jesus said, "If your eye be single, your body will be full of light," meaning if all of your vision, your understanding, your knowledge be one in spirit, then that great Light of Christ will surround you with its loving power and keep you healthy, wealthy, and wise.

Practice seeing this Light by using the knowledge given to you in the lesson on Meditation.

In Paul's experiences, Acts 9, it is recorded that suddenly a Light flashed from heaven, he fell to the ground and he heard a voice. Paul had received the first degree of illumination. His mind started to become spiritual and he was now born of the Light.

This Light is what is needed in us, then all other things in our rate of vibration will begin to glow and grow.

For light, even Spiritual Light, is issued forth from the Solar ray, and it is this ray that gives life to the planet Earth.

By understanding this we understand how God spiritualizes the Earth through His perfect manifestation, Man, who in reality is the image and likeness of the Creator GOD.

In first John is given this message, "We have heard from Him, and proclaim to you, that God is light, and in Him there is no darkness at all."

If we say we are in fellowship with him and we walk in darkness we lie and the truth is not in us.

Walking in Light is walking with God in that we are in time with the infinite Mind, our Father-Mother Creator. The Word of Power, the spiritual Word, is our Light and lamp.

King David mentions this fact in the most scientific book of the Bible, Psalms 119, where he states, "Thy Word is a lamp unto my feet, and Light unto my path."

If we follow this Light and become children of the Light we shall have fellowship one with another.

It is the purpose of this School to help you find Love, Light, and Truth through the teachings of Jesus Christ and all Masters and Saints, and especially through the physical sciences, in correlation with the Holy Covenants of all the world religions.

John concludes, as do we, with these words, "And we know the Son of God has come and has given us understanding to know Him who is true, and we are in Him who is true, in His Son, Jesus Christ. This is the true God and eternal life."

Now students find the Light. Share it with humanity. Watch, and pray.

Amen.

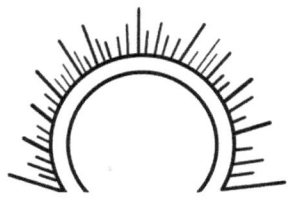

LIGHT THREE

NEW TESTAMENT

Matthew

4:16	which sat in darkness have seen a great light
5:14	Ye are the light of the world
5:15	Neither do men light a candle
5:15	gives light to all who are in
5:16	Let your light so shine before men
6:22	The light of the body is the eye
6:22	thy whole body shall be full of light
6:23	the light that be in thee be darkness
10:27	In darkness, that speak ye of light
11:30	yoke is easy, and my burden is light
17: 2	his raiment was white as the light
22: 5	they made light of it and went their
24:29	and the moon shall not give her light

Mark

13:24	and the moon shall not give her light

Luke

1:79	give light to them that sit in darkness
2:32	a light to lighten the Gentiles

8:16	they which enter in may see the light
11:33	they which come in may see light
11:34	the light of the body is the eye
11:34	the whole body is full of light
11:35	the light which is in thee be not
11:36	the whole body therefore be full of light
11:36	dark, the whole shall be full of light
11:36	a candle doth give thee light
12: 3	darkness shall be heard in the light
15: 8	doth not light a candle, and sweep the
16: 8	wiser than the children of light

John

1: 4	and the life was the light of men
1: 5	and the light shineth in the darkness
1: 7	witness, to bear witness of the light
1: 8	He was not that Light, but was sent
1: 8	was sent to bear witness to the Light
1: 9	That was the true Light, which
3:19	that light is come into the world, and
3:19	men loved the darkness rather than the light
3:20	one that doeth evil hateth the light
3:20	neither cometh to the light, lest his
3:21	that doeth truth cometh to the light
5:35	was a burning and a shining light
5:35	for a season to rejoice in his light
8:12	saying, I am the light of the world
8:12	but shall have the light of life
9: 5	the world, I am the light of the world
11: 9	because he seeth the light of the world
11:10	because there is no light in him
12:35	Yet a little while is the light with you
12:35	Walk while ye have the light, lest

12:36 While ye have the light, believe in the light

12:36 that ye may be the children of light

12:46 I am come a light into the world, that

Acts

9: 3 round about him a light from heaven

12: 7 him, and a light shined in the prison

13:47 set thee to be a light to the Gentiles

16:29 he called for a light, and sprang in

22: 6 shone from heaven a great light round

22: 9 that were with him indeed saw the light

22:11 could not see for the glory of that light

26:13 I saw in the way, a light from heaven

26:18 to turn them from darkness to light

26:23 and should show light unto the people

Romans

2:19 light of them which are in darkness

13:12 and let us put on the armor of light

I Corinthians

4: 5 will bring the light to hidden things

II Corinthians

4: 4 light of the glorious gospel of Christ

4: 6 commanded the light to shine out of

4: 6 to give the light of the knowledge of

4:17 our light, affliction, which is but for a

6:14 communion hath light with darkness

11:14 is transformed into an angel of light

Ephesians

5: 8 but now are ye light in the Lord

5: 8   walk as children of light

5:13   are made manifest by the light: for

5:13   whatsoever doth make manifest is light

5:14   and Christ shall give thee light

Colossians

1:12   the inheritance of the saints is light

I Thessalonians

5: 5   Ye are the children of light, and

I Timothy

6:16   dwelling in the light which no man

II Timothy

1:10   brought life and immortality to light

I Peter

2: 9   of darkness into his marvelous light

II Peter

1:19   as unto a light that shineth in a dark

I John

1: 5   declare unto you, that God is light

1: 7   if we walk in the light, as he is that Light

2: 8   past and the true light now shineth

2: 9   He that saith that he is in light, and

2:10   loveth his brother abideth in the light

ILLUMINATED

Hebrews

10:32   in which, after ye were illuminated, ye

REGENERATED

Matthew

19:28   the regeneration which the Son of man shall

Titus

3: 5   he saved us by the washing of regeneration

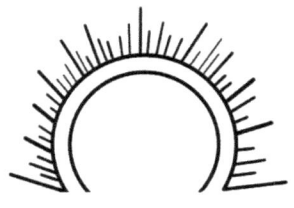

Life One

Of all the Bible teachings the most misunderstood is life. When someone says life the first thing a person thinks of is this world and the things they have encountered while they were in this world.

To a carpenter life would consist of him getting up at a certain time each morning, eating, and going to the job, finishing his work in the evening, going home, having his dinner meal, and then having an evening of TV or something of that sort.

To most people life is a combination of experiences which lead to their understanding of other people and other places. When in reality this isn't life at all, this is their understanding.

Life is movement of power within your own body. Life is a force and not concepts or understanding.

Jesus said in the Bible if you lose your life you shall have eternal life. When a person gives up the idea of his having his personal time, his personal understanding of things, he lets it all go and gives himself totally over to the Creator. Then he will feel the surge of power run through his whole being, then he'll begin to live of the Creator.

The great Christ, the Son (Sun) of God, is the source of all life. The Christ gives life to the animal kingdom, to the vegetable kingdom, to man, and to all other kingdoms. Plants definitely have life for they grow and they propagate themselves but they do not think, they do not build their own mental concepts, so life is not a mental concept.

It is the living, moving, dynamic power and force running through your body without thought, without concept.

The biggest trouble man has is his own opinions. He will, with his half-blinded physical eyes, see the world and proclaim his opinion on things he only half sees and he will label these things scientific facts.

Life is universal because it has one great source, therefore, all things that contain life are truly linked together. When you let go of your opinions of a race, a creed, or color and look into or at another man without labeling him with any of your biasness or narrow-mindedness and just take him as he is, you will feel, see, and know that you two aren't as separate as you feel and look. This does not mean that you are him and he is you. This is the explanation of unity and brotherhood of man that, as cells within the body, are closely knit together. So you and all of mankind are closely knit together through the Christ.

St. John 10:9, "I am the door; by me if any man enter in, he shall be saved, and shall go in and out and find pasture. But the thief cometh not but for to steal, and to kill, and to destroy: I am come that they might have life, and that they might have it more abundantly."

The great Christ permeates the earth with light, life, and love through the Lord Jesus. Jesus is the channel of life for the earth. Man must become conscious of this reality for until man becomes conscious of this he will remain dead.

In the Bible Jesus talked about the living dead. These are the people who walk and think, but who have not the power of the Christ running through their bodies. For it is this force and power that regenerates your physical body.

Due to the lack of life-force and power man is plagued by the disease of old age. For old age is deterioration of the physical body due to the lack of the life-force.

He who knows God and knows our Lord Jesus Christ will never grow old because he will have the life-force running through his body continually which will keep him healthy, wealthy, young, and wise.

Tree of Life, Volume One

The teachings of Jesus Christ are real and those who do a lot of talk, their fruits you can see by the shape of their physical body. If they are growing old they haven't known Jesus or the Great Creator, or that would never have taken place.

LIFE

For what man looks at these rolling spheres
After through life he has tread this Earth in pairs
And thinks to himself all the time that he has been away,
Away in mind, when life I was looking to express.

Another body I sought
That I might the Creator's works have wrought
In the dayless, nightless march of time
Tis but the following out of the pattern in your God's mind
Science but knows the things it finds
On the narrow band of the spectrum line.

But the mystic scientist, when his light shows strong
Seldom upon a path goes wrong.
For the range of his spectrum is wide and bold
And its evolution can be foretold
Man, Oh Man, the crawling ant
With the power so great, so small

According to his understanding of it all
Reach out and observe these moving orbs
For as you do in your brother, you'll become absorbed.

For thus we have but one Law to work,
Be it English, Russian, or Turk
When man creates, he is enfolded
In GOD'S great world of work unfolded.

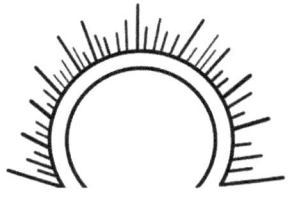

LIFE TWO

Life is the Force of Spirit. Life is the Divine Emanation.

LIFE IS GOD IN ACTION.

In Genesis, Chapter 2 verse 7, "then the Lord God formed man out of dust from the ground and breathed into his nostrils the breath of life, and man became a Living Being."

The Creator gives unto every creature this divine emanation, to prove His existence and Manifestation. It is through Life that the Word becomes manifest into flesh and dwells amongst us.

Life also has three stages of Manifestation, as does every other facet of Spiritual existence. These three stages are formation, growth, and perfection.

The Lord formed man from the dust of the Earth. The dust of the Earth symbolized the unmanifested Word of God, the idea.

The creator forms the idea in Universal Mind. Universal Mind, the unmanifested and the dust of the earth, are all one and the same thing. They are all form, the first stage of formation.

The breath of God is Spirit. It is the office of the breath of God as Spirit to create a pattern which can be filled in. Once the pattern is created man enters into life, becomes a living soul, and the stage of growth has been achieved.

The second chapter of Genesis goes on to tell us that our Creator the Lord God planted a garden in Eden and there He put man that He had formed. Eden represents Nirvana, the highest state of Universal Mind.

The Garden planted there represents our heavenly existence, our own heavenly life in that state of mind.

Genesis tells us that the Lord God our Creator made to grow every tree that is pleasant to sight and good for food. Trees represent and symbolize the many ways of life in which the individual manifestation of man can express itself.

Genesis also tells us that these trees or ways of life were pleasant and good, both to our sight and for food. Providing to us who understand that all the ways of life are to be visualized and are to be partaken of each in accordance to the Individual's Desire.

Genesis tells us that the Tree of Life is there. The Tree of Life symbolizes the main- stream of existence or the unlimited source of pure Spirit—the Truth and the Self.

The Tree of Knowledge of Good and Evil also grew there. This tree represented duality. The Tree of Knowledge of Good and Evil was purely symbolism. It was male and female.

Man had only just arrived at this stage of growth. He was unable to eat of this fruit in his current state of mind, the state of mind that he was in at the time of the Garden incident.

Therefore, the Lord Creator forbade him to be so tempted by the serpentine force of uncontrollable desire to attain. Man violated the Law of nature and unnaturally created a false image of himself because man had not grown to perfection and attained Lordship. He was unable to control his creation. This was the original sin.

In this new age of the Lord of Life, the Great Christ Power, man has grown to perfection and is now ready to dominate life. We stand by the threshold of pure life, not bound by handicap nor by inhibitions and fears. We walk in Liberty of the Christ and demonstrate through Truth, which makes us free. We are told that there is a river in Eden which waters that Garden. This river is the Spiritual Life. It waters the highest state of Mind in which God dwells.

The river was divided into four rivers. The four rivers plus the original river equals five. We are told about gold being forced into the Garden, Genesis 2 verse 11. Gold is the materialization of God's pure idea. Gold symbolically represents man, when the alchemist says he turns base metals he is in reality saying that he is forming man out of the dust of the earth and making him a living soul.

He is also transferring him out of the Kingdom of darkness into the Kingdom of God's dear Sons.

We are told in the gospel of John 1:4-5, "In him was Life, and the Life was the light of men. The light shines in the darkness, and the darkness has not overcome it."

Meaning that in him there is life and Life is also Light. After the divine alchemist the Creator has formed the Golden Force of God. That Golden Sun of God became the Life of the World. He became that power which brings forth many other sons through right understanding of the Self and the Self oneness with Life.

There is only one life and one Self, the primordial force for good. This primary force for good, infinitely indwelling, full of divine Wisdom and Knowledge is incapable of transgressing the Law, for the Law is part of its nature.

Jesus Christ was the first-begotten of many brethren, the divine Son of God. The Scriptures say in him was Life. He is a personification of divine life. He transmitted that Life to us through the divine bloodstream of Spirit.

That is why scripture declares in John 1 verse 7, "He came for testimony to bear witness to the Light, that all might believe through him." The blood of Jesus Christ is the Divine Life of Spirit, not any of the denser forces.

As it has been related before this life is incapable of sin. Therefore, we to whom this Life has been imparted are also incapable of sinning, because we are partakers of his blood, his Life.

Now we can rightfully understand St. John 10, verse 10. The thief comes only to steal and kill and destroy. I came that they may have Life and have it abundantly. Let us not forget we are partakers of the Father-Mother God, divine Love and be anointed of water and spirit, partaking of a new Divine Life.

Using the Law through form and pattern let us be forward and grow into perfection and stand fast in that liberty wherewith Christ has set us free. Otherwise that liberty is divine life in yoke of bondage.

For those yokes of bondage are in reality false ideas and images created by the only devil that actually exists—Mass Mind.

THE KEY

The center of life is neither in thought
nor in feeling nor in will, nor even in
consciousness, so far as it thinks, feels
or wishes.

For Real Truth may have been penetrated by a
man and possessed in all these ways, and
escaped us still.

Deeper even than consciousness there is our
being itself, our very substance, our nature.

Only those truths which have entered into this
last region, which have become ourselves, which
become spontaneous and involuntary, a part of the
instinctive and unconscious.

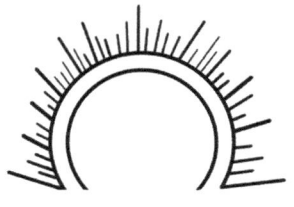

LOVE ONE

LOVE is a source of power though it of itself has no power. Love is the reciprocal action of give and take. Love creates a vacuum that necessitates reaction. Remember, Nature abhors a vacuum, but Nature does not repel love. Nature merely says that if we love, we must be loved.

The Creator naturally loves his creation, and this love keeps the creation satisfied in all of its many facets of Life.

Jesus said, "If you love me, keep my commandments." Now we see that the requirement of loving Jesus is the keeping of his commandments. All of his words and sayings are his commandments. As we grow in Love we automatically shall keep every one of them.

THE LAW OF LOVE

Love is a part of the Law, the same Law that runs the Universe. Love is a divine attribute having its origin in the act of creation. The creation must automatically manifest it since the creation is nothing more than the materialized substance of the Creator.

Therefore, Truth says divine Love always is, always has, and divine Love always will supply our every need.

Love is functional in the Law. It is the generator by which Law works, as we have said, the source of Power.

RIVER OF LIFE

Love is also the River of Life that flows from the throne of God.

Without Love we cannot see God. For we have to reach to God, the act of Love, to see the Creator as the Creator functions through love action.

LOVE — BIBLICAL REFERENCES

In Psalms 31, verse 23, "Love the Lord, all you his saints! The Lord preserves the faithful, but abundantly requites him who acts haughtily. Because it is the Lord of Love who preserves the faithful."

In John 15, verse 17, "Greater love has no man than this, that a man lay down his life for his friends." In loving one another we love the Creator for the Creator is present in each and every one of us.

Love necessitates giving and sharing without hope of reward, as we see in John 3, verse 16: "For God so loved the world that he gave his only Son, that whoever believed in him should not perish, but have eternal life."

In John 4, verse 19, "We love, because He first loved us." We see here that our love is the result of the Creator's Love and the manifestation of all our love is nothing more than the effect of God Loving all His creation.

In Romans 8, verse 35, "Who shall separate us from the Love of Christ? Shall tribulation, or distress, or persecution, or famine, or nakedness, or peril, or sword?" Paul desired to know who was able to separate us from the Love of God. The only answer to that question is we ourselves. Because we are more than conquerors through Him that loved us, and neither death, nor Life, nor angels, nor things present, nor things to come, nor powers, nor height, nor depth, nor anything else in all Creation will be able to separate us from the Love of God in Christ Jesus our Lord.

In Romans 13, verse 10, "Love does no wrong to a neighbor, therefore, Love is the fulfilling of the Law."

The night is far gone, the day is at hand. Let us then cast off the works of darkness and put on the armor of Light and we will demonstrate Love.

In I John 4, verse 18, "There is no fear in love, but perfect love casts out fear. For fear has to do with punishment, and he who fears is not perfected in love."

In Galatians 5, verse 22, "But the fruit of the Spirit is Love, joy, peace, patience, kindness, goodness, faithfulness."

In Ephesians I, verse 5, "He destined us in love to be his sons through Jesus Christ, according to the purpose of His will."

In I Corinthians 13, verse 13, "So faith, hope, love abide, these three, but the greatest of these is Love."

In I Corinthians 13, verse 1, "If I speak in the tongues of men and of angels, but have not Love, I am a noisy gong, or a clanging cymbal."

In I Corinthians 8, verse 3, "But if one loves God, one is known by Him." Here again that love of God, he has knowledge of God.

LOVE THROUGH KNOWING

Love of the Creation gives us knowledge of the Creation. Love of man gives us knowledge of man. It is spiritually correct to say that we cannot know anything without loving it. Love is a controlling factor. It restrains in many instances from doing damage to creation of God, and His Creation as seen in 2 Corinthians 5, verse 14: "for the love of Christ controls us, because we are convinced that one has died for all, therefore, all have died."

ITS VALUE

Truly Love is a thermostat and keeps our vehicle of expression well under control.

Let us pray for Love, let us seek Love, and when we receive it, let us exercise it, let us hold fast to it.

For it is a precious stone, a valuable part of our functioning here.

Jesus said in John 15, verse 5, "As the Father has loved me, so have I loved you; abide in my love." So Jesus stated that he loved mankind in the same respect and regard and in the same manner as the Creator loved it. This is the secret of true loving.

It is not something that is simply there to be used but it is something we ourselves create through proper use of Universal Mind.

GOD LOVE

The Creator creates the creation, and in turn the creation continually recreates the Creator.

This is the Father-Mother-God having divine activity of give and take within its own androgynous Being. This is Love expressed cosmically.

In reality this is what man and woman experience sexually on the individual level.

This, too, is an expression of the divine Will of the Father.

Whether it is expressed physically, mentally, spiritually, or materially, it is never sinful, but always virtuous.

Our prayer for you is that you allow the Love of God to be shed abroad in your heart in perfect peace.

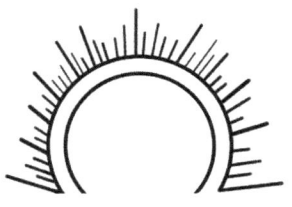

LOVE TWO

St. Matthew

5:44 But I say unto you, love your enemies, bless them that curse you, do good to them that hate you, and pray for them which despitefully use you, and persecute you.

5:46 For if ye love them which love you, what reward have ye? Do not even the publicans the same?

19:19 Honour thy father and thy mother; and thou shalt love thy neighbor as thyself.

22:37 Jesus said unto him, Thou shalt love the Lord thy God with all thy heart, and with all thy soul, and with all thy mind.

22:39 And the second is like unto it, Thou shalt love thy neighbor as thyself.

24:12 And because iniquity shall abound, the love of many shall wax cold.

St. Mark

12:38 And he said unto them in his doctrine, Beware of scribes, which love to go in long clothing, and love salutation in the marketplaces.

St. Luke

6:35   But love ye your enemies, and do good, and lend hoping for nothing again; and your reward shall be great, and ye shall be the children of the Highest: for He is kind unto the unthankful, and to the evil.

7:41   There was a certain creditor who had two debtors: the one owed five hundred pence, and the other fifty.

7:42   And when they had nothing to pay, he frankly forgave them both. Tell me, therefore, which of them will love him most?

11:42   But woe unto you, Pharisees! for ye tithe mint and rue and all manner of herbs and pass over judgment and the love of God: these ought ye to have done, and not to leave the other undone.

16:13   No servant can serve two masters; for either he will hate the one, and love the other: or else he will hold to the one, and despise the other. Ye cannot serve God and mammon.

St. John

8:42   Jesus said unto them, If God were your Father, ye would love me: for I proceeded forth and came from God: neither came I of myself, but he sent me.

10:17   Therefore, doth my Father love me, because I lay down my life, that I might take it again.

13:35   By this all men know that ye are my disciples, if ye have love to one another.

14:15   If ye love me, keep my commandments.

14:21   He that hath my commandments, and keepeth them, he it is that loveth me: and he that loveth me shall be loved of my Father, and I will love him, and will manifest myself to him.

5:19 If ye were of the world, the world would love his own: but because ye are not of the world, but I have chosen you out of the world, therefore the world hateth you.

21:15 So when they had dined, Jesus saith to Simon Peter, Simon, son of Jonas, lovest thou me more than these? He saith unto him, Yea, Lord; thou knowest that I love thee. He saith unto him, Feed my lambs.

Romans

5: 5 And hope maketh not ashamed; because the love of God is shed abroad in our hearts by the Holy Ghost, which is given unto us.

5: 8 But God commendeth his love toward us, in that, while we were yet sinners, Christ died for us.

8:39 Nor height, nor depth, nor any other creature, shall be able to separate us from the love of God, which is in Christ Jesus.

12: 9 Let love be without dissimulation. Abhor that which is evil; cleave to that which is good.

12:10 Be kindly affectioned one to another with brotherly love; in honor preferring one another.

13:10 Love worketh no ill to his neighbor: therefore, love is the fulfilling of the law.

I Corinthians

8: 3 But if any man love God, the same is known of him.

II Corinthians

2: 8 Wherefore I beseech you that ye would confirm your love towards him.

5:14 For the love of Christ constraineth us; because we thus judge, that if one died for all, then were all dead.

8:24 Wherefore shew ye to them, and before the churches, the proof of your love, and of our boasting on your behalf.

Galatians

5: 6 For in Jesus Christ neither circumcision availeth anything, nor uncircumcision; but faith which worketh by love.

5:13 For, brethren, ye have been called unto liberty; only use not liberty for an occasion to the flesh, but by love serve one another.

5:22 But the fruit of the Spirit is love, joy, peace, long-suffering, gentleness, goodness, faith.

Ephesians

1: 4 According as he hath chosen us in him before the foundation of the world, that we should be holy and without blame before him in love.

2: 4 But God who is rich in mercy, for his great love wherewith he loved us.

5:25 Husbands, love your wives, even as Christ also loved the church, and gave himself for it.

Philippians

2: 2 Fulfill ye my joy, that ye be like-minded, having the same love, being of one accord, of one mind.

I Thessalonians

5: 8 But let us, who are of the day, be sober, putting on the breastplate of faith and love; and for a helmet, the hope of salvation.

II Thessalonians

2: 9-10 Even him, whose coming is after the working of Satan with all power and signs and lying wonders, and with all deceivableness of unrighteousness in them that perish; because they received not the love of truth, that they might be saved.

I Timothy

6:10 For the love of money is the root of all evil; which while some coveted after they have erred from the faith, and pierced themselves through with many sorrows.

II Timothy

4: 8 Henceforth there is laid up for me a crown of righteousness, which the Lord, the righteous judge, shall give me at that day, and not to me only, but unto all them also that love his appearing.

Hebrews

6:10 For God is not unrighteous to forget your work and labour of love, which ye have shewed toward his name, in that ye have ministered to the saints, and do minister.

I John

2: 5 But whoso keepeth his word, in him verily is the love of God perfected: hereby know we that we are in him.

2:15 Love not the world, neither the things that are in the world. If any man love the world, the love of the Father is not in him.

3: 1 Behold what manner of love the Father hath bestowed upon us, that we should be called the sons of God: therefore, that world knoweth us not, because it knew him not.

3:18 My little children, let us not love in word, neither in tongue; but in deed and in truth.

4: 7 Beloved, let us love one another; for love is of God; and every one that loveth, is born of God and knoweth God.

4: 9　In this was manifested the love of God toward us, because that God sent his only begotten Son into the world, that we might live through him.

4:17　Herein is our love made perfect, that we may have boldness in the day of judgment: because as he is, so are we in this world.

LOVED

John

3:16　For God so loved the world, that he gave his only begotten Son, that whosoever believeth in him should not perish, but have everlasting life.

LOVETH

Hebrews

12: 6　For whom the Lord loveth he chasteneth, and scourgeth every son whom he receiveth.

I John

2:10　He that loveth his brother abideth in the light, and there is none occasion of stumbling in him.

Lesson 4: Spiritual Body • Soul • Flesh Body

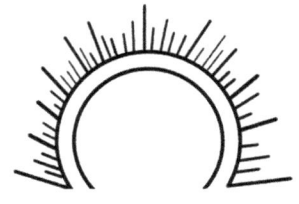

LESSON 4

SPIRITUAL BODY ONE

Among the many vehicles of expressions used by the life force the most important is the spiritual body of man. For it is the preparation of this body for the coming of the Christ in your dense physical body.

I Corinthians 15: 42-46

So it is with the resurrection of the dead. What is sown is perishable, what is raised is imperishable. It is sown in dishonor; it is raised in glory. It is sown in weakness; it is raised in power. It is sown a physical body; it is raised a spiritual body. If there is a physical body, there is also a spiritual body. Thus it is written, "the first man Adam became a living being." The last Adam became a life-giving spirit. But it is not the spiritual which is first, but the physical, and then the spiritual. The first man was from the earth, a man of dust: the second man is from heaven. As was the man of dust, so are those who are of the dust. And as is the man of heaven, so are those who are of heaven.

We call the spiritual body the first foundation or the primary body, because it is the body which holds the visible, physical, chemical, and material matter together, giving us our visible form of man. The spiritual body is the cover of the Spark of Life or SELF.

Thus it is that man has three bodies: Physical, Spiritual, and the Soul body which is around the Self. These are referred to in the Bible as Mental Body, Terrestrial Body, and Celestial Body.

As the Spiritual Body descends and accepts cosmic energy it increases both in density and intensity. The Divine Spark within it begins to evolve and the memory of the Soul starts forming a physical body as it approaches incarnation, physical birth.

As the Spiritual Body evolves and the Power of the Sun (The Christ) is accepted into it, it enlarges and becomes less dense. The Spiritual Body, like all other bodies, goes through stages of growth and formation towards absolute and perfect form. The Spiritual Body is symbolized by the circle and a dot. This symbol is part of the three basic symbolic forms in our present embodiment. This is introduced as part of the basic thinking in this School and the simplicity of the great reality of the Mystic Father, Son, and Holy Spirit.

The dot within the circle represents the Divine Spark. The circle around it represents the emanation of the body that St. Paul called the Divine Spark, the life-giving spirit or the lost atom.

This is the understanding of Adam and Atom. In the case of the lost Atom, they are symbolizing the same, one scientific, one spiritual or religious.

Scriptures declare the lost Adam to be Jesus Christ. We believe these sayings represent the Divinity of Man and will be covered more in the New Age.

Paul says in I Corinthians 15:51-52:

"Lo, I tell you a mystery. We shall not all sleep, but we shall all be changed, in a moment, in the twinkling of an eye, at the last trumpet."

We are being changed in the twinkling of an eye and the realization starts in the Spiritual Body.

The Divine Spark (the primal logistic meaning of Logos, logistic force, called by the Ancient Mystics Fiat) burns its way through the Spiritual Body, and removes all semblance of dross till it amalgamates Itself with it. The Spark of Life and the body become one.

When this happens on an individual basis we say that the Self is found. The seeing consciousness of the vehicle permits the individual to actually see the Self and the radiant being. The finding of the Self is what the Scriptures declare as the Great Awakening, the last trumpet. This is one individual at a time.

Through the Spiritual Body the Perishable Nature of man becomes the Imperishable Nature of God.

So Paul says the corruption must put on incorruption, because this is an immutable law of the Spiritual Body.

Each of the three bodies have their own laws which function in them, but are coalesced in the Law of Cause and Effect.

The first man Adam was like the awakening, only in a state of formation. As this man grew in knowledge of the God Self the physical vehicle at this stage was strong enough to contain much of the Divine Spark and its emulation.

So we have allegorically the fall of Adam.

The Spiritual Body has the potential of tuning itself with other bodies and making itself one with them.

It is important to remember that God gives us a body as He chooses. That which He determines (God chooses) we call Karma. It is the effectual reaction of the law of cause and effect. And thus we call it God's Choice because the Father is the basic or causeless cause.

Scriptures declare that Christ shall be made alive and that a quickening of the Spirit takes place. This is made possible only through the Spiritual Body.

Thus in each incarnation the Spiritual Body grows stronger. The Spiritual Body provides food for the inward growth for the other bodies making them inter-dependent upon each other.

The Spiritual Body is responsible for the care of all things contained in all three bodies.

In the next lesson we shall deal with the Soul.

Please read and analyze the 15th Chapter of I Corinthians (KJV). Note the Spiritual insight it conveys to us. It will help you to understand the Mysteries in Christ.

Peace Be Unto You,
As Your Teacher Is With You!

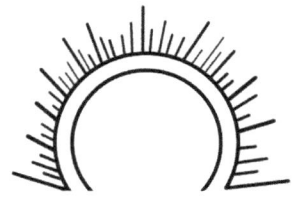

LESSON 4
SPIRITUAL BODY TWO

L et us approach the understanding of the Spiritual Body by putting together a series of parts, so to speak, different phases of life that will manifest the vehicle and its reality. Basically let us understand that when we use the word "spiritual body" we are talking about an electrical matrix which really exists, even though most people do not see it with their physical eyes. But there are many things in science of medicine and the experience of surgeons which go to show the existing function and manifestation of the spiritual body and its work through the physical.

One of the things which is quite evident in various forms of healing, such as medicine and electro-therapy, is that the physical body often-times makes its greatest recovery after therapy has been stopped. This shows that there is some agent other than the applied therapy functioning in order to bring this about. It is not only a potent but an intelligent force and pattern working upon the diseased or depraved part needing the healing.

First let us relate to the Self, for first and foremost is the Self, which lays within the Spiritual Body but whose form reflects through the physical. We begin with the Self in trying to bring about the reality and knowledge of the Spiritual Body. The Self is surrounded by the Soul and it is through the record of the Soul and its memory that man, in his travels from life to life, is able to improve and change the physical archetype of the physical body. In this way the physical body may be adapted to the conditions of the world in which he is incarnating.

This Self and Soul are the eternal which we are now and always will be from century to century to the ends of time.

We must necessarily begin here at this point because it is the infinite relationship of man to God (our Creator) that when we have attained and acquired divine rights, raised ourselves and our vehicles to that level of reality, we will be both at and of it. This is our conformance with the first commandment to love the Lord God with all thy heart, with all thy Soul, with all thy being.

The Soul, which is the sheath around the Self, is the collective impressions of energy from the blood, or its vibration, which will fill in with our emotions, acts, deeds, and leave their karmic record in the Soul.

The Soul is that which brings to this body the form and pattern which we must follow in our future life and is impinged on the negative pole of the Self. For the Self is a cell in the body of the Father and shines forth into the physical vehicle and to everything around us. Thus every organ that we find manifest in the physical body, or vehicle, and in accordance with the strength and perfection of its function, tells us of the closeness we are manifesting with the rhythm of the universe and the basic form of the body which God created.

Therefore, when we manifest a weakness or imperfection in a physical organ, or human body, it tells us that in some way in the past we have broken down through misuse of this organ. Or, perhaps we never have gained mastery over the body. We may have even tried to separate ourselves from the basic form of Creation, or God, by cutting off the life force and reality from our spiritual body, or what is sometimes called the vital body. From this vital body flows the vital life force into the material world of the physical body, giving it impetus and manifesting life, movement, creation, and function. When an organ is not functioning properly you have broken down its potential normal strength, the electrical strength of the spiritual body.

Thus the molecular structure and cells are not functioning intelligently according to the intelligence of the form of the spiritual body. The spiritual body is perfect.

For example, if the liver is functioning poorly and we are not assimilating food properly then this means that the liver in the spiritual body and the psychic stuff from which it is made does not have the electrical strength to cause the physical organ to take care of its normal functions.

When a person receives the Light of Christ, the Illumination, the spiritual body of man becomes charged up. This is why, when he receives this, if he has any physical infirmities they will show up. This is also why you will call down the Light, the Spirit, upon the student when he has physical infirmities. They will increase the potential of the physical body where it is, one might say, under-charged. When these organs in the spiritual body are brought up to charge then any foreign pathology, infection, growth, so forth, will immediately start to be drawn out and destroyed because they are not part of the basic pattern of the spiritual body. In other words, broken up into electron particles and radiated out. The cellular structure of the physical body will reorganize itself to reflect the perfect pattern of the spiritual body and reabsorb the spiritual body's intelligence.

The spiritual body's intelligence consists of the nature of attraction, repulsion, adhesion and cohesion of its molecular parts. Some writers cover these various functional parts of healing force as being sentient energy. The intelligence reflected from the spiritual body determines how an organ functions through the reflex systems of nerves in the physical body and are merely the reflection of those in the spiritual body. Due to the fact that the true memory and operation of the physical being as a whole is in the mind of the Soul, it is re-associated to its perfect function, and thus a healing is perfected.

On the other hand, those things which the Bible terms as evil, not good, materialistic, destructive, selfish, and the violations of the Ten Commandments, or the two great commandments which the Master

Jesus gave us, these create a lower frequency of vibration and thus crystallize to a certain degree the density of the Soul energy. They do not permit the passing of the power, Light and cosmic vibration of the Self, which is of God. Some Light passes but not in its pure state. This is the aging process.

Jesus Christ, our Lord and Master, promised us eternal life. This means that we must have perpetual life regardless of whether we are thinking of a physical or spiritual state. It would not be in one state and not in another.

When we try to divide this world on the physical level from that of the next level, then we are not having eternal life. Due to the fact that all vibration and energy received passes through our atmosphere, not all comes through in a pure state. This emanates into the body and is not correctly in harmony with the perfect creation of the spiritual body of man. Thus we have dis-ease.

We will talk about dis-ease not just alone from the medical scientific nomenclature such as chicken pox, arthritis, etc., but as a basic cause and how your fears and other things cause illness. Illness is a manifestation in the physical part of man which works into the being of man and becomes part of our individuality.

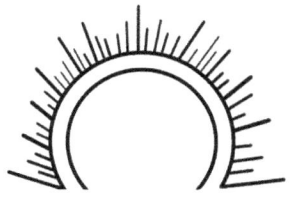

LESSON 4

SPIRITUAL BODY THREE

We have been talking about the vital body or spiritual body of man, or prime body of man, and relating to the function which the Soul, or second part of the Self, actually plays in the maintaining or functioning or control of the physical body. It is the resultant of the collective energy from the blood stream, or its vibration, which are filled with our emotions. The emotions of our acts and our deeds help to cloud and crystallize to a certain extent the peripheral area of the Soul.

As we have said before in the previous lesson, the Soul is that which brings to us and determines our future life pattern. It is the negative pole, so to speak, of the Self. And the clarity with which the God Force shines forth from the Self is determined by the density and vibration of the Soul. In other words, these patterns of life are impinged on the negative pole of the Self and they determine what shines forth and comes through them. The good, positive things give a more even flow to the perfect harmony that is manifest in the physical body.

The spiritual body of man (his prime body or form) is never affected by any disease, or accident, or problem of man in any way. The exceptions are that the potential God Force and Life Force of the Sun (which is stored up) manifests in the physical vehicle (the reactions which we see in the physical body) and we refer to these actions for natural healing. In other words the spiritual body has every organ, cell, and tissue in a colorless perfect form in the physical body.

When an individual has disease which the medical physician might term arthritis and so forth, it is because of the negative state of mind of the individual is blocking the radiation from the Self. The Self is primarily seated in the spiritual body. Thus the spiritual body spends its force in trying to maintain health in the organ affected, or the process impaired, so that it cannot maintain the chemical balance in the physical.

Thus it is then at this time that the medical physician says "Yes, Mr. Jones, you have arthritis," or you have a cancer, etc. It is then that the physical, chemical structure of man forms what the physician calls a pathological deposit in the physical body. The perfect physical form is distorted.

We have previously stated that the Self lies in the spiritual body but it is also dimensionally seeable in the physical. Now there is no such thing as a diseased Christian or a sick Christian. The reason for this is that the Christ-man has assumed And Taken

On The Aspects Of The Lord Of The Sun and he does not impair in any way the perfect flow of the life force and healing forces of the Christos.

There are many people who believe in Christ Jesus, many who believe in Jesus, and there are many more who believe only in God. These people who believe and are seeking God, who are followers of the Christian doctrine and faith, they may be good people and may manifest many righteous things.

Perhaps through ignorance they have not sought the fullness of the Christ and, therefore, have ills in the process of living and paying off their karmic debt.

The existence and manifestation in the physical body of a pathological deposit manifests sometimes as an eliminative or cold process. It is not necessarily disease and in these days it should not be recognized as such. It does show one thing: it manifests the existence of a powerful healing force of the Christ that is eliminating negative material and forces from the body. It also eliminates some foreign things you pick up in foods which are not adaptable to the body but clog the eliminating processes. For instance, water which is filled with pollution and extremely poisonous elements in the air which we breath are being thrown off.

It is true that once we have been exposed to the basic laws and principles of Creation, and how the tools given to us by the Creator may be used, we can then use this knowledge to perfect our own universe, and detect and screen out all derogatory substances.

As we become more like the Christ, or Christ Jesus, we will not need as great a quantity of food and thus will be exposed to much less impurity. This contact will have taken control of our Minds and thus minimized the flow of negative forces into our bodies. We will have reached the condition of what is expressed in one of the olden-time hymns, "resting in the arms of God." Then we will have reached the stage of letting go and letting God.

Let us pass on to what has been known or expressed as the psychic body because it is not a true body and not a distinct physical substance. It is highly effluvious and reactive to emotion and sound.

Light has a great effect upon the psychic body as it causes it to become less reactive. This is because the Light of the Sun is uniform and the same in all substances whether it is here or somewhere else, or in one organ of the body or another.

This substance, the Light of the Sun, is a mediator between the physical world and the psychic. This borderline is termed by our Catholic Brothers as "the soul in limbo." The psychic world is an intermediary state between the dense world and the lower heaven world. These lower states of vibration are part of God's Creation and it is the substance which motivates and gives to a Being in the physical form the flesh of the spiritual body in its lower form.

The psychic body is the thing which can be used as a reflecting substance or teleports the images and figures of a higher state to earth and man's other five senses. It is mostly a negative force, potentially. As I word it, the flesh also of the vital body.

Its formation, construction, and relationship to the spiritual life will be related a little later in these lessons. Let us note here that man is and can be master of the elements in his body and thus becomes the master of spiritual attainment through the power of God manifest in the Light of Christ.

Let us not sell short the spiritual function and control of the psychic body, the magnificence of its creation, and absolute enthralling simplicity in operation of what appears to be a most mysterious miracle of creation.

Without drugs or knife the science physician can perform the healings and surgery to himself and his brother man as a servant of God.

Man in this age becomes in reality a brother in Christ.

Man has been living in this age with a vastly different problem from 150 years ago. He is walking down the street with masses of wires around him, breathes air full of atomic energy, drinks water full of atomic energy or fluorides, eats food that has phosphorous poisoning in it, and works at a high pitch all the time. He is under great stress.

The normal tension level of nature by evolution to change its natural cell functions takes about 150 – 200 years. We are striking a new cell cycle and it is necessary to break down the tension level. Sometimes it is necessary to take the meat away for a few days or to fast. Some students react differently to different foods and you should watch their chemical balance to see whether they should set aside some foods temporarily. Until one has accepted oneself as a perfect being you cannot keep your own body in balance.

You will notice changes in the time of new moons and full moons. You need not set up charts as astrologers but it is good roughly to know the stellar forces or influences in the background of your life.

Let us finish by saying that if you will use these thoughts in observing your life daily you will come to a more comprehensive understanding of the reality that you are in control and feel less like a ship in the ocean tossed about by the ravaging waves.

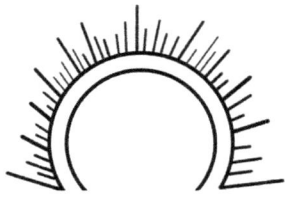

SPIRITUAL BODY FOUR

We have given a number of names to this vital body. One of my favorites is the electrical structure. Another is the spiritual body and of course the one we have just used, vital body. Each of these terms describe the nature of certain things about this body. It is the vital body because of the energy and vitality that is sent through it into the physical structure. It is the spiritual body because much of the higher frequency-activated spiritual forces feed this body. It is the electrical body because of its energy and the energy that comes through it. It is invisible, the same as electricity to the physical eye, but yet has a distinct structure which determines the physical form.

Certain scientists formulate quite lengthy investigations of this, the nature of the radiation of the human body. The inventor of the new term "Bio-radioactivity" called it this because the human body contains an average of 40 grains of potassium, causing the emitting of some 80,000, so they claim, body particles per second, and this radiation of particles contains electrons moving with considerable high velocity, more than 100,000 miles per second.

It is at this point that I ask a question: I wonder, are we talking about fourth dimension? Possibly.

These tiny body particles go down through all parts of our body at this tremendous speed but of course the length of their flight is all but infinitesimal because the space between, presumed to be solid objects, is very short. Such is the component parts of tissues and so forth.

The occasion of every encounter, or encountered object of this flight of body particles, incidentally gives rise to a minute flash which proclaims the formation of an x-ray or, one might say, package of x-rays.

Most of the experiments on the physical body that study with nerves in connection with electrical impulses which travel over them have been made by the aid of galvanic currents of considerable potential in comparison with the actual electrical potential of the human systems.

Both the current and the action of these currents are entirely different. We learn that every electrical current will produce a stimulus along the nerve trunk and will produce certain muscular contractions or reactions. Of course they are very incomplete and are entirely unlike what takes place in the human organism during life. It is not a smooth action.

Let us have a clearer view of this complex action, both chemically and thermodynamically, and its radiation. Metabolic reaction also comes into this field. We must take into consideration electrolysis and electro-chemical action. This in the final analysis forms the fundamental factors: the presence, quantities, and kinds of electricity which perform all of the changes.

It is a fact that one of the great forces in the human body is what is now called nerve energy. Its source is in the vital force of life. Science has recently tried to rename this energy and now calls it electrical nerve energy because it is found to be vibratory in nature like electricity.

It is entirely foolish to think that every energy that is vibratory is electrical simply because electrical energy is vibratory. Nerve energy is a wonderful force vibrating from place to place just as an electrical wire is used in a building to convey the current or power from one place to another. So do the nerves conduct this energy.

There are certain spots in the body where electrical or vibratory nerve energy manifests its strength. The energy flows hard and passes, or escapes, at what might be called the terminals of the nerve trunks.

We can now find this at the two principal nerve terminals of the body: the hands and head. In fact the tips of the fingers have been long used by the mystics as terminal points of radiation.

* * *

MAN'S BODY: Adaptation in Evolution—Water, Exercise, Breathing

The ability to comprehend, reason, and think. In the past, thinking by man has been unconscious and unguarded.

Those in the tropics developed dark skin. Those in the woods grew taller and stronger.

Those living on vegetables grew differently from those who ate meat alone.

Man's body changed in accordance with his use of feet, hands, and limbs.

Man physically is a water animal, conceived and born in water, and has a natural liking for water.

His admiration for mountainous country is a subconscious remembrance of the necessity to seek protection and hunt in them.

Man is essentially a water and air creature—water adapting to air. This should be remembered in connection with healing or analyzing man's health.

Man is renewing his every cell, as well as his whole skin, hour by hour. (50,000,000 explosions inside the human body.)

He throws off water and perspiration through skin, urine, and breath.

Water is the main essential element of man in health. In some things man uses psychic force in healing.

Exercise is needed for balance. It relaxes the physical, lets the spiritual express itself, and regulates glandular functions.

Three phases of elimination are needed for kidneys, bladder, and bowel treatment. (Dissolved tissue thrown off through bowel tract. Triangle of elimination of body.)

We question and through a question we are given a guidance rule. Why have we invented so many diseases since most, in fact all, can be traced to faulty thinking?

Proper breathing:

 1) It affects the flow of spirit.
 2) It affects the cosmic body. Ethereal stuff.
 3) It affects the electrical structure, the spiritual body itself.

MAN'S BODY

God took the body from which He built up man from those things which He created from nothingness into something. That mass of something was the extract of all creatures in heaven and earth. It would be the same as if one should extract soul or spirit, and then take that spirit or that body.

For example, man consists of flesh and blood plus a soul, which in the man is much more subtle than the former. In this manner was extracted that which was most subtle and most excellent in all creatures, elements, stars in heaven, earth, properties, essences, and natures. This was united into one mass. Afterwards from this mass man was made.

Second Day

Hence man is now a microcosm, a little world, because he is an extract from all the stars and planets of the whole firmament, from the earth and the elements, and so he is their quintessence. The four elements are the universal world and from these, man is constituted. Therefore, in number he is fifth, that is the quintessence. He is beyond the four elements out of which he has been extracted as a nucleus.

But between the macrocosm and the microcosm this difference occurs. That the form, image, species, and substance of man are diverse therefrom. In man the earth is the flesh, the water is blood, fire is the heat thereof, and air is the balsam. These properties have not been changed, but only the substance of the body. So man is man not a world, yet made from the world, made in the likeness, not of the world, but of God. Yet man comprises in himself all the qualities of the world.

Whence the Scripture rightly says we are dust and ashes, and into ashes we shall return. That is although man indeed is made in the image of God, and has flesh and blood, and yet is not like the world, but more than the world. Nevertheless, he is earth and dust and ashes. And he should lay this well to heart lest from his figure he should suffer himself to be led astray. But he should think what he has been, what he now is, and what hereafter he shall be.

Matter is not limited to the inorganic since it manifests in the organic as well. But what differentiates the inorganic from the organic matter and how does this matter manifest?

MAN'S BODY: Cosmic Consciousness—the Reality of the Soul.

Without a great deal of research, it is plainly seen that inorganic matter is lifeless. That is it cannot assimilate, grow, and reproduce itself. On the other hand, the organic is the same matter, either in simple or complex combinations, infused with the force of life, i.e., animal and vegetable, and this matter continually assimilates, grows, and reproduces itself.

In other words, the mass of one is increased by external action almost entirely, while the other assimilates matter within and grows or evolves externally from the single cell to the complex organism of the human body.

MATTER CANNOT MAKE MATTER AND LIFE CANNOT MAKE LIFE, for MATTER EXISTS AND LIFE EXISTS. Life utilizes matter in making the proper vehicles for itself, but it never uses crystals in body building if it can avoid them.

Organic matter which is constructed and used by the force of life, follows a definite law which is based upon the point and curve constituting the center and circumference of a circle. THUS MATTER

MANIFESTS ACCORDING TO THE TRIANGLE, AND LIFE ACCORDING TO THE IDEAL OF THE CIRCLE.

* * *

Let us remember one thing Brothers, the spiritual body functioned the same way 20,000 years ago, 10,000 years ago, 5,000 years ago. And when we think of it like this, as in the foregoing lesson, I wonder if we adore our Creator enough?

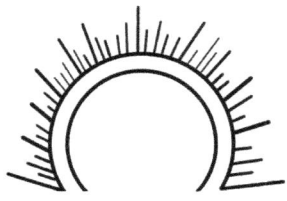

SOUL ONE

The Soul is the shell of the Self and that which protects the Self from all interference from ill development. Psalms 42:2, "My soul thirsts for God, for the living God. When shall I come and behold the face of God?"

The Soul is akin to the emotional body and affects it through development, thirsting after God, which unfolds the Soul and reveals itself.

In Judges 5:21 we find the Scripture, "March on my Soul with Might." As the Soul marches forward the Self advances. The soul produces of itself intense protections for the Self.

There are spiritual qualities within the Soul that bring about almost instantaneous illumination when the outer man lets go and lets God. We develop Soul through meditation and Bible study, especially the New Testament.

In Revelations we find that the Way which is readily seen preserved is Soul or sheath of the Self because here is the record of past life.

This is so because the Self which the Soul encompasses is the cell, the body of the Father. Its ever-effulgent revelations carry with it the universal knowledge of the existence of the Way, for it was the Father's Creation.

Man asks of the immortality of the Soul and the employments of heaven, or as one might put it, the state of the sinner in relation to it. This is another reason why these questions go unanswered until one has reached through the Self the Akashic records, or the Mind of the Father.

Revelation 20:4, "Then I saw thrones, and seated on them were those to whom judgment was committed. Also I saw the souls of those who had been beheaded for their testimony to Jesus and for the word of God, and who had not worshipped the beast or its image and had not received its mark on their foreheads or their hands. They came to life, and reigned with Christ a thousand years."

Unless the Soul is maintained by prayer, meditation, and Bible study, the Self cannot find illumination or realization. Its potential must be activated by thought.

All material endeavors must be put to one side until the Soul is enriched to the point where it begins to expand its activity of life.

Then the Self will be realized and illumined and found through the enriching of the Soul.

This is because the Soul is and functions on the plane of the heaven world.

The Father tells us in Ezekiel that all souls are His. Ezekiel 18:4, "Behold, all souls are mine; the soul of the father, as well as the soul of the son is mine; the soul that sins shall die."

In Psalms 33, "Our Soul waits for the Lord."

The Lord is a consuming fire. The soul waits for that fire to burn out the dross and then elevates itself and the Self is realized. All power is contained in the Soul that has realized the Self because its karma is paid off.

The great Soul force or substance is Infinite, indestructible, and has a very high rate of vibration.

It came into the human body at birth and leaves it at so-called death. Before it came into the body this soul substance or force existed somewhere and manifested in some nature.

When it leaves the body, it does not die. It cannot cease to exist. It cannot remain on the earth plane without a vessel or vehicle, a means of material manifestations, so it must return to its original source.

During its temporary residence in the human body this great Soul substance keeps in touch or attunement with the great Divine Source from which the Soul came and to which it returns. Therefore, all Souls on the earth like all Souls on the Cosmic Plane are in constant attunement, one with the other, and each with all.

You make tests to show that the minds and intelligence of departed Souls can communicate with the minds of Souls here on earth.

It is because man's Soul is attuned with all other Souls that thought vibration operates at great distances and thus makes possible telepathy or mind reading.

The subjective Mind is the mind of the Soul.

Music we can understand because it is God's language of the Soul.

The difference in the expression of my Soul makes up my Personality.

Individuality is a material manifestation of earth habits and life.

There is that part of the Soul which makes it the Soul, that something which one does not say it is but which makes it so. It is the quality which is likened unto Grace. It is that which is above the Soul essence itself. It is simple, it is impressionable and pure nothing, yet is the All, the totality of your life and mine.

There is no name for it this pure nothing, unknown and yet closer than breath. I can call it receptive power, this Divinity of man. It is the uncreated Light of the Christos.

This is the absolute, free from all names and form, just as God is free from all names and is all that there is in our life now. It is pure God with our life representation.

This the body of Soul above love, higher than grace and knowledge, for these are distinguishable.

It is in this power that God does blossom and flourish with the Holy Family, through which the spirit of God blossoms forth and its actions are visible in the dense world. It is in and through this power that the Creating God bringeth forth His only begotten Son, the

Christos and the essential part of Himself, and in the Light of this is cast the shadow of the Holy Ghost.

PEACE BE WITH YOU.

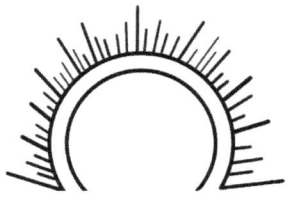

SOUL TWO

Tonight, we shall touch the first part of the study on the Soul. I think the question probably most important in your mind is to say what is it? Let us learn first what, or how—what it is.

It is so important that we realize the Soul is not of such a material nature that we can hope to sense it just by looking at it alone. This is part of the job of the teacher. It is there—the Self and the Soul. It is part of the objective and subjective of this School. This School seeks to bring each man and woman, at their wish, into the realization of the Self. Therefore, the teacher touches upon the sense of Soul.

We have a material body, we have a spiritual body, and we have a Soul. We have come to see that even the blood, visible to us in an objective sense, contains that which is not seen or perceived objectively. We have come to understand the blood cells and plasma of the blood in man is easily seen and recognized by physicians, doctors and scientists. It is the only medium for carrying throughout our system the real power, energy, and force of the Light of Christ.

One great fact is quite evident, it is an unquestionable reality, we can see the Self. It can be done. We will also usually notice around the Self that there is a Soul. We can understand it and learn to work with it but only through its functions and its manifestations. We can see it. The functions and manifestations are so definite and distinct that we can make no mistake about its presence.

We can easily mark and define that function of human existence which belongs to the Soul exclusively just as we can define any other function or attribute with which we come in contact during our spiritual endeavors and seeking. We can define those things which belong to the heart of man. Furthermore, these clear and unmistakable functions of the Soul cannot possibly belong to any other part of man's existence. The Soul and the Self, they are YOU.

As one great mystic once said, "If we had never been told, had never even heard or read about the existence of the Soul in man, the Soul would have forced us to create or invent a Soul to account for what we had observed through our studies, experiments, working, existence, life and living. This includes our observations of the Soul's multiple functions in the human body."

The Great Creator God created man out of the dust of the earth, breathed into his nostrils the breath of life as said in Genesis, and man became a living Soul. We truly do take this statement literally.

I believe the teachers of this School have shown us that the first part of this statement is absolutely true. Every form of science is proving to us that man's material body is composed of earthly substance and elements. Man's material body, materially and physically, is of the negative elements of the earth. Man's body is made of dust. It is like the clay images molded as some of the gods. It is like a pot in the potter's hands. It is the pot in our hands which we mold and form as we go along in life.

We compare the lifeless body of a man with that of a man who is lying beside it asleep. What is the difference? So far as the objective sight is concerned, they are similar. They both have the same organs, both spiritual and physical, and same material forms. Each is the identical replica of the other.

The spiritual essence is there in the man. But in one there is life. In the other there is not. In one, breath is passing to and fro. In the other is no breath. We also note that in the one something is absent while it is still present in the other. Our conclusion is that the Soul is absent in the lifeless body.

We know at this time in our studies whether or not there is a Soul. But we do not understand its functions necessarily. We do know that there is something of us which goes from life to life. Our work should prove to us that this is so.

There is a very close relationship between the breath and the psychic aura of man, between the breath and the psychic body of man, and the spiritual body and its being charged energetically.

This relationship is evident in the writings of the old mystics and philosophers. In fact there is evidence of the Soul and breath relationship in writings that remain practically since the dawn of civilization. They include going back to the Zen Vesta, the languages of the Atlanteans, and the languages that followed it: Sanskrit, then Greek, Roman, and many of the some fifty-odd tongues.

We find in dictionaries of these languages the word Soul and breath are synonymous, using the same root. We find also that in the Soul quality of being they were using the same words that they used for breath. But most of them made a distinction between spirit and Soul.

This we find is just proof that the old thinkers knew the functions that the Soul and breath maintained toward man's manifestation. Some of the ancient Stoics held that the divine principle, the first cause of the universe, was from the breath of God. It permeates all things. This breath manifested in a series of creative laws and matter. It is what we term Spirit. It became the physical laws which science knows and studies.

This is the logos, the law, and in man this breath becomes Soul and draws together that which man does, lives, breaths, thinks, prays, manifests, lets go, and allows the Great Power to come through him. It moves man in his spiritual senses.

In the Soul around the Self is etched the experience of man from life to life, from era to era, age to age as he goes down that long path, as he climbs the ladder of Life, and as he goes up the bootstrap path through the center of all Being.

Even though we are engaged and agree on the teachings that the Soul and the breath are closely related, we have discovered little regarding the Soul in a concrete manner, except those things which we have seen and have changed in relationship to that experience. This we must try to do more. We must try and we can only hope to know the Soul a little better through experimental work, through working with the Self, and through other things of this nature.

We cannot demand to know for it is that part of us which has nothing to do with our objective material lives directly, with the exception of control over the body systems. A knowledge can be based upon objective senses, but we must depend upon the sensing of the Soul subjectively and the Soul essence. In working with the Self if we have gone through God-Realization we will notice that there are things that take place and there are changes in the perimeter of the Self around it. The very first point we discover about the Soul is its divine nature, that it is of God. We are sure, so naturally the question arises, "What do we mean by God?" That is why our first lesson of this particular subject and level of work in the lessons of the Golden Dawn are devoted entirely to the subjects of God and the Soul.

If we recognize God as the Great Divine Power and Intelligence which animates the universe, we can readily see and understand how the Soul is then a part of this Intelligence and Power. God and the Soul are divine because both represent the infinite and supreme, the everlasting, the ever moving, the records of all being, and the first Great Cause and Principle of all creation to the mystic. That is, this supreme is infinite, a part of the first Great Cause. It is Divine.

In no other sense do we mean this word. In no other sense is it applied. Therefore, we say that the Soul of man is a part of Divinity. Why is it there? How did it come to be there? What is its part of the scheme of Creation? These questions are the next important parts. What purpose does the Soul serve as a divine and immortal element residing temporarily with the human body? This is a question which should be profoundly followed up.

In looking at man's existence from a purely materialistic standpoint of view the Soul, granting its existence in man, serves no purpose not already served by all of the physical functions and attributes of the material man. That is of course the very foundation of why the Soul is there. Here is the infinite man in memory although this is not from a material point of view.

The attempts several years ago made by the University of Columbia to create living organisms artificially by the process called spontaneous generation proved that living organisms could not be artificially created, except so far as to produce or bring together the necessary material elements as needed was concerned.

The life and vital force that animates such an artificial generation organism was not created and remained unknown in growth. However, such experiments often repeated seemed to prove that life is purely a chemical action, something which resulted from the action of several groups of elements upon one another under certain conditions.

Such a theory would bring the question of vital life free of principles of divinity and man's brain would be all there was in intellectual reactions. Consciousness would then become something that would simply be action and reaction, or reflex action due to the materialistic stimuli of minerals and elements. Life would come primarily and principally from the air breathed into the lungs bringing with it a certain vitalizing element of a chemical nature, just as an electrical current animates a motor with nothing divine, nothing super physical, nothing pertaining to the Soul.

Such a chemical materialistic theory of life is still propounded by men of science. The Soul was not placed in the scheme of things and, therefore, the Soul did not exist. They had not reached that level of thinking in its reality.

Even the theological explanations for the existence of the Soul and its purpose in the human body did not make the Soul a necessary attribute. Thus in the earthly existence and development of man there was no propagation of life after life because they left out reincarnations. They left out the experiences of those who had experienced the present existence and lived before.

Here again was called into existence the problem of the Soul because something had to move from this life to another. Something had to, just had to, know and understand how this body worked so that its automatic systems would work readily, freely and in perfect rhythm. That rhythm, that perfection, came out of the divine essence within man's Soul, the divinity to make him simply an image of God and nothing more.

It also had its affect upon man's morals or development. It has also failed to fulfill the unknown purposes designed by God if the Soul were placed in man simply to give him an immortal attribute, something to live after and await a day of spiritual existence. This is not practical. The only purpose served by such an example of reason for the Soul's existence would be to foster the theological idea of the final judgment. That is the day when all the Souls released from the earth from millions of years would come together to be judged and to suffer punishment or receive reward.

This theological idea has long since been shown to be illogical. It is not in keeping with nature, its laws and principles. Therefore, it couldn't be of God. There is another reason for the existence of the Soul.

We may consider the mystics, philosophers, and even Spinoza which said that he affirmed that when man is self-conscious, that is, when he is aware of his own existence, which Soul makes possible, then man realizes himself. This is because the Self of man is the Self of God, a part of it, a great cell in the being, form and body of our Great Father.

We shall contemplate upon the reality of God and see what our consciousness of Him is when we exist in that consciousness in tune with Him.

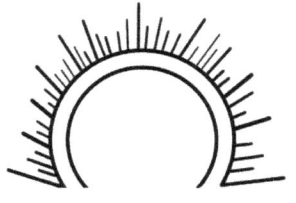

LESSON 4

SOUL THREE

One of the most confusing things any student has to contend with is when somebody starts talking about soul, and then the individuality, reality, actuality and all the other "alities." One sort of feels that he has been subdivided, divided, and re-subdivided. Well this is not wholly so. You are all one in God.

We discuss now for a moment those conditions of which we call Personality and are often confounded with that which is called Individuality by some. These two terms are often used interchangeably and should not be so. They are not the same condition and state of manifestation.

But to us they are much like the terms reality and actuality often used by schools of thought. In reality there is a definite distinction between these in the sight of God.

The English dictionary makes these two words almost synonymous. We read that Personality is "that which makes for personal existence, or identity, or that which constitutes the distinction of a person." Individuality, we are told, is "the characteristic peculiar to the individual and some of the characteristic traits.

Now let us take this point of view and define it in light of life and reality of God's creation. Personality cannot pertain solely, or even partially, to one's physical countenance, material body, or appearance. One's personality may reveal itself, or even veil itself, in the clothes one wears or in the manner of a physical expression and likewise one's home, furnishings, books, friends, hobbies and pleasures. Personality may be revealed or veiled. Personality is that subtle quality of the inner man which reveals itself at times in those material elements of the human manifestation in earth which we notice as characteristic traits and groups in mass individuality.

Actually the personality of man is the sum total of many lifetimes brought together in the soul which is around the Self. It is the reflection and reaction of man from his many lifetimes and his much learning, error, and development. It is not really something that has anything to do with his outer man in a sense, except that it is reflected there.

Individuality on the other hand pertains solely to those materialistic qualities, attributes and expressions which constitute characteristic traits. The individual, the outer manifestation, plus education, habits, thoughts and creeds, is the wearing of the physical body and the physical world, so to speak. I use the word wearing because we are wearing a body. It is a vehicle which is carrying you, the Self and the Soul.

To continue this simple explanation, you might say that the personality is the naked body under the unchangeable cloak of Soul. It is YOU. The individuality is a cloak which you have taken on and give your personal appearance to.

An important matter to be considered here is what constitutes the personality of man. It is the personality of man, the soul-personality as we call it, which is most concerned with all earthly existence through its reincarnations of man's soul. As we shall see reincarnation is the purpose of the evolving of the soul personality. This we may attain so that we may attain a certain goal.

But by the lessons we learn by the soul-personality it is the process of evolution which is going on. It will bring us into the things we need to learn our lessons by. This is because whether we know it or not the subtle forces of the soul are in function as long as we are in this functional body.

Only through his personality does Man express in each incarnation. He brings with him the knowledge of the material body functions. In a few words, personality may be said to be the mind of the soul in reality. It is and carries that record of wisdom and knowledge.

Just as individuality may be said to be a brain in the sense of the material body, in using the word "mind," in this case, a distinction is made between mind and brain. This is a little different. It should be familiar to all students. The subjective faculties and attributes of the mind are particularly referred to in all references as the mind of the soul.

Personality, as it is used in the principal elements, is the soul storehouse of memory. If we assume or believe that it is in a single incarnation the lessons learned today are preserved for us tomorrow, a year or 10 years hence, we must admit that the memory has its faults as a storehouse of facts and experiences, pictures and impressions.

The materialist will claim that the memory and its possible storehouses are faculties and functions of the brain, a physical thing associated with a subtle mind of an unknown soul.

We will point out the fact that the brain will prevent the brain from remembering a past impression. It is a fact that an injury to the brain will affect recollection and conscious memory. It is a fact also that a blow on the head or an injury to the brain may remove or affect the desire to eat or drink. But not even the materialist would claim that this proves that the injury to the brain removes or destroys the existence of hunger or thirst in the body.

The brain is an organism of the body through which all the emotions and desires are consciously realized and find their power to function or manifest outwardly. To injure the functions of the brain is to affect the conscious objective realization of facts and impressions.

The brain is very much like a prism, or a group of should we say cells, brain cells. They are like tiny reservoirs that pick up impulses and pictures. Then, they are reshuffled, like a little computer.

We may close or obstruct the threshold which leads from the inner subjective to the outer objective chamber, but such shutting off of the free passage of thought does not destroy the thought. And most certainly the blockade does not prove the non-existence of the chamber beyond. That memory is stifled or stuck in the non-manifest by an injury to the brain does not prove that the memory resides in the material outer chamber of the brain.

Paralysis may mute the activity of every human faculty and muscle of the human body to an extent that not a sign or signal of intelligence may be expressed. But the mind will and does continue to think and have within its chambers many thoughts unable to manifest objectively.

The reality is that the mind we use is part of the Mind of God the Creator. If we admit the possible existence of this storehouse of memory in which all facts and impressions consciously realized are stored away for future use, it is just a little point to yield that this Great Archetype of the structure of the human body is a functioning part of and reflection of the temple of experience. Wherein this temple is contained the chamber of pleasures and sorrows, the school of lessons learned, the chart of likes and dislikes, the encyclopedia of facts, the court of justice and retention, the record of impression, the resort of test and trial, the tribunal of decision between rights and wrongs. These combinations constitute in each existence the personality of the Human Being. This is his or her being alive in this particular existence.

But he could be alive in another existence, in another world entirely, and still use the same function, the same mind. He might even be in another type of body but the mind would be the same.

Now let us explore the subject of the soul concerning personality or character of being. This would include the study of its purpose and function. The religious tendencies of the Egyptians relating to theories and explanations of man's physical and spiritual existence contained nothing that could be interpreted as belief in the existence or possibility of the soul.

But this was true only of the popular religious beliefs and principles. This was not true of the tenets and beliefs of several religions and cults which existed in Egypt as far back as 1500 BC and later.

These Egyptian cults or religious bodies were the forerunners of all modern secret cults of a semi-religious and philosophical nature. In their peculiar symbolism were ceremonies and rites copied and adopted even to this day. There is much evidence not only of belief in the soul but considerable understanding of its origin, nature and purpose.

In fact, the learned Egyptians definitely recognized the duality and reality of man's being. They said duality because he had two bodies—the divine nature and material body. He has four: the Soul, the Self, the spiritual, and the material.

The inner divine nature of man, his soul, was known to them as RA, or BA. RA was the sun and life force coming in, the inevitable. It was principally symbolized in the form of a bird. This material symbol represented the flight into eternity of the soul after death, after the transition of the body.

At times there were many other gods or spirits known. Soul was symbolized by the lotus flower as the unfolding, the everlasting, the white, the being, the perfect, and the unblemished which flourished in the rich soil along the Nile. These symbols and flowers go further and further into reality. The concepts of the ancient Egyptians were highly evolved in religious matters and many of them were mystics.

In the Orphic religious cults of the 6th century BC the soul was considered a divine element which was evolving through earthly expression. We read that the soul was a part of the divine, universal soul. The body of man in its limited and moral conditions was but a womb or prison. The continuous existence of the soul and the body together was a punishment for sins in a previous condition.

The Orphic principle and rites tended to establish a belief in the homogeneity of all living things. In this particular doctrine, or in many doctrines of original sin, was the transmigration of the soul. For instance, John Milton in his English manuscript on the Secret Laws of the Orphic Rites said it was taught that the soul was entombed in the animal, earthly body for that length of time which would enable it to gradually attain perfection during its contact with matter. It was the same way by which your dog or mine learns to know us and assimilate our actions. They get to know even what you say. They realize the symbol and the sound of the word.

When the soul has attained perfection, it is freed from the cycle of generation and no longer requires contact with these conditions, tests, trials, and re-cycling. It again becomes a pure and evolved soul which returns to its divine source as before its first imprisonment.

The oldest rite in early philosophy shows that belief in the soul was a part of the principle of primitive culture. Furthermore, it has always been believed by nearly all of the primitive and modern philosophies. Our mystic cults said that man's soul is a divine essence and is rarely associated with the material body.

We find much in the writings of many great people and the historic philosophers born in the Taurus about 301 BC. They held that the sun was the abode of God. From the sun radiated a divine essence, the soul of God. This soul pervades all space and in separable segments entered into the human body to be born on the earth. The soul, or god-man essence, was the revivification of the fire and universal emanation of the intelligence providence of God.

In addition, the degree of the validity of the soul after so-called death depends upon the degree of vitality in its life while in the body. Arguments in favor of this believe that the soul is a divine element or entity having its origin in God, residing temporarily in an earthly body, and freed at the dissolution of the body to return to its original source.

To really understand what life is, we must begin to see and know that all of the great wonders which we see around us must have something that remembers from life to life. We are. We are going to be, but we are not going to be just a man. We are going to be a Being. We are going to be a highly intelligent individual. If we listen to the words of the inner voice we reach a state of spiritual consciousness where we follow the direction from within. We will soon realize that there has to be a soul. For many of the answers and things we get will be impossible without a record brought forward.

Even if we recognize the soul, we may also admit that a man might still not think about the things which might come from the soul.

Plato voiced this same idea in the words: "As manifestly as the human soul is, by means of the human senses it is linked to the present life, attracting itself by reason of concepts, conclusions, anticipations and efforts, to which reason leads it to God and eternity."

We see that the human mind not only conceives the existence of the human soul, but that the duality of man's earthly existence is at once made apparent by our recognition of such concepts of the soul. It is not possible after considerable thought to conceive of a man as having a soul without conceiving that man's expressions on earth is in the form of body and soul. The material form enclosing the immaterial form which has continual existence.

Consider the Soul as a separate part and shell of the Self, the immaterial parts of the dual man. Mind must naturally be considered the immaterial entity of the being immortal, divine and immanently from God. This the reality. This is the actual heritage which God has left us with, that we can take with us: our life history, our life library from one life to another without hesitation.

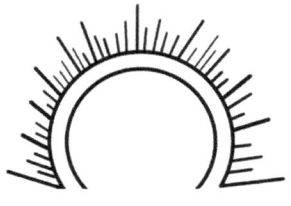

SOUL FOUR

THE INDIVIDUALITY OF OUR PERSONALITY

D own through the years and in the course of our striving to attain initiation to obtain illumination by the Light of Christ and the divine Christos through our Lord Jesus Christ, we have heard many instructions about letting go and letting God. This includes our killing the ego and many other things of this nature. This would be a very sad thing because we would not be worth very much to Jesus Christ, the glorious Creator, or the Nameless One.

That which is real and within this physical body of ours is an inseparable part of an infinite soul. Your soul is in attune with the Mind of God and a part of it. This oversoul is in all men. It is the bridge to all space and time. The Soul is the sheath of the Self and is in the body of our Lord Jesus Christ. It is a part of the body of God, His Mind, what we call the Akasha. If we are part of the body of Christ we cannot help but be a part of our Nameless Creator.

The intelligence and substance of the earth has helped and aided us in producing our physical bodies. This body is sometimes called a body of clay because of the way we have used it. We have allowed it to hamper and master us rather than we master it. The body is actually the temple in which we, as the Soul and Self, reside. And it is within this Soul and Self that dwells the record and memory of our many lifetimes. This includes the demonstration of our attunement with the pure consciousness of our God and our Master Jesus.

As we take on the illumination of the Light of Christ that Light becomes so infused into our physical substance that the temple of our body becomes transmuted. The degree to which it is transmuted is determined by the amount of light we receive and the degree to which we permit it to take over our body. This is the degree to which we get ourselves out of the way.

What I am saying in the words of the old masters would be that to the degree that we can become and attain self-mastery will determine the transmutation from the normal density of people's physical bodies to where their bodies are partially light. This is to the extent that we can see it and anyone can see it with their physical eyes.

In the holy testament Jesus prepared himself after the resurrection and then he ascended. It was in a pretty completely transmuted body. He rebuilt his physical body when he returned and arose after the crucifixion.

The soul in you or me will express itself differently in my body than it would in your body. This is through habit, education, temperament, and the effect of many lifetimes of learning. I may through habit and education prevent my soul from demonstrating the same degree of purity needed for the understanding of our Father's creation and word.

Your soul may receive the same words, facts, and educational material in Christianity but due to the fact of your experience, you may not be able to pick them up and receive them in the same way as I would. This is my personality which expresses my soul. It does not have anything to do directly with my individuality which expresses my likes and dislikes in the material world, a passing thing that I can change at any time.

This individuality is something that I leave behind when I pass through transition into the other worlds.

That which is a part of God is infinite and is not separated, a unified part. It is not independent but dependent. This is the foundation and basis for the term unity, brotherhood, fellowship, of God and man, of man and man. For my individuality are the forces which I set in action, I determine the nature of, and are totally of my own creation. This is a term used by many of the churches which are called the sins of the flesh.

Both personality and character are ever in the making. In our evolution we find the true purpose of the existence of the soul. Through spiritual reflection and the growing light of the soul of man man's personality slowly evolves. That which is recorded in the soul slowly evolves within him. That evolution manifests itself not only in the spiritual sphere of the unmaterial to which the soul belongs, but right here on the earth plane while the soul is within the body. When it is unhampered, the eternal light of man is a pure and radiant light of God, God's firstborn Son, Lord of the Sun, and in us the Light of Christ.

All colors are vibrations of the same white light but appear different in each personality when filtered through an earthly medium. The soul remains distinct with its personality, which it never loses, while the essence of the soul is always a part of the cosmic soul. The cosmic soul essence manifests in millions of expressions which separates and represents a part of this cosmic personality. Each of these expressions represent another person, another personality.

This cosmic soul cannot be lost because the essence of these personalities blend into one complete cosmic soul. Just as the many colors of the spectrum cannot be lost when they are again assembled, passed through a prism, and they blend into pure white light.

Man studies the cosmic arts and very often, as he reads and studies their mysteries, he gets so complicated that he loses the simplicity of God's great creation. He starts to separate one art from the other, like astrology. He separates it from the testament and philosophy. This is a fallacy because there is only one God, one creation, and one basic truth. It has to be part and parcel of the same truth totally united with all other facets of truth and creation. The basic patterns and symbols must be the same.

So let us now look at the ten planets of this solar system to which we attribute certain functions or personalities. For instance, to the planet Mars we say that it has an effect upon red blood cells, the temper or disposition, the volatile disposition of an individual. Therefore, it is a force in action.

We say that Venus is the planet of love. Here is a perfect example of personality and individuality. For when the planet Venus is rightly aspected, meaning it has a good relationship to our sun sign or some aspect, it brings an adoring nature. It has the tendency to give us a great deal of love for humanity. It increases the potentials of our physical love. But when it is badly aspected or influenced by another planet, we would find that our love influence was not as pure and as selfless as it was when it was well aspected.

Here in this explanation of the aspect of planets we have the demonstration of personality and individuality. For the Planet Venus is the planet of love. That is its personality. But the way we use it or the way it is aspected in accordance with the other heavenly bodies, what their electro-magnetic influence is on that planet in their birth chart, this and the pattern of it denotes our individuality. It is the individuality of the planet Venus at the time of our birth.

Therefore, souls on the cosmic plane never leave it except to reincarnate here in an earthly body, but they can and do project their personalities to other personalities on the earth plane. They do this in an effort to help those whom they are able to reach here. This is assuming they are highly enough evolved to receive the help constructively.

Let us take this from another standpoint. The personality is to the soul as the psychic body is to the physical body. For the psychic body is the effluent material which fills the spiritual body and gives effervescence through the physical. In fact, the personality is the psychic body, one might say, of the physical.

The soul does not lose its personality through the change called death or transition. Neither does the being, in communicating with those on the earth plane when the personality is extended, does it have any change. One does not take or extend the soul with it in that extension or image.

Even as two earth beings in separate locations communicate by extending the personality through mind while the soul and the body and spirit remain where they are. Even as one projects his personality over the Zoom screen or cell phone while remaining physically where he is.

The dictionary defines personality as the habitual patterns and qualities of behavior of an individual as expressed by physical and mental activity and attitudes. Also the quality or fact of being a person, not an animal, not a demon, not a stone, and that which constitutes a person. Here is a very interesting fact that in the Latin word "persona" the meaning is given as "mask," so you might say that the personality of the soul is its mask.

For instance, let us take individuality as that which distinguishes one person from another, and that personality is really the naked body under the changeable cloak of individuality. This reverses in a sense the Latin origin of the meaning since the latter originated from the Latin word meaning not to divide and indivisible. But when you look at this carefully you will see that individuality is not divisible because it will not move from this plane to another world and still be intact.

The personality of man goes with him the same as the Self and the Soul. This is why Jesus said, "He who saveth his life shall lose it, but he who loseth his life shall save it." For when we let go of what we think we are, our actions, our individuality which we see in the mirror of our memory, only then may the pure being of our personality show forth. Those things of the greater realization will become a real part of our physical being and be taken on by our personality. Then and only then may we be reborn.

Within the personality of man is the storehouse of our memory. Our memory is the combination of impressions accrued through many lifetimes with the purity we have been able to accept of the Great Mind and our Lord Jesus Christ. This constitutes the existence of the personality of a human being. A human being existing within the mind and body of Christ.

Here we have a picture of cosmic forces in action. We have personality forces in action blending together creating an atmosphere. This is the atmosphere of our own personal universe. Be it sunshiny weather, rain, or cyclone depends upon our approach and our acceptance of what Jesus said, "I am the way." You are traveling this Way. Your individuality becomes His personality. His personality becomes the total overshadowing mask of your life.

YOU are not the outer physical form or color or size. This will help you in identifying yourself to others on the physical level. No longer will you bother to judge, no longer will you bother to be heard or to listen to others' comments. You have a greater realization, and this realization is of your-Self. You are different from every other individual. Therefore, there is no comparison. Nothing to be drawn alike. This is because everything you see and experience is filtered through and experienced by this knowing. Therefore, life is colored differently for you.

If you become dominated by any one or two major emotions or sentiments the personality will reflect these, especially if they are untrue. Look at and take on these reflections. Their aggregate is individuality. The finer and more delicate your thoughts the more attractive and harmonious your personality. The more you devote time to thinking that which arouses the gentler emotions, you will experience a most beautiful transformation of personality and will be able to take on the mask of the Lord Jesus in a brief time.

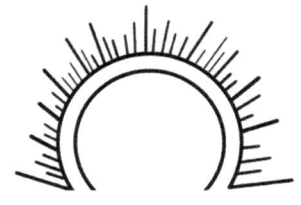

LESSON 4

FLESH BODY ONE

In Leviticus 17:11 we read, "For the life of the flesh is in the blood; and I have given it for you upon the altar to make atonement for your souls; for it is the blood that makes atonement, by reason of the life."

The flesh body is the lowest descent of God's manifestation in the living bodies of Earth. But this flesh body is still the temple of God.

In Corinthians 3:16-17 we read,

"Do you not know that you are God's temple, and that God's Spirit dwells in you? If anyone destroys God's Temple, God will destroy him. For God's temple is Holy, and that temple you are."

The blood circulates through the body, feeds it, and carries the vibratory energy which keeps the reconstruction process up, and provides God with an excellent means of communication with this denser world Earth.

The blood also carries the record of life to the three seed atoms of life. The flesh body and its desires are not evil.

In this New Age, this School shows how to reconstruct the flesh body. By applying Bible truths to our consciousness, we are able to attune our bodies to higher rates of vibration.

The flesh body is just raw or plain matter and needs to be clothed with immortality of pure thought vibration. Thus the flesh is renewed and transmuted from mortality to immortality by the renewing of the Mind.

In Romans, Chapter 12:1-3 Paul says,

"I appeal to you therefore, brethren, by the mercies of God, to present your bodies as a living sacrifice, holy and acceptable to God, which is your spiritual worship. For by Grace given to me, I bid everyone among you not to think of himself more highly than he ought to think."

The law of the flesh body must vigorously and diligently be observed if they are to reconstruct and control the Kundalini force, thus the flesh body may enter into the realization of the existence of itself, the Self.

The Laws of The Flesh Body are:

1. Right body function.
2. Right breathing.
3. Right thinking.
4. Right action.
5. Right pride-less humility.
6. Right mindfulness.
7. Tolerance in love.

The flesh body discipline must be only as rigid as the student needs to be stimulated into Spiritual action.

In the eighth chapter of Romans, we find the transmutation of the physical body through the Spirit of Christ and the redemption of the physical body or flesh body through the Spiritual nature of the Divine Christ.

It is emphasized and reemphasized that there is no condemnation in Christ Jesus but that the nature of man's carnal body is at constant variance with the Laws of God.

The flesh body will transgress the Law, or sin as we call it, because in this stage it is carnal. The carnal mind expresses the erroneous concept of sin which believes what you see is all there is. This is in the physical section of the mind. We prefer to call this the physical misconception of Universal Mind by man's finite and non-illumined brain, the Mass Mind. Mind rules the flesh body.

Often the spiritualization of Man's mental concepts of the Creation of the Flesh Body becomes Sanctified, or separated from Mass Mind, through the illumination of the Christ Light.

The Flesh Body then becomes controlled by the Father Creator. There is nothing evil in the interpretation and concept of the Flesh Body, as believed by Mass Mind.

The Flesh Body is the vehicle through which the Father Creator manifests Himself. It is continually creating within.

Power is made ever present in the Flesh Body. The power for the Sons of God is generated in the Spiritual Body which transfers the Father Energy into the Physical Body.

Every organ of the Flesh Body has both a physical and spiritual function.

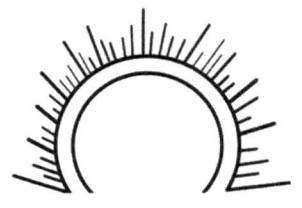

FLESH BODY TWO

ST. MATTHEW

5:29-30   And if thy right eye offend thee, pluck it out, and cast it from thee: for it is profitable for thee that one of thy members should perish, and not thy whole body should be cast into hell. And if thy right hand offend thee, cut it off, and cast it from thee: for it is profitable for thee that one of thy members should perish, and not thy whole body should be cast into hell.

6:22-23   The light of the body is the eye: if, therefore, thine eye be single, thy whole body shall be full of light. But if thine eye be evil, thy whole body shall be full of darkness. If, therefore, the light that is in thee be darkness, how great is that darkness!

6:25   Therefore, I say unto you, Take no thought for your life, what ye shall eat, or what ye shall drink; nor yet for your body, what ye shall put on. Is not life more than meat, and the body than raiment?

10:28   And fear not them which kill the body, but are not able to kill the soul: but rather fear him which is able to destroy both body and soul in hell.

14:12   And his disciples came, and took up the body, and buried it, and went and told Jesus.

26:12   For in that she hath poured this ointment on my body, she did it for my burial.

26:26   And as they were eating, Jesus took bread, and blessed it, and brake it, and gave it to his disciples, and said, Take, eat; this is my body.

27:58-59   He went to Pilate, and begged the body of Jesus. Then Pilate commanded the body to be delivered. And when Joseph had taken the body, he wrapped it in a clean linen cloth.

ST. MARK

5:29   And straightway the fountain of her blood was dried up; and she felt in her body that she was healed of that plague.

14: 8   She hath done what she could: she is come aforehand to anoint my body to the burying.

14:22   And as they did eat, Jesus took the bread, and blessed, and brake it, and gave to them, and said, Take, eat: this is my body.

14:51   And there followed him a certain man, having a linen cloth cast about his naked body; and the young man laid hold on him:

15:43   Joseph of Arimathea, an honorable counsellor, who also waited for the kingdom of God, came, and went in boldly to Pilate, and craved the body of Jesus.

15:45   And when he knew it of the centurion, he gave the body to Joseph.

ST. LUKE

11:34 The light of the body is the eye: therefore, when thine eye be single, thy whole body also is full of light; but when thine eye is evil, thy body also is full of darkness.

11:36 If thy whole body, therefore, be full of light, having no part dark, the whole shall be full of light, as when bright shining of a candle doth give thee light.

12: 4 And I say unto you my friends, Be not afraid of them that kill the body, and after that they have no more that they can do.

12:22-23 And he said unto his disciples, Therefore, I say unto you, Take no thought for your life, what ye shall eat; neither for the body, what ye shall put on. The life is more than meat, and the body is more than raiment.

17:37 And they answered and said unto him, Where Lord? And he said unto them, Wheresoever the body is, thither will the eagles be gathered together.

22:19 And he took bread, and gave thanks, and brake it, and gave unto them, saying, This is my body which is given for you: this do in remembrance of me.

23:52 This man went to Pilate and begged the body of Jesus.

23:55 And the women also, which came with him from Galilee, followed after, and beheld the sepulchre, and how his body was laid.

24: 3 And they entered in, and found not the body of the Lord Jesus.

24:23 And when they found not his body, they came, saying, that they had also seen a vision of angels, which said that he was alive.

ST. JOHN

2:21 But he spake of the temple of the body.

19:38 And after this, Joseph of Arimathea, being a disciple of Jesus, but secretly for fear of the Jews, besought Pilate that he might take away the body of Jesus: and Pilate gave him leave. He came, therefore, and took the body of Jesus.

19:40 Then took they the body of Jesus, and wound it in linen clothes with the spices, as the manner of the Jews is to bury.

20:12 And seeth two angels in white sitting, the one at the head, and the other at the feet, where the body of Jesus had lain.

ACTS

9:40 But Peter put them all forth, and kneeled down, and prayed; and turning him to the body said, Tabitha, arise. And she opened her eyes: and when she saw Peter, she sat up.

19:12 So that from his body were brought unto the sick handkerchiefs or aprons, and the diseases departed from them, and the evil spirits went out of them.

ROMANS

4:19 And being not weak in faith, he considered not his own body now dead, when he was about an hundred years old, neither yet the deadness of Sara's womb.

6: 6 Knowing this, that our old man is crucified in him, that the body of sin might be destroyed, that henceforth we should not serve sin.

6:12 Let not sin, therefore, reign in your mortal body, that ye should obey it in the lusts thereof.

7: 4   Wherefore, my brethren, ye also are become dead to the law by the body of Christ; that ye should be married to another, even to him who is raised from the dead, that we should bring forth fruit unto God.

7:24   O wretched man that I am! who shall deliver me from the body of this death?

8:10   And if Christ be in you, the body is dead because of sin; but the Spirit is life because of righteousness.

8:13   For if ye live after the flesh, ye shall die: but if ye through the Spirit do mortify the deeds of the body, ye shall live.

8:23   And not only they, but ourselves also, which have the first fruits of the Spirit, even we ourselves groan within ourselves, waiting for the adoption, to wit, the redemption of our body.

12: 4-5   For as we have many members in one body, and all members have not the same office. So we, being many, are one body in Christ, and everyone members one of another.

I CORINTHIANS

5: 3   For I verily, as absent in body, but present in spirit have judged already, as though I were present, concerning him that hath so done this deed.

6:13   Now the body is not for fornication, but for the Lord; and the Lord for the body.

6:16   What? know ye not that he which is joined to a harlot is one body? for two, saith he, shall be one flesh.

6:18-20   Flee fornication. Every sin that a man doeth is without the body; but he that committeth fornication sinneth against his own body. What? know ye not that your own body is the temple of the Holy Ghost, which is in you, which ye have of God, and ye are not your own. For ye are bought with a price: therefore, glorify God in your body, and in your spirit, which are God's.

7: 4   The wife hath not power over her own body, but the husband: and likewise also the husband hath not power of his own body, but the wife.

7:34   There is a difference also between a wife and a virgin. The unmarried woman careth for the things of the Lord, that she may be holy both in body and in spirit: but she that is married careth for the things of the world, how she may please her husband.

9:27   But I keep under my body, and bring it into subjection: lest that by any means, when I have preached unto others, I myself should be a castaway.

10:17   For we being many are one bread, and one body: for we are all partakers of that one bread.

11:24   And when he had given thanks, he brake it, and said, Take, eat: this is my body, which is broken for you: this do in remembrance of me.

11:27   Wherefore, whosoever shall eat this bread, and drink this cup of the Lord, unworthily, shall be guilty of the body and blood of the Lord.

11:29   For he that eateth and drinketh unworthily, eateth and drinketh damnation to himself, not discerning the Lord's body.

12:12-20   For as the body is one, and hath many members, and all the members of that one body, being many, are one body: so also is Christ. For by one Spirit are we all baptized into one body, whether we be Jews or Gentiles, whether we be bond or free; and have been all made to drink into one Spirit. For the body is not one member, but many. If the foot shall say, Because I am not of the hand, I am not of the body; is it, therefore, not of the body? And if the ear shall say, Because I am not of the hand, I am not of the body; is it, therefore, not of the body? If the whole body were an eye, where were the hearing? If the whole body were hearing, where were the smelling? But now hath God set the members every one of them in the body, as it hath pleased Him. And if they were all one member, where were the body? But now are they many members, yet not one body.

12:22-25 Nay, much more those members of the body, which seem to be more feeble, are necessary: And those members of the body, which we think to be less honourable, upon these we bestow more abundant honor: and our comely parts have more abundant comeliness. For our comely parts have no need: but God had tempered the body together, having given more abundant honour to that part which lacked: That there should be no schism in the body; but that the members should have the same care one for another.

12:27 Now ye are the body of Christ, and members in particular.

13: 3 And though I bestow all my goods to feed the poor, and though I give my body to be burned, and have not charity, it profiteth me none.

15:35 But some man will say, How are the dead raised up? and with what body do they come?

15:37 And that which thou sowest, thou sowest not that body that shall be, but bare grain, it may chance of wheat, or of some other grain.

15:44 It is sown a natural body; it is raised a spiritual body. There is a natural body, and there is a spiritual body.

II CORINTHIANS

4:10   Always bearing about in the body the dying of the Lord Jesus, that the life also of Jesus might be made manifest in our body.

5: 6   Therefore, we are always confident, know that whilst we are at home in the body, we are absent from the Lord.

5: 8   We are confident, I say, and willing rather to be absent from the body, and to be present with the Lord.

5:10   For we must all appear before the judgment seat of Christ; that everyone may receive the things done in his body, and to be present with the Lord.

12: 2-3   I knew a man in Christ about fourteen years ago, (whether in the body, I cannot tell; or whether out of the body, I cannot tell: God knoweth) such as one caught up to the third heaven. And I knew such a man, (whether in the body, or out of the body, I cannot tell: God knoweth).

GALATIANS

6:17   From henceforth let no man trouble me: for I bear in my body the marks of the Lord Jesus.

EPHESIANS

1:23   Which is his body, the fullness of him that filleth all in all.

2:16   And that he might reconcile both unto God in one body by the cross, having slain the enmity thereby:

3: 6   That the Gentiles should be fellow heirs, and are the same body, and partakers of his promise in Christ by the gospel.

4: 4   There is one body, and one Spirit, even as ye are called in one hope of your calling.

4:12 For the perfecting of the saints, for the work of the ministry, for the edifying of the body of Christ.

4:16 From whom the whole body fitly joined together and compacted by that which every joint supplieth, according to the effectual working in the measure of every part, maketh increase of the body unto the edifying of itself in love.

5:23 For the husband is head of the wife, even as Christ is head of the church: and he is the savior of the body.

5:30 For we are members of his body, of his flesh, and of his bones.

PHILIPPIANS

1:20 According to my earnest expectation and my hope, that in nothing shall I be ashamed, but that with all boldness, as always, so now also Christ shall be magnified in my body, whether it be by life or by death.

3:21 Who shall change our vile body, that it may be fashioned like unto his glorious body, according to the workings whereby he is able even to subdue all things unto himself.

COLOSSIANS

1:18 And he is the head of the body, the church: who is the beginning, the firstborn from the dead; that in all things he might have the pre-eminence.

1:22 In the body of his flesh through death, to present you holy and unblameable, and unreproveable in his sight.

2:11 In whom also ye are circumcised with the circumcision made without hands, in putting off the body of the sins of the flesh by the circumcision of Christ:

2:17 Which are the shadow of things to come; but the body is of Christ.

2:19 And not holding the Head, from which all the body by joints and bands having nourishment ministered, and knit together, increaseth with the increase of God.

2:23 Which things have indeed a shew of wisdom in will, worship, and humility, and neglecting of the body; not in any honour to the satisfying of the flesh.

3:15 And let the peace of God rule in your hearts, to the which also ye are called in one body; and be ye thankful.

I THESSALONIANS

5:23 And the very God of peace sanctify you wholly; and I pray God your whole spirit and soul and body be preserved blameless unto the coming of our Lord Jesus Christ.

HEBREWS

10: 5 Wherefore when he cometh into the world, he saith, Sacrifice and offering thou wouldst not, but a body has thou prepared me:

10:10 By the which will we are sanctified through the body of Jesus Christ once for all.

13: 3 Remember them that are in bonds, as bound with them; and them which suffer adversity, as being yourselves also in the body.

JAMES

2:16 And one of you say unto them, Depart in peace, be ye warmed and filled; notwithstanding ye gave them not those things which are needful to the body; what doth it profit?

2:26 For as the body without the spirit is dead, so faith without works is dead also.

3: 2-3   For in many things we offend all. If any man offend not in word, the same is a perfect man, and able also to bridle the whole body. Behold, we put bits in the horses' mouths, that they obey us; and we turn about their whole body.

3: 6   And the tongue is a fire, a world of iniquity: so is the tongue among our members, that it defileth the whole body, and setteth on fire the course of nature; and is set on fire of hell.

I PETER

2:24   Who his own self bare our sins in his own body on the tree, that we, being dead to sins, should live unto righteousness: by whose stripes ye were healed.

JUDE

1: 9   Yet Michael the archangel, when contending with the devil he disputed about the body of Moses, durst not bring against him a railing accusation, but said, The Lord rebuke thee.

Flesh Body Two

Lesson 5: The Word • Mind • Faith

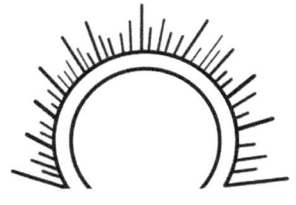

LESSON 5

THE WORD ONE

The Word is ever present, ever misunderstood, ever in action and rest, and gives when understood Life unto the Dead, Strength unto the Weak. Pronounce it not, for it is worthless unto any who know not its correct pronunciation or manner of such, or when and how it should be used.

The Word is worthless unto any who knows it not as the finest Ruby which is so overlaid with incrustations that its Light cannot be seen. In Egypt that Word was known and its action joined hands with others and they as one invested earth and other places with its Sound and its Perfume.

Stand in awe in its presence; one humbles their heart when seen. Gaze upon its Ineffableness and ask that The Highest may assist thee.

Held within the Hidden Universe is all this. And Peace which comes through the Enlightenment is Great. Slowly unfolds the Rose, in Color seen, the Perfume sensed, the properties held within each when seen, known and understood. The Soul becomes as its Origin.

Silence then becomes known, the red Ruby shines in its Might, the Right encircles the Inspiring, and Love comprehends. As Dawn in its Radiance, the Color of the Ruby sheds its roseate over the falling and rising of all things. Hast thou, O reader, comprehended? All writing is far from plain, for language conceals more than it reveals.

The heart throb is unknown unto any but the one. A smile may linger on the lips and the pain be concealed from any and all except the one!

The tragedies of Life are but moments along the mighty Way. Each and all serving as lessons and they who make their Mark when passing down the Mountain will see them on their return. Then has your accomplishment begun for Recognition is first when in the ascendant.

Before we pass from this we do so with all kindness for those who see not nor know. The Voice of a God may be so great as to deafen some and awaken others. Then it becomes necessary to use other means than the Voice, although they are the same but appear different.

When considering anything repugnant to the reader the first consideration to have settled is the accuracy of the statement made. It is impossible in some cases to demonstrate the accuracy to anyone who presupposes that he is receptive to some extent. What to one is folly is logic to another.

In such a condition as has so far been set forth, proof is only such when the mind and all its faculties are receptive to the Truth. That means that all preconceptions are placed in abeyance at least.

We now enter into another point which briefly is this: the passions of mind are not always demonstrable to the reader. Mind attempting to fathom mind is often an impossibility.

It can only be conceived through control. To conceive of anything there must be a lower and a higher. The lower cannot be expected to receive the higher in its completeness, but the higher can and does conceive of the lower in its many parts.

Any lesson of any height will necessarily be found to be hard to grasp by brain, for brain is a falling Force and not an ascending one. Mind, the attribute of Soul, debased by the Fall, cannot completely conceive of Soul, its parent.

Mind has become so enmeshed in this lower materiality that to see and to conceive it must be penetrated by Higher.

As we look at mind there comes to view its progenitor Self, that part which has been abolished from the House of its Origin and has become a wanderer. Wandering to find its plane of action it has taken refuge in many kinds. One is mankind, using the physical organs of expression known as brain in mankind with accessory organs in other parts of the body.

Between the mind of man and that of other kinds there is of necessity a link, strong in some, weak in others.

We take up for consideration mind in mankind, Mind saying unto the brain: "I have taken refuge in thee, O physical organ of expression, for to me thou art capable of much. And I tarry along the Way, and thou art now my instrument of expression, but at some time I will leave thee and go unto another which will suit me the better, for I cannot remain with thee longer."

The physical organ responds: "I accept thee as thy home for a time for I, too, am not to be without a tenant, for the blankness of non-occupancy is very hard on me; as to thee thou must make of me as thou canst, for I am very finite."

The two are not at all times in harmony for the brain often fails to register and transmit what mind wishes. Then comes a conflict which disorders both physical and mind, and the many organs having relation with them. Then one has so-called insanity which is but discordant impulses due to faulty registering and transmission.

Between them there is induced a condition strong in effects on the many organs forming mankind. This faulty registering is sometimes due to a poorly evolved brain, poorly conducting apparatus, and poor receiving in its more peripheral parts. Add to this the confusion in higher ethereal parts which causes the many impulses to be faultily impacted upon the brain.

These are not all the elements to be taken into account in such cases. Within mind there is a small element in ascent. This has little affect on mankind until that one individual is well enough evolved to receive. These are few indeed.

With this as our basis we proceed to demonstrate how mankind struggles against such adversity and passes upward in spite of such drawbacks. These many inequalities lead to traits of character, all of which play their parts.

Some are called good, some bad. The differences cause many actions which are judged by those, or others of the same kind, as crime, and judged by many others by whatever name may be appropriated to them. When the philanthropic and proactive instincts meet, you have genius.

When a certain level is achieved and on a high plane you have one who is no longer reincarnating. These are the ones who become Masters. Their plane is so high that they function evenly, balance is maintained.

Such a one passes to higher Heights and soon becomes emancipated from earth's thrall. Such are rapidly elevated for they have overcome inertia and are passing swiftly into such Heights as are beyond the cognizance of mind.

Mind has then ceased to be the great functioning part and occupies a subordinate position. It is required to do but few of the acts, and they are the ordinary ones needed to meet the requirements of life as known on earth. The receptive being non-homogenous, the acts of the receiving, or caused by it, are also such.

We deal not so much with the brain as we do with the factors influencing it. As we proceed with this subject, let us for a moment pause and visualize the many whose organ of reception and propelling function is not so highly evolved as the brain of mankind.

There is at the present nothing in the lower creations, such as plant life, which in any way approximates the brain of mankind, yet they perform the same functions.

The hand reaching out to take a glass of water is equaled by the plant reaching out to follow a course which leads it to the same object.

Within the leaves and other parts of plant life there exists a center, or more exactly, centers of reception and perception which perform the same function as in the body of mankind. Mind acts in each in the same manner.

There is the same difference and similarity in both species. Each acts and reacts in accordance with the selectivity accorded to each. The higher acting through the lower can only give as to the selectivity of the transmitting, which is also the receiving.

This also applies to all kinds irrespective of their origin and course. All kinds on earth are but parts of such and can and do and will change as the evolution of earth changes, which is continual.

Mankind in form is but a conglomerate of many kinds. Being such he is but a part of the many kinds and they of him. He who can reach, find, and know this consciously and not by rote or repetition of words, is and has become part of the University of Nature.

Having mastered he is a Master. As a Master he is one conscious part of the Whole and needs not to remain on earth except as a "sacrifice" to do the acts of greatness. These are seldom known and little appreciated by those of earth whose standards are different.

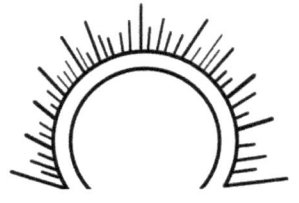

LESSON 5

THE WORD TWO

In the beginning was God. We are not interested where God began or when. But we are interested in God for it was the Word He gave that is the creative Cause, first started in function.

This is the beginning of any created thing, either of God, the Hierarchy, or man.

Perhaps one might say that in the beginning we have the springtime of the planting of the Seed of Causation, before any objective is created. This reality, to which we have given the name God, is an ever-present fact in every man's experience.

The Word as spoken by the Father, the infinite and universal Creative Spirit, is the activation of a symbolism which contains imagination, knowingness, and intelligence. This is coupled with what you will learn of as the Law in the second level of the tools of man.

This Law is the format which is the self-exacting intelligence of the Spirit. This is why we said that the Spirit was the personality of the Father in action.

Within this intelligence and its symbolic format exists the potentiality of the function of everything which exists. This is saying that God is absolute intelligence, limitless imagination, with the all-encompassing consciousness of complete self-expression.

For the Spirit makes things out of Itself, through the inner act upon Itself, which is the act of God's Word, being acted on in consciousness.

In other words, it is the inner consciousness of the Father acting upon Itself, thus releasing power into a given form or symbolism.

Within the nature of this spirit, its own nature, there is a law obeying the will of God.

Since we speak a great deal about self-contemplation, it is well to analyze exactly what we mean by it. Self-contemplation is an awareness of the core of Self, being conscious of its duality as absolute nothing and absolute everything. An inner sense of being, thus is the Word of the Father transmitted through us, and His Word must, therefore, be completed. For this is the original Cause working through the sound of our mind and voice.

Therefore, God must forever be expressing. God's expression must always be harmonious and perfect. And perfect are our answers, and they will be, that is self-evident, as they come from the Self in proportion to the original creative Cause. Were it to be anything but perfect, it would be self-destructive.

All words are symbolism, and when we use the Word, the First Cause becomes evident in the absolute intelligence of God. The Spirit motivates, and thus reality starts its process through our vehicles, conveying the intention behind the words. This means, and must be, that the Universal Creative Intelligence, never completely formed nor completely came into being, continues to create.

Jesus simplified this in his words, "For the words that I speak unto you, I speak not of myself, but the Father that dwelleth in me, He doeth the works."

This is the Mind of God working in us and through us, for God can work for us only by working through us.

The power of God, Creative power in the universe, manifests itself through imagination, will, and feeling. The Creative Mind of the Universe operates upon Itself through Its will, imagination, and feeling, It creates forms which are subject to It, and Its law, but which have no reality apart from the Mind which created them.

It is the creative Mind that Jesus used, and that we all use for conscious purposes and have the consciousness of self-knowingness.

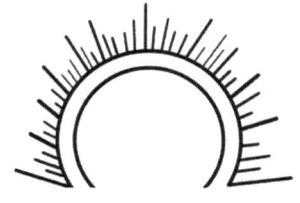

THE WORD THREE

The Word, as spoken of in Genesis and the first chapter of John, refers to the spoken Word of God. The Word can be either written or spoken with equal effect. So consider the following facts of it:

1. The written word is symbolic and conveys a message, and if properly written, will be recreated in your mind and effective.

2. The spoken word is a symbol with power, and has both the basic energy, and the creative "In the beginning was the Word, and the Word was with God." Or in John 1:14, "and the Word became flesh."

We, our beings, mankind are the manifestations of the active Word of God. God said it and it was done. We say it and it is and shall be done.

Jesus was known as the Logos of the Word. We in turn are the Logos (plural), the many-membered sonships of the Father.

We are the extensions of God's spoken word. When we reach the state where we speak from the Self then we become the Word of God in flesh.

The written word is merely the symbolic combination of power and focus of the spoken word to the person reading it.

In Genesis God said, "Let there be Light" and there was Light. Here we have the potential and the Spirit. It activated the Power in the voice and the Word of God was manifest.

Everything was created in the beginning by the great Word, or Logos, through projection into space of Divine Creative Power.

The Creator is God in the act of creating and is the supreme Uni-Being, nameless but with supreme Will, a Will-Power which the Egyptians called "RA."

The word "rite" is from Sanskrit *riti,* meaning a going-away, and from the Aryan *ri,* meaning to flow. In this sense using a writ is using the word since rites help to understand the way by causing a flow to the form which depicts the desired result.

Jesus said in Matthew 4:4, "Man shall not live by bread alone, but by every word that proceedeth from the mouth of God."

This gives us the evaluation of the statement made by the Master when he said, "Think not what goeth into the mouth, but what cometh out is what defileth the soul."

Jesus said, and many times spoke and things took place, but he told us in the Upper Room at the Last Supper, "All these things I do, so shall ye do also, and even greater than these."

In Matthew 8:16, "That evening they brought unto him many possessed with demons, and he cast out the spirits with a word."

This helps us to understand the reality of the Word, for in John 1:1, "In the beginning was the Word, and the Word was with God." So likewise is the word with you, if you are conscious of the Master. If you are conscious of God, it is with you.

An interesting fact of the Testament is that in the writing of the New Testament the term "word" is used better than 575 times.

The word comes as produced by vibration with form. As mankind has a desire so likewise does humanity give it form by assuming (by producing) the sound, over which the light travels.

In the art of healing, if one is being healed and hears the word, it works better, apparently, for the less enlightened. Then if there is that within him which can accept the words, and he does, this aids the healing. The word is projection into the physical realm of manifestation by the power of sound. Sound must have form and a force. Back of all of this is motivation of mind.

When one speaks the Word the one being healed responds to forms and the sound of letters and the conveyance, or package, that is sent out. The motivation of mind is important. If you merely repeat it the word drops to the floor. But if you give it Life with feeling, you send it out because you want it to take form and manifest.

It is something said. Because of the LETTERED Sounds, not as accidental mechanical sounds, the Word gains Life through the intelligence of Mind and thus it is so because at that moment there is but One Mind and One Consciousness.

The Word of the Father, He spoke the Word once, then has held it ever since in silent, everlasting prayer.

It had all the increments of sound, frequency, wavelength, power, force, and motivation of mind. It became flesh, because it carried all of the wave-lengths consistent with the chemical elements.

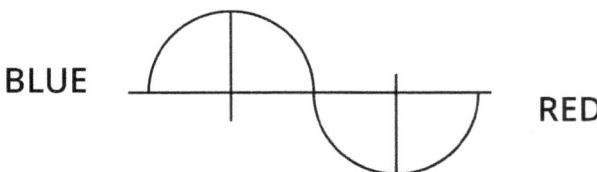

BLUE   **RED**

The cycle carries the two facets in the world of sound which is the Divine Fiat.

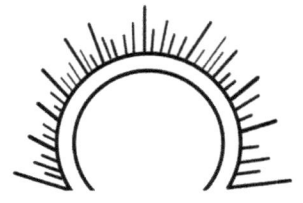

THE WORD FOUR

THE SPOKEN WORD

The tongue, the two-edged sword, with its vibration and the sounding box of the roof of the mouth, produces radiation or waves of sound. When words are spoken there is actual energy going out from the mouth emitting into the atmosphere as the mouth moves and forms the opening. This permits the wave vibrations to go out. They are neither positive nor negative.

Power travels along the soundtrack of the voice and no other way. The Word of God was sound-less because it was within Him. It is the same place, but another dimension within which we live.

Thus it is that the Word of God was left with man, for it echoes eternally with the Being of the Creator. The Spirit of God gives it Life. For this was God's feeling. The movement within God brings breath. The Great Self develops the form.

There are two ways of speaking, one through the lips, and the other is through the solar plexus where it takes on dimension. The solar plexus is taking the life force from the Self. For it is from the Self that we can gain God-consciousness.

The ability to make sounds is taken from the breath. The palate is vibrated, the muscle tissues vibrate, the entrance of the breath from the throat has two channels, and the sounds are both negative and positive.

They act as a modulator in radio receptors. All spoken sounds are nearly-rounded tops to the waves. The breath with its life force forms a carrier. The voice wave travels over it. The sound is consistent. Words without feeling are flat, not creative.

Words of anger with adrenaline motivation have feeling which vibrates. These create temporarily and this creative word has impact, but it returns to you because it is not male, it is all feeling.

The true creative word must have balance, both male and female. The first must be expressed.

SOUND

Any of a class of waves consisting of mechanical disturbances, which may be of varying pressure or alternating movement in an elastic field, such as air.

The auditory stimulation produced by waves of this type having frequencies between 20 and 20,000 cycles, or waves, per second.

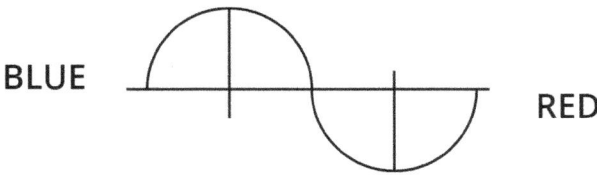

This is way down on the red side. Below 20 you could not hear it. (Six cycles per second with volume is lethal.)

Instances of this stimulation: the sound of a car, a speech sound. Normal hearing has a range of about 30 to 13,000 cycles per second.

MEASUREMENT OF SOUND

A science is a series of investigations in a specific field. The resultant of these investigations and their numerical values are summed together and the root of the mean is evaluated.

Sound is not measured by angstroms but by decibels, strength of impulses (a graph of intensity volume), a unit of sound, like the volt in electricity. Its pressure is measured by water, because water is the best conductor of sound.

SPIRITUAL FACTS OF SOUND

Sound in the Spirit is entirely reversed, as everything is reversed on the spirit plane, polarity and direction-wise, as to what it is on the material plane.

The speed of sound is about 741 miles per hour. The state in which the illumined being works is neutral in nature.

There is an interesting interrelation of sound, light, power, force, and energy.

The ability to make sound is taken from the breath. Also through the voice of the spirit, in deep contemplation.

Control of sound coming from mouth is also controlled by adrenals and mind. The negative forms are called the cries, and due to shock impulses.

When you speak, you use the same energy as when you create a child. Remember, the gas through which the Kundalini fire of the spine of man moves, the stuff spoken of in the 23rd Psalm, is the creative energy used by the brain and sex forces, the same force used in speech.

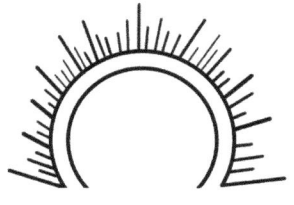

MIND ONE

All through the Holy Testament, all through all of the teachings of Jesus through the Testament and the ancient mystery teachings, runs the Great Golden Thread of the mental law.

Your ability to demonstrate the supremacy of spiritual thought force over all apparent material resistance must necessarily depend on your understanding of mental laws. We use the term mental laws because these will be your way of activating them, setting the patterns, because they use a mental medium, either yours or God's. He pronounced the Word and it still exists in His mind, therefore it is ever working because the spirit is ever-present here.

We must come to think of the mental medium, which is the principle or law governing the spiritual mind healing, in terms of exact law. We should think of it as the mind of God. We cannot think of it as the spirit alone. The spirit of God activates through the mental medium automatically, for the spirit acts as a self-knowing force. It carries within It the feeling, the personality of the Father.

Let us then consider this all-important idea of God in terms of an infinite knower, a limitless doer.

Though we repeat this idea many times, we are merely reaffirming the thought that the universe contains the pure spirit. This spirit is filled with warmth and color, which is the material demonstration of the love of God for Its creations. It is illumined through the Christos by the divine presence. It is filled with the divine idea.

In other words we are surrounded by an atmosphere, a presence in the universe which is conscious, alive, awake, and aware, like that of our own atmosphere, of which we must be conscious.

In this divine presence we live and move and have our being. This is the medium upon which inspiration, intuition, and the three aspects of the Christos called Light, Life, and Love, are conveyed to us.

It is this presence of God in which is the living spirit, eternal reality, and supreme being with whom we communicate in prayer and meditation. In Its combined composite form It contains the ever-present silent receptive place, the Akasha or soul of the Father. When we ask a question, it is from this soul that floods through mind into our brain or Self, and the divine infallible answer is given. This might be called the divine influx of divine mind working through divine principle.

It is the achievement of the divine communion of God. This is what man has been attempting to call Being.

This is the office of prayer, the office of intercession of the saints throughout the ages.

It is the divine inspiration being transmuted into our vehicle as a voice of the invisible. It is the emanation from the burning bush in the wilderness to which Moses responded. It typifies the unproduced, unproductive, uncultivated place of mind. It is the need of mankind met by the consuming fire of love descending from the Father from heaven.

Moses had gone out into the wilderness to meditate and pray. He was in need of conviction and inspiration that somehow in his meditation or prayer he so completely left the human will behind that the divine mind spoke and made itself heard. For the pure reality of pure voice, or sound vibration, would be very painful to man's physical being, thus it came through the burning bush which had no personal will of its own.

In this way the most humble event may proclaim the omniscience of God or good.

The weakest link of any chain of cause and effect may be so tempered by the flame of a new concept that it may have sufficient strength to bind a complete sequence together.

It is necessary that we be careful not to confuse divine presence with the universal law. The law is a principle, the immutable cause and effect. As we examine this objectively, we find that it is both intelligent and conscious without knowing that it is intelligent and without being self-conscious.

The universal mind in its subjective state is what we refer to when we speak of the Law of Mind.

One of the most difficult things for us to understand is that while we may consciously deal with the law, we may even definitely direct it, and set its creative intelligence into motion for good, yet the law is not self-conscious.

In other words, even though this law is creative and intelligent, even though it is conscious of our desire, it has no self-consciousness, no self-choice with regards to such a desire. It must execute the directions given it by our self-knowing mind. It must respond to our word.

Jesus said, "Heaven and earth shall pass away but my word shall not pass away." This is a wondrous concept of unity with God and the command of the law. This shows the difference between a schoolteacher and a teacher. He taught as one having authority, not as one repeating the words of others. This is why the wind and the waves obeyed him.

We receive the inspiration from the spirit, but we command the law. In the common occurrences of our everyday life in dealing with the laws of nature we are so accustomed to the reactions of these laws with which we are familiar.

We never stop to recognize that in using any law of nature we are dealing with the creative agency which knows what to do and how to do it but it cannot have any self-choice. That choice is ours.

In other words, electricity does not know whether it is furnishing motive power to a streetcar or boiling an egg but when the switch is turned on, in that certain sense, it knows what it should do, what path it should follow, and it must do this. We must do the deciding and choose the pattern. This is why we put copper wires from the source to the equipment which we want the power to move through. It has the authority of the laws of nature but no volition.

It is energy, but itself remains undirected and is subject to our desires. If this were not true of the laws of nature we could not depend on them and we would be confronted with chaos.

It is because we can depend on the laws of nature that this is an exact science. It is the science of the mind of creation and your mind and it is subject to our conscious use, and it is a principle of nature just as the laws of infinity in chemistry.

Many times we say, how is a prayer answered to people who have no understanding of this law? But we forget that through pure faith a person with a great need arrives at a state, or you might call it a conclusion, which would permit the function of this law. But to reproduce this at will, to reduce it to a laboratory experiment whenever and wherever we desire, that is a different thing.

One is chance, the other science; one is ignorance, and the other wisdom; one is the path of the penitent sinner, the other is the way of the true Christian, the Law of Mind.

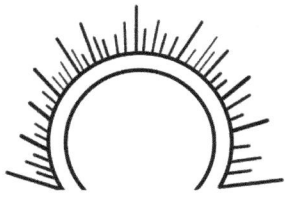

MIND TWO

The Law of Mind is absolutely impersonal. We might call it the way of the Word which works through the mind. Once set into motion it produces a logical result. It proceeds in a mathematical manner to create and, unless that tendency set into motion is changed, it will create a logical result whatever idea is given to it.

WE CANNOT DESTROY THE LAW BUT WE CAN RE-DIRECT ITS MOVEMENT. In this concept lies the possibility of freedom from bondage. Not that we can change the Law of Mind but that we can change its direction.

The spirit of man, as being a part of the Spirit of God, has self-consciousness and self-choice. The law having neither self-consciousness nor self-choice automatically reacts to the spirit. Therefore, when you are treating or saying a prayer for someone else, you are really treating yourself or praying for yourself.

It is well to understand from the start that this is exactly the way the law works. You will never have to go outside of yourself to treat any person, place, or thing. To think it necessary to do this would be to deny the unity of God, good, and your access to the universal law of cause and effect.

WITHIN THIS ONE LAW ALL EVENTS TRANSPIRE.

Ralph Waldo Emerson rightly said that history is the record of the doings of this Mind on our planet.

We must remember that the Law of Mind has a binding force. It is intelligent. No greater mistake could be made than to think that subconscious means unconscious. It does not. Subconscious means below the threshold of conscious Mind.

As a matter of fact the subjective laws of the universe with which we deal in giving treatments have limitless intelligence and that limitless power to proceed from cause to effect.

It is THE creative agency of this universe. When you give a treatment or pray to help someone sick or who is in need, no matter what the need may be, you must be conscious that you are making a definite statement in the Mind and that Mind is the sole and only acting agency or actor.

The principle acts upon your thought projected into the experience of the one toward whom you direct it. This whole mental-spiritual practice is what is meant in the Testament, "Be still and know that I am God."

It is back of the illumined thought of Jesus when he said, "You shall know the truth and the truth shall make you free."

We explain here the trinity as God is the three-in-one. For God is threefold in nature: God is spirit or self-knowingness, God is law or action, and God is form or result. It is the trinity which runs through all the religions of the world, and it is recognized in all the teachings. We might call it here the thing, the way it works, and what it does.

This is creation: whatever the spirit wills or knows as a result of creation, the law is set in motion and produces that which the spirit knows.

God knows no evil as the Testament shows, "Judge not that ye be not judged." This will help you to have an understanding of the nature of God, which must be truth, beauty, and peace. God is always in tune with His nature.

God cannot will evil. We know that it will disappear from our experience in exact proportion as we cease using destructive thoughts. Evil is merely a misconception, the wrong way of using good.

It is limitation which God knows nothing of because the nature of God is infinite and that which is infinite cannot will limitation.

Ralph Waldo Emerson expressed this beautifully. He said that the finite alone has wrought and suffered, the infinite lies stretched in smiling repose.

The law never initiates anything. It always reacts to the spirit. Let us realize the meaning of this marvelous idea. The spirit is both the circumference and the center of everything and that there is such a perfect completion within our own souls that we really do have access to the very soul of the universe.

The Law of Mind in action: we find when we study its reality that while there is no limit to law, there appears to be a limit to man's use of it, and I said "appears." This means that even though the law of creating is infinite, we shall draw from it only as much good as our measure will hold, no more, no less.

This brings us back to the central theme of universal creative spirit of God which creates by self-knowing or contemplation. Man being the image and copy of the creative spirit acts in accord with his nature. That is, he creates by contemplation or self-knowingness.

This is the explanation for the great saying of Jesus that you shall know the truth and the truth shall make you free.

It is evident that if the knowing of something can produce freedom, there must be a law which automatically reacts to our knowing. It is of great importance that the laws of creation given to man and spirit be understood.

When you treat or pray for a physical or financial betterment in some other person's experience, you must be conscious that his good is now made manifest. It will appear in his experience to the degree of your being aware of the good. Becoming aware of his good is an interior awareness.

It is something that the Mind does to itself and as a result of this self-recognition, self-knowing, or state of consciousness as it is often called, the law automatically reacts to this self-knowing and produces an objective form, a physical condition, that exactly balances and equals the self-knowingness. This would be the same as water reaching its own level by its own weight.

The spirit and law were never created. They co-exist. They are part of the eternal reality. The law which man uses, Mind which he uses, and the spirit which he is, are all one.

Let us also consider the fact that there is no such thing as my mind, your mind, his mind, or her mind. Mind is an eternal principle in the universe and when we think we are making use of it, and as we think we are individualizing it.

Just as all physical nature is made up of one ultimate stuff including our physical bodies, and just as each body is a peculiar individualization of that stuff, so all individual mentalities emerge from one universal Mind. We should think of ourselves as being in such complete unity with that Mind that there are no longer two, only one. As we think within our being, we think only of being.

MIND is the realm of causes; conditions are the realm of effects; new thoughts create new conditions.

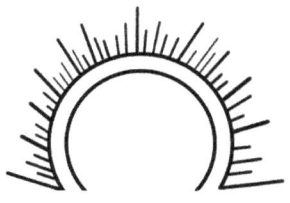

MIND THREE

There is but one mind and that mind is the Great Creative Mind and we live, move and have our being in that Mind.

Each one of us uses a part of that Great Mind and makes it a personalized part for our own use. In essence, we have put a wall around a part of that Mind. This is why we feel separate from God until we are in the lower stages of illumination.

The basis of all energy is in the mind of God, as God is Mind. Thus it is that we have the statement in Romans 8:5 & 6,

"For they that are after the flesh do mind the things of the flesh, but they that are after the Spirit mind the things of the Spirit. For to be carnally minded is death, but to be spiritually minded is life and peace."

II Timothy 1:7,

"For God hath not given us the spirit of fear, but of power and Love and a sound mind."

The awareness of the spirit of a sound mind is given to us by the Father through dedication and yielding up all unto Him.

We see in II Corinthians 8:12,

"For if there be first a willing mind, it is accepted according to that a man hath and not according to that he hath not."

This teaches us to be of willing mind. Without willingness nothing can be accomplished. God our Father will not force us to do anything. We must be willing of ourselves to do the will of the Father.

The reference of the term "to mind" is to pay attention to that which takes concentration. Using the mind function in concentration is the act of giving "life" to that which we are paying attention to. The way this works is that God Energy is the radiation of the mind.

IN THESE LAST DAYS

If we as manifestations of the Sons of God dare to operate in Carnal Mind we shall surely die or become separated from the God Energy.

To be Spiritually Minded is Life

The Spiritual Mind is the Mind of Christ and the Bible stands fast on this.

SELF DISCIPLINE

We must exercise the Mind constantly for God. We must be prepared to use the mind for God. In Philippians 2:5 & 6,

"Let this mind be in you, which was also in Christ Jesus,

Who, being in the form of God, thought it not robbery to be equal with God."

PEACE OBTAINED THROUGH THE MIND

Isaiah 26:3,

"Thou will keep him in perfect peace whose mind is yielded" to the Christ.

The Christ does the functioning. As mind is functioned by Christ it will begin to produce the Christ in you.

The doubtful mind is the mind of fear and has not been introduced to perfect love.

Luke 12:29,

"And seek not ye what ye shall eat or what ye shall drink, neither be ye of doubtful mind."

God is your source of your supply.

Romans 14:5,

"One man esteemeth one day above another. Another man esteemeth every day alike. Let every man be fully persuaded in his own mind."

In the study of any philosophy that is associated with the Soul, and based upon a thorough examination of man's mental and spiritual existence, mind is an attribute of the soul. The brain is not logically of the body of man unless we admit that the mind is an attribute of the Soul. This distinction between brain and mind is apparent as we study the mental activities and possibilities of man. The philosopher Baruch Spinoza and a number of other careful and unbiased scientists agree that:

"The human mind cannot be absolutely destroyed with the body."

Whether we accept the theory of other scientists, that man physically evolved to his present physical body because of evolution through all the lower forms of animal life, or refuse to accept it, the fact remains that primitive man, in his first phase of Soul-personality, evolved as an image of God.

It is also true that man's automatic functions of reflex and body type is recorded in the Soul Sheath.

OUR BIRTH IS BUT A SLEEP AND A FORGETTING, THE SOUL THAT RISES WITH US, OUR LIFE'S STAR HATH HAD ELSEWHERE ITS SETTING AND COMETH FROM AFAR.

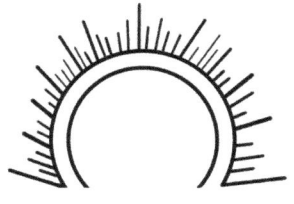

MIND FOUR

L et us now take up the attribute of reasoning. We seldom think of our reasoning abilities and take too much for granted. However, we hope to make plain to you some very interesting facts that will open the door to a great deal of thinking along this line.

If we divide reasoning into simple forms we find that we reason DEDUCTIVELY and INDUCTIVELY. Life, or rather self-living, is constituted by and embraced by the intentional or unintentional combination of these two elementary principles. They are known as the two processes of reasoning, either in balance or with one predominantly displayed over the other.

Therefore, we may say that self-living is the third point of the triangle. These two fundamental forms are the basis of all our reasoning. The triangle simply expressed is: DEDUCTIVE or structural reasoning is the function of the knowing mind; INDUCTIVE or genetic reasoning is the development of the cognitive mind; SELF-LIVING or the functional reasoning of mind is the part which knowledge expresses and plays in individual life.

The subject of reasoning would be very dry and uninteresting as a study were it not for the fact that so much of our work depends upon the strange reasoning done by the subjective mind. In fact, as you will find later on, most of the remarkable occurrences of a psychic or occult nature come from the distinctive reasoning of the subjective mind.

Reasoning in general is the analytical thinking we do. Our conscious reasoning is done by the objective mind, while on the other hand some of our most important reasoning is done in the subjective mind. The two are clearly defined.

When we analyze a statement or thought we use our ability to reason. If I asked you what qualities or colors compose the color green, you would hold the color green before your eyes mentally and examine it.

In this analysis your reasoning would tell you that since green has both blue and yellow in it, it must be composed of both blue and yellow. Such reasoning is analytical.

Analytical reasoning examines the idea or thought from every angle. It separates the idea into various parts or qualities and tries to find the cause. This reasoning leads back to the idea, thoughts, actions, and very principles which preceded the idea with which we started.

Now if I placed before you here on the table a very fancy cake which had the appearance of a birthday or wedding cake and asked each of you to step up before the cake and permit your reasoning abilities to influence your actions and thinking, there would be two things, one of which you would do. Either you would try to eat the cake, or you would study and examine it. Now the cause of your action would be found in the reasoning you did. Therefore, we will stop and examine the two methods.

Those who would examine the cake would reason **inductively**. They would note the finish of the cake first and try to reason out the recipe for making and methods for finishing it with filling and icing. All materials used would be studied and from each step would the mind travel, till the one doing such reasoning would see the cake in its first stages, in its ingredients and parts. By such a process of reasoning, from effect to cause, a person could tell how the cake was made. Some can look at a prettily trimmed hat or gown and by reasoning backward tell just how the hat or gown was made.

Detectives when called in to fathom the mystery of a crime look upon the result, the finished deed, and by reasoning backward are able to tell just how the crime was committed, and when and by whom. They go backward, step by step, to the cause and thus have a picture of every step that leads up to the crime.

All these examples are forms of INDUCTIVE REASONING, so please write in your notebook that:

"Inductive Reasoning is progressing from results to cause, step by step, logically."

Now those who would come up here and see the fancy cake and immediately proceed to eat it would reason **deductively**. Their reasoning would be as follows: "That is a fine cake, cakes are good to eat, this one was made to eat, it was made with great care so that it is especially good and palatable, I like cake and I can enjoy it by eating it, therefore I will eat this cake."

You can easily perceive that such reasoning is the reverse of the first method. This reasoning is done from the result forward to its ultimate end instead of backward to the cause. It embraces no question, no analysis, no examination, but is a mere chain of subsequent actions, each a logical result of the former. This is DEDUCTIVE REASONING.

It is the kind of reasoning which a criminal may use in committing a crime. The criminal may walk into a room and see a man counting his money. He would reason somewhat as follows: "I need money. There is plenty of it. I need some or all of that so I will take it. The man counting it is protecting it. Therefore, I will get rid of the man and take the money. To get rid of the man I will kill him. To kill him I will shoot him. To shoot him I will use my revolver. I will use my revolver to shoot him in the back. He will drop to the floor. He will be unconscious. He will die. I will take the money and run. I will get out of the window through which I came. I will have the money. Persons will hear the shot and come into the house. I will be gone with the money. They will find the body…"

In this way the criminal would plan every move until the time came to reason differently. He would reason deductively: how the persons would search for him, how the police would be called in, how his fingerprints would be examined, and so forth. Consequently, he would endeavor to do those things which would defeat their reasoning. This form of reasoning, reasoning deductively, is best defined in this way. So please write this in your notebook:

"Deductive Reasoning consists of logical steps forward from the primary idea to its ultimate conclusion."

Now these are very simple definitions and which our advanced students of psychology might qualify. But they will suffice to make plain to you what we mean by deductive and inductive reasoning.

When we reason over anything we wish to say or do, we reason both deductively and inductively. If we wish to take a journey to a distant city we might reason first in a deductive manner. We would figure out what our first move should be: the amount of fare or cost of the trip, the time it should take to get there, the inconvenience of the journey, the place we should eventually reach, whom we would see there, what we would do, what would be the expense while there, when we should return, and all other little incidents of the trip.

In other words, we would make the trip mentally from start to finish, from the going to the return. This is following out the idea to its conclusion, deductively. But if we should stop to say to ourselves: "Why should I go there?" Then we would begin inductive reasoning. We would reason backward to the cause of our taking the journey.

Now let me explain what all this has to do with our work. If we reasoned deductively always, we would make many mistakes but at the same time we would accomplish a great many things both good and bad. If we reasoned deductively only all our acts would be like starting a railroad engine moving forward on its track without an engineer. It would follow the track regardless of all obstacles and keep going to the end of the track. Signals along the way would mean nothing to the engine since its sole aim would be to keep going on the one track to the end. It would not stop and examine signals to see whether it should take a branch track or not, for that would require inductive reasoning.

Likewise, if we reasoned inductively exclusively, we would remain inactive in the constant process of analysis, reasoning backward to the causes and questioning the causes in turn. Thus we'd be lost in the fine threads of dim memory with hardly a recollection of the original effect which started the whole process.

Now God and nature have given us the ability to reason by all methods as a protection in order that we may progress, or go forward, and by means of our analysis of every act make no mistakes. Yes, God and nature have given us the ability to reason in order that we may make no mistakes. But it is evident that mistakes are made and each can ask the other, "Why?" Yes, WHY do we make these mistakes when we have such reasoning abilities? And if our reason is valid what must be the relation of the knowing consciousness to the object or experience known?

Logicians and scientists have concluded from observation that logic is either valid or invalid. They have tried to find and state the definite standard to which thinking must conform in order that it may be valid. But are they not taking the effect of the results as their premise, rather than going back to the cause and reaching an understanding of the principles of the causes themselves, which produce the effects? Here we find the principles of God and nature where they may more nearly approach the pure form of thought. It is too easy to begin with the created instead of the pure principles of creation. These have been neglected and lost to most of us through the past ages. This is because of our attempted separation from the Cosmic Mind and development of our selfish purposes.

Syllogistic reasoning based upon the two fundamental reasonings mentioned is the form of general reason employed by most of us. It is based upon a premise, a statement, and a conclusion.

This form of reasoning is found in the axiom expressed in the exact science of mathematics, that two things equal to the same thing are equal to each other. Thus it is seen that it is difficult to go astray in the conclusions, provided our premise is based on the truth and our statement is exact. However, we are all a little careless in the acceptance of our premise and with such a beginning it is little wonder that we arrive at so few valid conclusions. For instance, the form of syllogistic reasoning is expressed in the following statement:

"Stones sink in water. This thing is a stone. This thing sinks in water."

How simple this reasoning seems and how true, to all appearances. But supposing this thing we were using was a piece of porous pumice stone. It is a piece of stone, but when it is placed in water we find that it floats. What is wrong? It is our premise that stones sink in water. We might go a little further and show conditions where few stones would sink with any great speed in water. For instance, if the water is frozen we may call it ice, but it is still of the chemical composition of water and though stones, heavier than water, or rather heavier than ice, would sink in it. This motion would be so small as to be almost negligible. We have said, "stones heavier than water and heavier than ice," and herein we begin to see that we accepted as a premise an assumption based upon several observations but hardly based upon any laws.

Our premises are usually plain assumptions and hardly based upon facts at all, or more often probably related to facts only dimly. We must get back to the principles, laws, and proportions of all manifestations in order to perceive and explain the exact premise of truth.

Thus we see that the weakness or strength of deductive reasoning is in the premise. In the process there will be no mistake. The weakness or strength of inductive reasoning is in the process.

Our formal system of logic, which has changed but slightly with the centuries, was first introduced by the great philosopher, Aristotle.

He said that ideas or conclusions were higher forms of thought in comparison to the sense perceptions of experiences from which they arose. In other words, he meant that an idea or conclusion is a complete form and arises from the combination of two lesser impressions or thoughts.

These lesser thoughts may be complete by themselves, but in comparison to the thought, idea, or conclusion which arises from them they are incomplete. For instance, a syllogism is composed of three propositions. The first two propositions are called premises and the third coming from the first two is the conclusion.

The premises are major and minor and they have a common middle term. This common middle term forms the basis for a conclusion and after furnishing the logical connection between the other two disappears. For example:

"No finite being is exempt from error;
All Men are finite beings;
Therefore, no man is exempt from error."

The major premise we see is that no finite being is exempt from error. The minor premise is that men are finite beings. We have here two thoughts. What is the middle term or connection? It is that finite beings can err. What is the new idea, thought, or conclusion that arises from that middle term? It is that since man is finite and finite things err, so then does man. All logical and formal reasoning is done according to this method. You should practice this remarkable system.

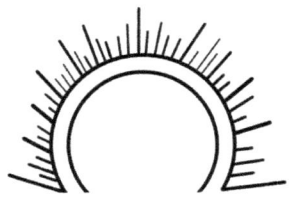

MIND FIVE

In the study of Mental Law, we are now considering one of the most vital of all the laws of life, except those which have to do with the creative function or use of the Mind of God. They will be covered in Lesson Mind Seven.

That Mental Law, your consciousness of it, ability to demonstrate it, and supremacy of spiritual thought over all apparent material resistance must necessarily depend on your understanding of these mental laws and how they operate. This is the canvas upon which we paint the scene of our life.

We must come to think of this mental medium and Law as the principle governing spirit mind control, brings to us our likes and dislikes, and is the foundation of spiritual healing and its many ramifications.

We must do one thing and this is to think in terms of this Law as an exact Law which does not vary nor does it err.

The law is in the mind of God. It was in His mind when He created this universe. It is in His mind yesterday, today, and forever.

The law is imprinted and is part of the nature of the spirit of God. It is a facet of God's personality.

This law functions automatically because the spirit is self-knowing and conscious of the things in the mind of God. It causes all mental patterns to be filled with the energy and force of Creation because of the self-knowing of the spirit. God also passed on the Word, His creative Word, to us through our Lord Jesus Christ.

Now let us consider this all-important idea of the reality of Him in terms of the Infinite Knower and a Limitless Doer. Let us assure you that here in this universe it is filled with the warmth and color of pure spirit.

The following are five steps to understanding and putting into use this mind function so that it becomes a part of your KNOWING.

These steps are not only the steps of a mental system of assimilation, digestion, and assumption but they are also the steps and pattern of the complete function of the Law.

1. DIGESTION: Digest = to assimilate mentally; obtain information, ideas, or principles from; to arrange methodically in the mind; think over; to arrange in convenient or methodical order; reduce to a system; classify; to condense, abridge, or summarize. From Latin, *digest* (us) = separated, dissolved.

2. ASSIMILATION: Assimilate = to take in and incorporate as one's own; absorb: to bring into conformity; adapt or adjust; to make like; cause to resemble; to compare; liken. From Latin *assimilat* (us) = likened to, made like.

3. ASSUMPTION: The act of taking for granted; or supposing; act of taking to or upon oneself; the act of taking possession of something; the bodily taking up into heaven of the Virgin Mary. From Latin *assumpt* (us) = taken up.

4. COMPREHENSION: Inclusion; perception or understanding; capacity of the mind to perceive or understand; power to grasp ideas; ability to know; the act or process of comprehending. Comprehend = to understand the meaning or nature of; grasp with the mind; perceive; to take in or embrace; include; comprise. From Latin *com* + *prehendere* = to grasp.

5. REALIZATION: The making or being made real of something imagined, planned, etc.; the act of realizing or the state of being realized. Realize = to grasp or understand clearly; to bring vividly to the mind. Real = true; not merely ostensible, nominal, or apparent; existing or occurring as fact; actual rather than imaginary, ideal, or fictitious; being an actual thing; having an objective existence; not imaginary; being actually such; not merely so-called; genuine; not counterfeit, artificial, or imitation; unfeigned or sincere. From Latin *re* (s) = thing + *alis* = pertaining to.

These steps are in reality the paths, rungs on the ladder, higher consciousness, and creation of a new life and new body. They are the reality of God. This is the way that the mind works from the dense to the less dense, from the small to the greater. This is the way of Mental Life.

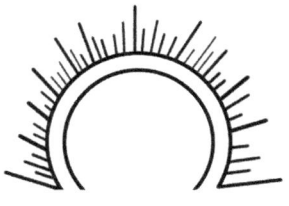

LESSON 5
MIND SIX

MIND—WHAT IS IT?

Our mind is part of the Mind of God into which the sentience of the soul and memories of the soul arise. Absorption depends on the level of the consciousness of the individual. This will determine the sharpness, purity of reason, and logic with which the individual operates. The individual, as he grows from childhood, does not reach the full consciousness of his level of purity in the Mind of the Father until he is 28 years of age.

The Subconscious Mind is that portion of the mind which acts below the level of conscious awareness. It is that part of mind which is constantly active and never sleeps but continues unfailingly in its operations. Subconscious mind has perfect connection with all points of the interims of time and space, and this perfect connection is the basis of telepathy.

It is also the Law and the way through which we are put in touch with our spiritual teachers. When the soul has become spiritually effervescent from the activity of the Light and Life of Christ within us then we are ready for instruction by teachers on the higher level.

Through this medium of mind, we are drawn to other persons and material. They come into outer manifestation once the call has been sent out in prayer or meditation and you know of their present existence. **We are not alone**, for our souls and our minds are not isolated. In the inner realm, Mind of God, all are connected to the one great reality, the One Great Sentient Mind of God. It is thus that our intuitions reach us from the great super-subconscious, passing into the conscious, and out into the thinking or conscious realm. On the other hand, instinct comes out of the subconscious itself, from the memory of nature and past memories of the soul.

Because of its retentive nature, in the sense of the holding of vibration and relative relationship of all that has been or now exists, the Cosmic Subconscious or what is usually termed Akashic Records, can be contacted and read by those who have developed this ability, those who have the aspect of the spiritual sight, or have had the veil removed from the Self. Thus it is that the individual's past life and experience may be read, even for the many previous lifetimes. This is difficult for most people because it requires complete removal of the mind itself when one is receiving impressions.

In the human body we have what is called the pituitary body, or gland, which acts as a sub-transmitting station through which cosmic thoughts are relayed to centers low in the body. These cosmic thoughts may be correlated with other experiences and things. It is considered that the moon symbolizes the pituitary body because of its reflective nature and it is sometimes pictured as a rolled-up scroll of all that has been written. It is associated with the element of water because of its psychic reaction.

One of the most useful ways of picturing our own subconscious mind is to think of it as a tilled and fertile field which is every moment receiving seeds dropped from the conscious mind. As you think, speak, and visualize so do you sow and so shall you reap. If you have feeling and desire attached to thought here the law of Karma works as surely as the function of cause and effect in action but more subtly. The out-pictured world in which you live and move is the result of many combined words, thoughts, and imaged pictures which you carelessly or knowingly dropped into the soil of the past.

It is like an orchard being harvested, some fruit is good and some is perhaps not. Dwell on the good and joyful, emphasize and magnify it, and give thanks to God continually. Do this not just because the past produced good fruit but so that each thought of thanksgiving, though it brings each kind word, though it brings a rebuff today, will bear in time fruit, unless the weeds of resentment of the rebuff outnumber and outweigh the good.

The subjective mind of man, unlike the objective mind, is the reasoning mind and reasons only deductively. Deductive reasoning is discussed in Lesson Mind 4. It has the ability to reason in no other way. There is a good purpose behind this for it has one mission in life. That mission is to obey orders and to do as it is told, or inspired to do, by the soul. For it has charge of involuntary actions.

The law of suggestion works through the subconscious. Suggestion is a very subtle command, request, a wish, or action of law of the subjective mind transmitted to the objective mind. The subjective mind has perfect memory. It is a complete storehouse of facts and experiences, well protected yet easily reached by the objective. It is like a vault with separate **entrances** for every field of knowledge. Each fact enters and leaves by the same door, let out as taught in psychology by a thought that plows a pathway of discharge through the mind by which it ever after tends to escape.

The subconscious mind is actually more impressed with the personality of the individual in his last life than by the personality in his new body in this incarnation. This is because the personality of this life is being formed now and much of it is in the blood and flesh.

As for the term Akasha or Akashic Records: The word Akasha is taken from the Sanskrit word meaning, "primary substance or that out of which all things were and are formed." They are the records maintained in the Universal Mind and are the forces of the Spirit or Universal Intelligence which is directing the Spirit.

Therefore, we can say the Akashic Records are the indelible or eternal record of the delicate or Divine Mind containing the knowledge of the past, present and future. They are not material records or written accounts, but they are the divine consciousness of past or future events.

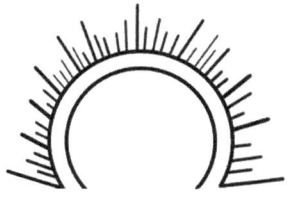

MIND SEVEN

In the previous lesson we spoke of mind and what it is. Now we want to talk of function or Use of Mind. I can hear my students asking, "What do you mean, use of mind? Here I've been working all this time to keep my mind quiet." Well, this is one of the uses. For in the use of concentration, you are attempting not to use the lower mind, the objective mind, but rather the thoughts and impressions which the subconscious is in contact with, even the Akasha.

Therefore, when we begin to have some degree of consciousness developed in us, we are establishing degrees of attunement with this Universal Mind and these Absolute Records, the Akasha. The use of your intuition, the facility of its use, is just the first manifestation that such attunement is being established. It is not until we reach a degree of control that the voices of the cosmic, that which comes through the subconscious, can whisper facts or knowledge through urges which arise within us when we are pondering and in doubt.

When we choose to use the brain and reasoning in any matter, the cosmic mind through the subconscious tries to set us aright. But we have gotten out of the habit of listening until reason gets the upper hand. Now let us put aside reasoning and listen to the still small voice until it again becomes automatic and of first importance to hear the Reality of Truth.

The subconscious mind has ways and means of collecting obsessive impressions independently of the objective mind, absorbing impressions of which the conscious mind would not be aware.

Certain things are not impressed upon the ordinary nerves or retina of the eye but upon extra-sensory nerves which are made to receive higher rates of vibration and by which impressions are carried to the subconscious instead of the objective mind.

In such cases the subconscious mind receiving the impressions, stores away the pictures or idea and they remain there. These are unknown to the objective mind until they come across the border of the objective mind and become known for a passing moment. We have a dual consciousness, either subjective or objective can communicate with it.

The purpose of concentration or meditation is to bring about a borderline condition like the balancing of the two arms of a scale. The student may look upon himself as being in an arena around which are numerous doors or cells like monks' cells. In each is the personality of the past.

As we gain inner consciousness and draw closer to the Akasha, our subconscious rises and we visit these alcoves. We look in, some we may like and some we may not like. We examine personalities and recognize that each carries with it the particular personality you had in a previous lifetime. Some might be male, some female. In accordance with these the level of cosmic consciousness is developed. Until we have acted upon our present life functionally, we depend on the past experiences which radiate on the soul because of the light from the Self.

TRIANGLE OF MIND

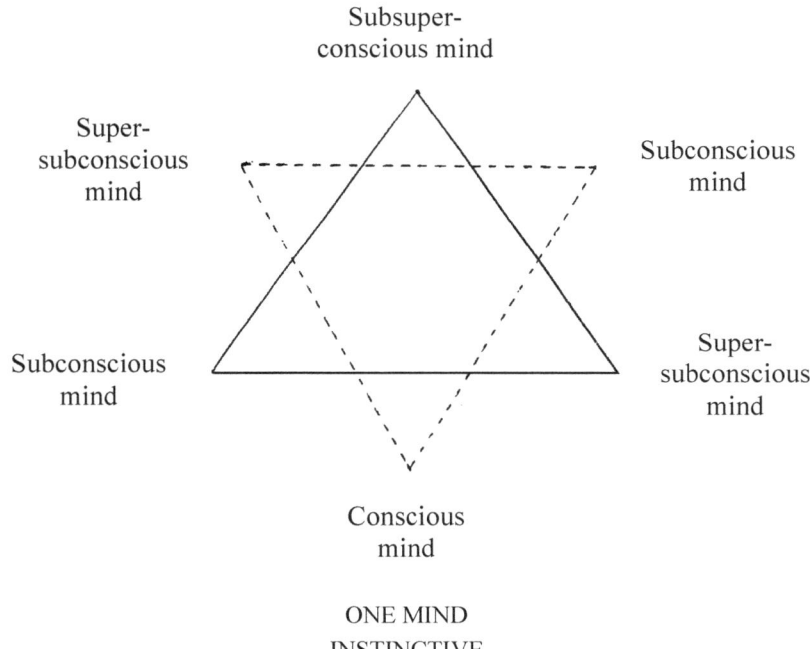

ONE MIND
INSTINCTIVE

-CONSCIOUS MIND = MATERIAL FORM
+SUBCONSCIOUS MIND = SPIRITUAL FORM

SUBCONSCIOUS MIND = MATERIAL FORM
SUPERSUBCONSCIOUS MIND = SPIRITUAL FORM

SUPERSUBCONSCIOUS MIND = MATERIAL FORM
SUBSUPERCONSCIOUS MIND = SPIRITUAL FORM

The table above depicts the maze and tangle of psychology, but added to it is an understanding of the fact that the inherent subconscious traits of the personality are often inherited from past incarnations. An outstanding trait from which we suffer deeply may be one which took many long years in previous lives to acquire so that it becomes deeply ingrained in us, a part of us.

We carry this totality in the Soul.

Sometimes as one gains the ability to look into the records of his past, he might observe blank spots signifying absolutely no action at fairly regular intervals. This shows the periods of rest or intervals between cycles of material manifestation or incarnation on a material plane, whether it be on the Earth or any other planet.

In some ancient writings the record of the past is symbolized by a rolled-up scroll, the entire memory of the individual. It oftentimes is said that he who becomes adept may read his history from the Akasha, be it pleasing or not. The subconscious is called subconscious because whatever it does occurs below the level of conscious-awareness. In other words, it is not on the material plane.

A good exercise to provide an example of what I have just said is to trace back all the words and thoughts of the last half hour and then read them over carefully and see if you like them. If you don't strike them out, wipe them out, and put a positive thought in their place. Thus the mind will harvest no unfavorable harvest in the future from the subconscious by receiving false or negative ideas. Let's have no garden of weeds for you to harvest.

The mastery of mind is the great objective and first step of those who would follow the Christ and Master Jesus. Once this is accomplished we have become master of our destiny insofar as it is not under a certain rational Karma or cosmic trend. We will be spreading positive seeds amongst all those with whom we come in contact.

The subconscious mind is an absolute subordinate to the conscious mind and thus is reactive to reasoning. It is amenable to suggestion and can be controlled. It is a feminine gender in action, whereas the conscious mind is masculine.

The mind originates and the subconscious creates. The mind makes clear good pictures in your mind and thinks positive thoughts. This must outweigh gossip, complaints and elaboration on the dirt someone did to you or the misery you have been feeling.

The subconscious mind does not know any better. It has been given the function of the ingredients given to it and does the job perfectly.

Whatever the ingredients given to it, it will give it back to you in outer circumstance. So get out your mental vacuum cleaner and give yourself a good mental housecleaning, ridding yourself of all negative thoughts, and turn your eyes toward God and towards Christ in the light of the Christos.

In Philippians 4:6 we read, "In everything let your petitions be known to God in prayer and supplications with thanksgiving." Instead of fault-finding, wait a minute and look for something to praise and give thanks for it. Look at it carefully, magnify it and soon you will see something to be joyous for.

Still more important is the thanksgiving of faith as Jesus, in multiplying the loaves, looked upward and gave thanks before the miracle had happened and became an event on earth. It had already been done in mind and perfect faith in knowing. So likewise, giving thanks to the Father for hearing does not mean he will dwell on the lack of your faith, for that would multiply lack.

In John 6:11 we read of how Jesus fed the five thousand with five loaves of bread and two small fishes, "And Jesus took the loaves; and when he had given thanks, he distributed to the disciples, and the disciples to them that were set down; and likewise of the fishes as much as they would." This is the only miracle reported in all four gospels. In the other gospels the word "blessed" is used in place of "thanks," as used by John. These are some of the tools that we use to keep the mind scrubbed up so that the subconscious is not growing tares in the wheat crop which we have planted for the harvest.

In order for those who live in this day to welcome the return of the Christ force and principle, which is present in the new earth as it is developing now, must keep a positive and clean mind. Unless the people of earth clean out the rubbish in their minds and bodies now there will be too much for the human body to clean out as the New Earth is built.

Look around you and see the rubbish and waste in the world today and it will tell you the rubbish that is in the mass mind today.

Let me remind you, again, to steady yourself so that you do not react to the negativity of the world or the acts of others. Thus we can go on in the future and not pass through transition now. As a new heaven and the New Earth are forming, do not hold any negation or sorrow within. Do not water them with a few tears occasionally to wash out your emotions. You will be blessed as the positive things grow. This is one reason that you bless them that persecute you and return good for evil. Although some enemy is tossing weed seeds into the garden of your subconscious, they never hit the ground unless your own mind accepts them.

You must not accept what you do not want mentally. If you are living in difficult circumstances you know they are not immaterial but that you must work all the harder to plan for the future by being Christlike today. There are other areas of the field that will come into fruition tomorrow through epigenesis and grace everyday.

IF YOU WISH TO SOW NEGATIVE SEEDS NOW, YOU WILL PAY LATER.

IF YOU WISH TO SOW POSITIVE SEEDS NOW, YOU WILL REAP THE HARVEST OF USEFUL FRUIT.

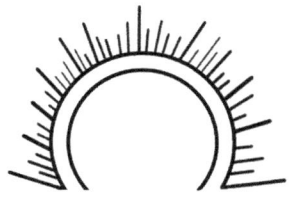

LESSON 5

FAITH ONE

"If ye have faith as a grain of mustard seed, ye shall say unto this mountain, be ye removed hence to yonder place; and it shall be removed; and nothing shall be impossible unto you."

In the Bible, the word faith is used many times, and in religious circles today, it is just a word. But faith is something that is very real and not just a word.

In business or on the stock market a person will take a look at the various companies selling stock and will decide which one will be the best for him to invest his money in. He has faith in that company because he put his money where his mouth is.

When you have faith in God that means you stopped talking and started doing.

When you have faith that you can heal, you have started putting your hands on people and asking for healings either by direct contact or the word. Faith is an action word. Without faith you couldn't move a muscle.

A newly born baby learns how to walk through faith. That new baby has seen those around him walking and by those around him saying you can walk. By faith he stands on his feet, he puts one foot in front of the other. He may stumble and fall a few times, but he will walk.

If he would have sat and thought within himself, "I wonder if I can do it," he would have been sitting there for ninety years wondering if he could do it.

When a person has faith, this means that he'll get up and try doing that which is there to do and he will keep right on trying until he succeeds.

The term faith came about because most of the world we live in is unseen and it will remain unseen until a person moves out (for example, tries spiritual exercises). Then the unseen for him will be seen. The seen world is just the result of the unseen world. The reality isn't in the seen but in the unseen. The only reason it is unseen is because man has lost the consciousness of God. The greater part of His Being is in the unseen world.

Something may be unseen but if you take the step, it will then appear and the taking of that step is faith.

This whole world, this whole physical world moves and runs on faith for when a person makes a contract to buy a house he has stepped out on the faith that he will keep his job which will let him bring in the money to pay the payments each month.

The term unseen world doesn't mean unreal world. It just means to a person who hasn't developed his full range of sight that it isn't apparent. The unseen world is as much "here and real" as the seen world. The difference between unseen and seen is that in the unseen is the source of all power.

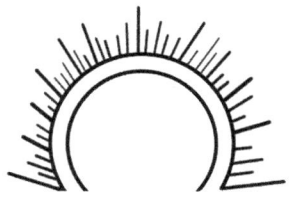

LESSON 5

FAITH TWO

The act of faith is an act which unleashes tremendous power into action. It is not the act of blind belief or hopes but the act of knowing that it is now or is going to be done and that the prayer will be answered.

As we have learned by the use of the Law that Jesus taught, the first thing to know is to become close to God. Matthew talked of the Manna of God in Matthew 6:11,

> "But if God so clothes the grass of the field,
> which today is alive and tomorrow is thrown
> into the oven, will He not much more clothe
> you, O men of little faith."

Here we see that even the grass has a pattern set by God. It is provided for. Again, in the world around us Jesus said in Matthew 17:20,

> "Truly I say to you if you have faith as a
> grain of mustard seed, you will say to this
> mountain, Move hence to yonder place...and
> it will move and nothing will be impossible to you."

This shows the unlimited power of man through the power of God and the tool of faith. Jesus also said in Matthew 21:22 that whatsoever you ask in prayer you will receive IF YOU HAVE FAITH.

In Mark 11:24, Jesus said that whatever you ask in Prayer believe that you receive it and you will. We have a definite lead to the lesson on the Law. YOU ARE TO BELIEVE THAT YOU HAVE ALREADY RECEIVED WHAT YOU ASK. This is so because you have set the pattern in the Mind of God.

In the story of the woman who touched the hem of his garment, Jesus said, "Take heart daughter. Your faith has made you well." Here we see that we need to have a feeling with our faith especially when we are dealing with the physical body.

In Acts 3:16, Peter says, "By faith in His name has made this man strong whom you see and know; and the faith which is through Jesus has given this man this perfect health in the presence of you all."

In I Thessalonians 5:8, Paul says, "But since we belong to the day, let us be sober and put on the breast plate of Faith and Love, and for a helmet the Hope of Salvation." This is the knowing that nothing may touch us when we have faith, that we are protected.

"Faith is assurance of things hoped for, the conviction of things not seen." (Hebrews 11:1) Note that assurance is used here for the word assurance is a felt guarantee of performance while in the word conviction, we have knowing of its reality.

"Looking unto Jesus the author and finisher of our faith, who for the joy that was set before Him endured the cross, despising the shame, and is set down at the right hand of the throne of God." (Hebrews 12:2) This is an explanation of what was accomplished on the cross in the way of perfecting our faith through His death and resurrection, or a seen performance. Faith is a part of what motivates the Epigenesis of all deeds.

"For by faith we understand how the world was created by the Word of God, so that what is seen was made out of things which do not appear." (Hebrews 11:3) Here we are told that what appears in the dense world, all things, they were made out of the substance of the unseen world.

Faith is a most important spiritual teaching. But before we proceed any further, let us use Webster's New World Dictionary for a definition of the word "faith." Faith: To trust or confide in; unquestioning belief in God; anything believed; childlike reliance.

Yet we who are spiritual have seen a deeper understanding. "Faith is the substance of things hoped for..." Substance is the real or essential part or element of anything; essence, reality, matter. It is something that has an independent existence and is acted upon by causes or events, "...the evidence of things not seen." Evidence is the condition of being evident. It is something that makes another clear or evident sign, something that tends to prove ground for belief, indication, or sign.

We can see that normal church teaching on faith is lacking. Here is our understanding of faith. It is that which is real or essential. It exists independently of our senses and is acted upon by causes and events. Faith is that which creates a condition of being evident, a realistic sign that tends to prove ground for belief.

"...and He said unto them, Why are you afraid, O men of little faith?" In Romans 1:5, we find that grace is given for obedience in faith, or with faith. In Galatians 2, we find that we live by the faith of the Son of God. In Romans 10:8, we find that we preach the word of Faith, or in essence the Word of substance or reality.

In II Timothy 4, Paul says he has kept the faith meaning that he was faithful to the substantial reality of the Christ. In Romans Paul tells us that that which is not of faith is sin. Thus, if it is not real or substantial, if it is not self-evident or essential, it is sinful or a transgression of the Law which states that all things truly spiritual are self-evident, eternal and realistic.

We find out what actually happens to us when we continue in the faith by reading Colossians 1:23,

> "And you who were once estranged and hostile
> in mind, doing evil deeds, he has now
> reconciled in his body of flesh by his death,
> in order to present you holy, and blameless,
> and irreproachable before him, provided that
> you continue in the faith, stable and steadfast,
> not shifting from the hope of the Gospel
> which you heard, which has been preached
> to every creature under heaven, and of which I,
> Paul, became a minister."

We have been told that faith is essential to our Salvation. Let us say that faith and confidence are the reality of our Salvation. It is one of the many vehicles through which the Great Light of the Christ travels.

When we have true faith it is solid and substantial. It is so real that we can feel it and see it with our spiritual senses. It is sometimes so real that it will manifest physically and our faith in it is so evident that no man or beast can deny it.

THE GREAT GIFT

> Not more of Life, Oh Master, do I ask
> But faith of thy Presence, ever near to feel,
> Not better sight,
> But to see in my brother that which is real,
> Not better ears to hear,
> But faith the Cosmic Voice to be ever near.
> I need not courage when Thy Presence I do feel,
> For through Faith I live and have my being
> In my mind year by year.

But one gift do I ask,
Faith to be of service with a task,
Never ending until the time,
When by Faith
I leave this earthly vehicle behind.
Then to rest and start anew,
To help some other, through lack of faith have but few
Of these precious gifts thou givest me.
Through Faith
I might have Love, Wisdom, and Charity.

Lesson 6: Awakening • Return • Feast

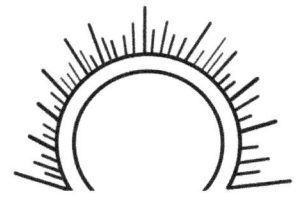

LESSON 6

AWAKENING ONE

"I am the way, the truth, and the life," said Jesus.

All religions, arts, and sciences are branches of the same tree. The aspirations of every individual directed through his life basically are the ennobling of man regardless of his profession.

They lift him up to a better physical existence and experience and slowly but surely lead him toward the reality of what is so frequently said, "Man, know thyself."

It is by no means a measure of chance that our present educational system in schools has developed out of the ancient mystery schools and that sciences were first known by the old mystics and teachers.

It would be much to man's greater development if both churches and universities, insofar as they might live up to their true functions, should seek to prepare men and women to stand on their own two feet as a counterpart of the great creative mind and power.

As man looks at his brother, he sees those special persons who stand out in the ranks of humanity as having something that the rest of the masses do not possess.

It is the calmness of this human that is the one thing that attracts people to them, along with the possession of that firm but gentle attitude, they each one of them know themselves and the power they possess.

Some of the teachers were called mystics and some were called just philosophers, but there was something these men had that seemed to endow them with spiritual abilities that other men did not have.

This apparent difference was not an inequality of God's doing but they had earned this endowment by their working with the law and order of things, and abiding by the laws of creation.

Actually these men and women were so close to nature and themselves that they were, in reality, natural scientists.

Then we have the lamas, the priests, the disciples, and let us not forget the Apostles of our Lord and Master. All were alike except they had made up their minds that the way of attaining and manifesting the perfection of their deity was of greater importance than anything else in their life.

They had come to the great realization that only when they were able to find God or the understanding of the great creative intelligence would they be able to help their one thousand and one brothers in the world which had not come to that point of awakening.

This School and its teachings take the mystery out of the mysteries in this new age. It has already added to it the sciences of the outer material world and the mysteries taught by our Lord Jesus Christ, Buddha, and many others.

This School, with its insight and direct revelation of our Master Jesus Christ, not only teaches but practices the esoteric teachings. It has realized these teachings at a level or state of consciousness and vibration which brings to light the commandments in their reality. It also brings a consciousness of the one "Way" or universality of all peoples' soul growth.

The awakening to the reality of the Way makes it possible for them to function without dogma or creed, regardless in which group, church, or mystical group in the body of Christ exists within which they are working. This is because they revert to the infinite information of the Self and the Law of God, which directs one regardless of his position on the golden stairway.

It is through his becoming acquainted with and knowing how to use the tools God gave him that he is able to work with any and all people and he senses and sees existence of the greater light.

He is somehow conscious of the Way, the ultimate path of attainment, which you must travel in peace so that all the world may have peace.

This is the Way traveled by the great ones. On this path you find no differentiation in race, creed, or color. It is long and becomes very narrow the further one travels along it. It is also very satisfying. It brings inner peace and security regardless of the turmoil and strife around you.

This School has no new philosophy except to unite ourselves with all humankind. It is this School's only wish and striving to put these tools of the great Creator into the hands of each brother and sister on earth. This allows one to work with the great White Brotherhood to bring the earth in its entirety into the light of the Christos.

To be a real brother in this School is to be under the direct guidance of the Great Teacher, striving to understand your brother and sister, not just agreeing to be sociable or at peace with them.

One of the first commandments, if you wish to follow or put your foot on this Way, is don't try to convert a man to your philosophy or religion. Instead try to understand his philosophy or religion. Do all things in service for your brother and sister that will help to raise him to your own level of appreciation of God.

Remember man only learns to know himself by knowing the Creator he lives in and working with It. While walking the face of the earth and among all people without fear, want, in joy and gladness, only then can we serve God and humankind alike.

Remember that it takes a brave man and woman to be an individual and work in the body of Christ to live his Way. Grow with them and grow with us in this Age of beauty to share the glory of the Christos returned to earth. It takes a brave heart to attain his and her Godhood.

For man consciously started on the path of involution into dense matter and is now evolving out of dense matter to attain his mastership and Godhood.

> Set your face to the Sun
> Never Run
> Use spear of Mind
> Which is thought
> To stop what negativity has wrought
> Be a "Brother"
> Help another.

The most important thing that could ever come into a spiritual person's life is the awakening of the Soul.

Let us before going on see what Webster's New World Dictionary has to say about the meaning of the word awakening, "A waking up, an arousing or reviving, as of impulses or religions."

Since a revival is indicated, something must be there which was awake but now sleeps.

Let us search the scriptures on this subject. Mark 4:38, "They awoke Jesus and said unto him, Master, don't you care that we are drowning?" This is the awakening of fear. Jesus rebuked them for their unbelief.

In Luke 9:32, we find the awakening to the Glory of God, "But Peter and his companions had been overcome by sleep, and it was as they struggled in wakefulness that they saw the Glory of Jesus and the two men standing with him."

It is in awakening to the fact that all around mass mind is asleep. Mass mind has lulled us into sleep so that we are righteously angered into awakening enough to see the Glory of Jesus, which is the Glory of the Father. Jesus reflects the Father's Glory.

In John 11:11, Jesus states that he is going to awaken Lazarus. "Our friend Lazarus has fallen asleep, but I am going to wake him up." We need to be awakened to the Christ.

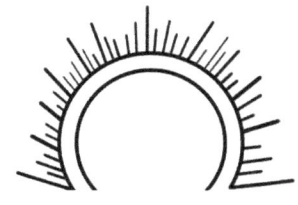

AWAKENING TWO

"AWAKE, O sleeper, and arise from the dead, and Christ shall give you light."

Before one may go forth and serve his fellow man, the spiritual part of him must be born. It has lain dormant for centuries as a fetus within—alive, and developing, but not delivered. First the spiritual child is born and then he grows to manhood to serve with Christ.

As Jesus said, "Behold, I stand at the door and knock". One may think of the Lord, coming with a flashlight to the door of someone's individual temple, and knocking to awaken him, saying, "Turn on your light within the temple, so you may see to rise. Then, when you are fully prepared, I shall return to pick you up to come and help me."

As Peter said, "You will do well to pay attention to this as to a lamp shining in a dark place, until the day dawns and the morning star rises in your hearts."

The divine Child, the Son of God, is born within man in one of his rounds of incarnation. When his consciousness has been lifted and he has become amenable to and capable of functioning as a superman in righteousness and selfless love, then for the good of all, he arrives at the capacity to serve God with utter devotion.

The more single your eye is in this respect the less you look at the physical life you have stepped out from. The more pure your motives are, the more you will develop the light of the Sun within.

God becomes the universe, the blue sky, in which the golden sun/son swims and functions. You are immersed in God and dwell in Him. Collected together in you are innumerable particles of Light which are as invisible as the Father, being all pervading.

But when the particles of light gather together in one strong focal point of Force and Energy they become the warm strong light around which the lesser beings gather. They look for strength and guidance to the true Son of God.

The Child is born in the very Bethlehem of our bodies in the approximate area ruled by Cancer, plus Gemini and Leo. In the zodiacal sign of Cancer is a configuration called the "manger."

That is to say the Self is located behind the heart area near the spine. It is as though, speaking imaginatively, the twins Adam and Eve of Gemini in their home nest of Cancer become parents giving birth to the divine Child, who is the Sun. The Sun rules the sign of Leo which rules children.

Paul Case said, "Spiritual consciousness is an awakening to the meaning of what material consciousness supposes to be nothing but physical existence. It is a recognition of the spiritual substance of this world which ignorance calls matter.

The wisdom which results from new birth shows us that we are truly Children of the Sun even now. When this knowledge comes it wells up in our hearts as a song of Joy and we turn from the limitations of the senses to the freedom of spiritual knowing."

In Malachi 4:2, the prophet said, "For behold, the day comes, burning like an oven, when all the arrogant and all evildoers will be stubble, the day that comes shall burn them up, says the Lord of Hosts, so that it will leave them neither root nor branch. But for you who fear My Name, the Sun of Righteousness shall rise, with healing in its wings."

The Sun when it comes, and the Christ with His Spirit returning to earth will be so dazzling as to destroy all the darkness before it. It will burn the dross and only the gold, the righteous, shall remain.

When the Christ Spirit comes to show us the way by its very brightness, the negative shows up the more prominently. As the brighter the light, the darker and more defined the shadow cast by an object.

If you placed a light within your body so strong it will make all transparent except that which is foreign to its inherent nature, the evil tendencies would show out stronger and have to be faced. There would be no nice dense place to hide the faults.

As long as there is no light mankind can hide their sins. When they show up they have to get rid of them or leave the scene.

On the other hand, to those who love God and want to do well and turn to Christ, then this merciless spotlight becomes the healing Sun of Righteousness.

Just so, a great teacher who comes to emulate Jesus Christ on earth, to bring men to the Light and to God the Father, has to first **flush** all negation to the surface. Then it can be gotten rid of before he can work with the True Son within the man. He has to rout out all anger, hatred, dissipation, the lies and stealing. He has to make the subject face them and consciously turn from all attachment to them.

Jesus healed many people and performed many miracles. He woke Lazarus from the sleep of death in order that the faith of many might be strengthened.

Paul promised that he would wake us all when he comes, in Cor. 15:51, "Lo! I tell you a mystery. We shall not all sleep, but we shall all be changed, in a moment, in the twinkling of an eye, at the last trumpet. For the trumpet will sound, and the dead will be raised imperishable, and we shall all be changed."

The Psalmist declares in Psalm 27, verse 1,
"The Lord is my Light and my Salvation."

The awakening comes from the Lord through the Scriptures as Psalm 119 proves, when David says that, "Thy Word is a lamp to my feet, and a Light to my Path."

The Scriptures declare the Glory of God.
Some people awake and find their Soul empty.

Isaiah 29, verse 8,
"But he awaketh and his love is empty, but he awaketh and he is faint."

Others wake up as if they were once dead.

Ephesians 5:14,
"Awake thou that sleepest, and arise from the dead."

After the Great Awakening the Light of Christ comes. In other words, "Awake, thou that sleepest, and arise from the dead, and Christ shall give thee light."

Nothing can progress spiritually for us 'til we are awakened by Christ through the Light of his word in us.

In Acts, chapter 16, verse 27, the following is recorded, "When the jailer awoke and saw that the doors of the prison had been opened, he drew his sword and was on the point of killing himself." The jailer is mass mind. When mass mind sees the arousing of the believer it will destroy itself.

In Romans 13, verse 2, Paul says, "Because as I think you have realized the present time is of the highest importance, it is time to wake up to Reality. Every day brings God's Salvation nearer."

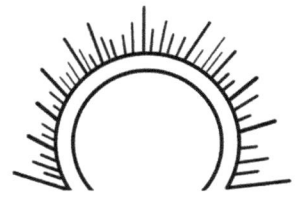

LESSON 6

AWAKENING THREE

Once when my alarm clock had accidentally not been set at the precise hour of the early morning when it should have rung, a soft voice whispered my name, and I awoke in time to get to a new job. Physically there was no one else in the house. Perhaps a friendly entity decided to give a helping hand or perhaps my own inner Self took a hand.

When it is time for the spiritual awakening no alarm has been set but in the realm of God consciousness it is known that this soul has slept long enough. There is work to be done and unless he wakes to the realization of this some Brothers and Sisters in the higher realm of Spirit may gently nudge the person into awakening.

His Spirit was born of God originally. As it became more and more engrossed in physical activity and worldly interests, God seemed farther and farther away until many even have claimed not to believe there was a God at all. Else why all the suffering and sin of the earthly plane?

God made man in His own image. Surely God never sleeps. Yet man has spent one third of his life physically asleep and most all of it asleep spiritually. He wakes up a little on Sunday if he goes to church. He lifts up his heart to God when he sees the stars, hears a bird, or finds a blossom in spring.

He glimpses God in a baby's eyes and assumes some of His quality in an act of selfless love. Otherwise most of the time he sleeps except when he gets a serious problem. Then he wakes up to the hope that God may, **must** hear him and help him.

Man slept first in the Bible when God caused a deep sleep to fall on man while he removed a rib in order to create his mate from his own flesh, so that they might truly be one, and not separate entities in nature. Man woke to find himself with a beautiful wife and she must have given him great joy, but she also diverted him from his one-pointed attention to God.

Attention can only serve one master at a time and if people are giving whole-hearted attention to providing all the things needed to preserve (and to serve) their bodies, how can they be thinking of God?

Our spiritual awakening must be first of all to the realization of God as a reality. We must acknowledge Him in all we do. We must keep in remembrance the first Commandment, Thou shalt love the Lord thy God with all thy heart, and soul, and mind, and thou shalt have no other gods before Him.

We awaken to the fact that He really IS, and always has been, and always will be. He is more than a Being Who once created the earth and everything else and talked with people for a while and then got discouraged with that. He finally sent down His only Son in a last great gesture to salvage whomever would listen to him and believe he came from God. Then He went into retirement letting men learn about Him from books.

When spiritual awakening comes, we know without being told that not only does God live NOW, continuously, everywhere, but that He loves us almost beyond imagining. This is even to the point where He is willing to accept us as His sons/suns (by adoption, as Paul said). He chooses us when He feels we are ready.

When we are reborn to a new consciousness of Him we gain a certainty that we have been given a chance to dwell with Him forevermore. We know He expects us to measure up as His children, as inheritors of His Grace. Then we must accept the commission to represent Him.

God is Mind, the totality of Mind, where all things are created. To reach Him we must elevate our own minds to something approaching His consciousness else how can He reach us? We must move very close dropping away the earthly attentions, the concentration on those things which are below us in the sphere of creation.

We have to reach above, as high as we can reach and that means within as far as we can go, paradoxically. Within to the point of absolute zero, past all that can be seen or imagined, there God is.

In all action refer first to God. Go to sleep thinking of Him and on awakening in the morning present Him with your mind, letting Him take it over and thus become cooperative with Him in all you do.

You know that when you think mean or ugly thoughts you are separating yourself from His presence and heading for trouble on a downward path. If you can give up concentration of that meanness and surrender to Him **all** your thinking, you will eventually become worthy to become a co-creator with Him as He yearns for you to be, having conquered your own mind.

To start out all things with God is like starting at the top of the ladder but we have to place our mind at the top of the ladder or our feet would never know enough to start climbing, much less reach the top.

We are gods of our own universe. Until we awake within our minds and inmost beings, how can we wake up the dormant faculties within us? How can we move inert matter or stir the consciousness of lower stages of life from their comparative stupor, into living function?

Psalm 139:18, "When I awake, I am still with Thee."
The night is gone and the new Day is almost dawned.

We must awake to the fact we are living in a new age, one that has never appeared on the earth plane before.

The new Jerusalem is coming down from God today not tomorrow.

The words of John the Baptist ring true today,
"Prepare ye the way of the Lord. Make straight His Path."

The great Preparation can only take place after the awakening of the Self into full realization.

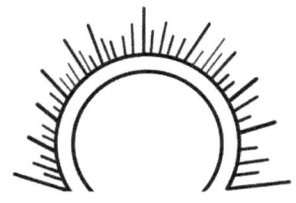

LESSON 6

AWAKENING FOUR

A sleep in the deep are those who are steeped in the waves of one phase or another of Neptune's illusions.

The psychic "waters" are attributed to Neptune and many a spiritualistic medium seems content to remain submerged in the shimmering semi-realities which are sometimes true, and sometimes quite misleading.

Entities which have left the body to pass beyond dwell in this region, as well as the thought forms which have taken form and are now filling with substance prior to appearing physically.

Some persons have slept the sleep of Neptune via drugs. Some enjoy it in night clubs or other glamour spots, where they are dazzled by the rhythmic music, plus the colors, bright lights, and the ultra-glamour of persons "putting on" the evenings glittering personality.

The sleep which comes from the alcohol absorbed need not be mentioned. Any wino asking for the price of a bottle is so sadly asleep that only the most intense desire or motivation can inspire him to wake from the dreary nightmare of his existence, to cease from the false sleep by which he seeks to escape.

Many of these will perish in their self-induced sleep to wake elsewhere another day.

But for those who are ready and eager to awaken from the "sleep" of earth's hold on them into the higher spiritual Realities, the psychic waters act as the media through which the spiritual beings may act to reach through to the physical to bring about that awakening.

This is the passageway, the meeting ground where the spiritual may reach down to function and the astral or psychic body of a person may reach up to meet the spiritual and gain thereby.

By means of the psychic world and its tools, discarnate teachers may cause phenomena which aid in teaching an aspirant, or in bringing him to an earthly teacher.

By these means the student is helped before he has gained his inner sight or hearing. The Teacher is thereby able to bring to him from the outside many lessons or eye-opening experiences which he will not need once he gains his spiritual sight and hearing.

In Canticles, or Solomon's Song, 5:2, we read: "I slept, but my heart was awake. Hark, my beloved is knocking."

God knocks when the body is asleep but the desire for Him is awake. Later, He'll expect you to be awake, expecting Him.

Water conducts electricity and Uranus of the heavens is the "great awakener." Uranus rules electricity. In that sense, awakening comes out of the water, too, the water of the heavens as lightning comes out of a storm.

Lightning represents Truth, spiritual truth, and the Bible says, "As the lightning flashes from the East, even unto the West, so shall the coming of the Son of Man be."

If strange things happen which can hardly be explained by ordinary means it may well be the gathering of the "waters" of the heavens through which the Lightening of Truth will flash to you. Nothing will ever again be the same for the Spirit of Christ shall have arrived in your consciousness.

To quote Dr. E.W. Blighton, "Awakening comes to individuals when processes, actions, and desires of the physical body both mentally and emotionally have reached a point where they totally recognize total failure.

"This is the time when the awakening comes. Not desire. Your whole body cries out. Nothing you have can satisfy that great ache within you, that great vacuum. Words and books will stand for nothing."

And again, he said, "In conquering death, Life begins! As Jesus did."

Every winter the tree seems to die giving up its robe of green. It endures bitter, crackling cold until the warm sun of the Spring appears, when then sap stirs in its roots, and soon begins to flow upward to its topmost branches, bringing a beautiful return to full life.

With the warm sun of spring, the whole world wakens. Again speaking astrologically, the first day of spring occurs when the sun enters the sign of Aries where it is at its place of exaltation. It is also a sign which energizes and acts.

Is it any wonder then that the water, which had been frozen and held in abeyance all winter on the mountain tops, begins to thaw and tumble down the mountain sides, to fill the brooks and water the fields and valleys below.

In this same way the coming of the Sun of Christ at the dawn of the spiritual awakening within us melts the long-frozen stream of consciousness within us so that it feeds the seedlings of new spiritual fruitfulness.

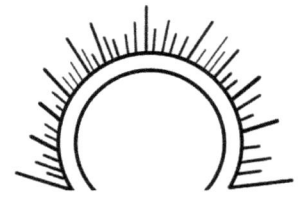

Awakening Five

In waking we *emerge* from the corridors of sleep. Consciousness *comes out* from the dark places.

In sleep the body is there alive but quiescent. The consciousness is somewhere alive. But the two are not functioning together.

It is when the bodies all *unite*. When the reasoning mind, the body and all the rest come together and work together all in one piece, then do we awake.

In sleep the eyes are closed to outside things. The first proof of waking is the opening of the eyes. The first proof of the spirit's awakening is the *seeing* with new eyes so that all the things seen before now look new and different.

Ordinary man is in a deep sleep. He has come down from God and entered the house of his body and becomes heavily involved with its needs and desires. HE HAS PULLED THE SHADES. He is walled in by thick flesh and has become involved in serving the temple rather than its indwelling Spirit.

The body needs food, drink, and warm shelter. It needs a place to rest. Primitive man worked at supplying all these and little more. They are essentials to the physical upkeep or maintenance of the "house."

Man nowadays has acquired unnatural tastes and has to work harder to supply these complex wants. He keeps in a dither doing so and becomes involved in a tangle of bills and jobs and charge accounts.

It's time somebody told him it's morning. Christ has returned and the energy of the Sun is pouring into our beings. Let's arise and use this energy. Let's stir ourselves and do something to feed the **Spirit** that dwells in the temple and the cells which comprise its walls.

The whole symbolism of Easter and spring refer to the awakening of the earth and its creatures to the return of the Sun's warmth. Bears go into hibernation in winter to escape the snow and long period of cold but they come out as the sun grows warm in spring. So too do the crocuses, tulips, and baby chicks. Similar to this is the entombment and resurrection of Jesus.

The awakening of the human consciousness to God-realization, as the awakening of the seed below the earth, begins below the level of conscious awareness. It stirs deep down in the sub-conscious REALMS of mind and being. Toward morning while we still sleep, certain sounds or movements bring us almost awake yet drowsiness holds a curtain about us.

It may take an earthquake to rend the veil of the temple, an inner jolt, with the accompanying flash of realization of God's Truth. That's the alarm clock of the Spirit.

It may be hard to topple out of bed, but once out we begin to bloom as the fragrant daffodil in the early morning sun. Birds begin to sing in the flowering trees, and we come outside to breathe the wonderful scent and yawn, breathe deeply to take in more of the oxygen of God's own Life-Breath, the pure air.

As the animal having spent the winter in hibernation comes forth to frolic on the spring meadows, as the seed unfurls its embryo to push up and show itself above ground, as the chick and baby bird pecks its way out of the enclosing shell, so the locked-in spirit of man will burst his bonds as the solar energies within him get rid of the dross and open his eyes to the true nature of his being.

One *lives* by being awake. Being asleep is like existing only in Nature bound by time processes. But awaking is a miracle of God which overlooks time and takes on eternity. Awake and living one also chooses and acts freely to change his or her own destiny.

Rocks and minerals apparently sleep in their slowness of evolvement. Man is the most awake creature because of his high intellect.

SLEEP: is a state of reduced physical and nervous activity, accompanied by suspension of voluntary movements, and a complete or partial unconsciousness. To be dormant, inactive.

WAKE: is to emerge from sleep. To become active or alert after being inactive or dormant. To keep watch or guard at night. To rouse, stir up, excite.

All the waking of earth corresponds to the timing of the Sun except for certain night creatures which use night as cover. So does the waking of the Spirit of Man correspond to the coming of the Christ, the Son-of-God consciousness, to his being. Thus he is reborn to this state through Grace.

Isaiah said, "Thy dead shall live, their bodies shall rise. O dwellers in the dust, awake and sing for joy! For thy dew is a dew of light, and on the land of the shades thou wilt let it fall."

Paul wrote in Thessalonians 5:6, "But you are not in darkness, brethren, for that day to surprise you like a thief. For you are all sons of light and sons of the day; we are not of the night or of darkness.

"So then let us not sleep as others do, but let us keep awake and be sober. For those who sleep, sleep at night, but since we belong to the day, let us be sober, and put on the breastplate of faith and love and, for God, who died for us, so that whether we wake or sleep, we might live with him."

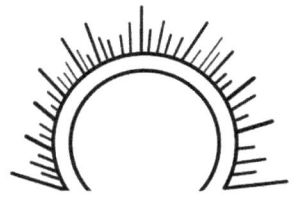

Lesson 6
Awakening Six

The Way, the Truth, and the Light is the Path to eternal peace. There is nothing in the pattern of Creation about Catholic, Protestant, or Judaism. All of these are creations of Man's Ego but are and have been used for the advancement of Man.

There is however in the Plan of Creation a set of steps they might be called which Man must climb if he is not going to lift himself by his bootstraps.

These set of steps are related to the set of tools which the Creator gave to Man so that he might attain Godhood.

When we look really close at the Universal Picture to see what really is there and what can be put to use, we find most interesting that the tools of Man are closely related to the various religions. These tools come from his experiences from using the universal pattern of creation and the Law.

The principle religions are:
Christianity • Islam • Buddhism • Judaism • Hinduism

The following illustration shows the attributes of Creation. In this figure is the monogenetic expression of Universality.

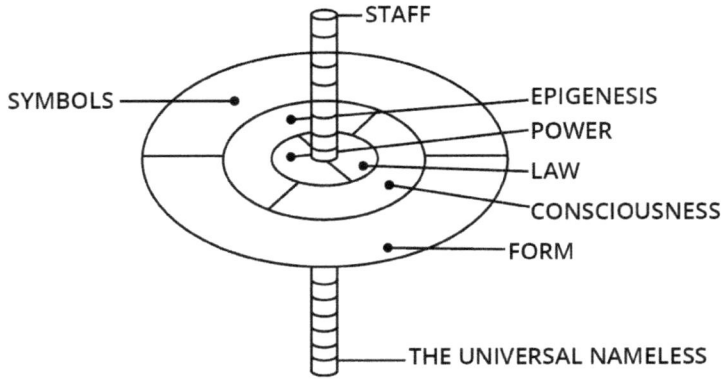

In the figure are the secrets of all Creation. It is the dynamic force of God demonstrating its Power of progenity in bilateral action.

This also illustrates the polarities which will produce action, growth, and balance. Starting at the center the three polarities are: Power and Law, Epigenesis and Consciousness, Symbols and Form. It is the whole bag of tricks of Nature in action from the primordial state to Godhood.

It illustrates all the chemical, mechanical, electrical, and philosophical conjurisms in existence from the beginning to the end.

The simple magnificence of the All Mighty, SELF in SELF.

GLORY GLORY GLORY

To the all-pervading intelligence of all creation.

Let us now go back and look at the tools of man as they are grouped together.

We have what might be called in the language of the past age the invisible tools which are:

1. Symbolism
2. Power
3. Law
4. The Way

Then we have the triangle of MA:

FATHER –
EPIGENESIS

UNIVERSAL VEHICLE –
HOLY SPIRIT

SON –
COMMUNICATION

You can see that if these are assembled together, we have the Universal Tools of Man, our Level 2 classes in the Tree of Life:

1. Symbolism
   Communication
   Power

2. Universal Vehicle = Man Material "Staff"

3. The Law
   Epigenesis
   The Way

By looking at the other diagram, we see that the staff and the Nameless One correspond. Two Attributes of the One Force are RA and MA. RA is the mind of God, which is positive. MA is the substance, or being of God, which is negative.

In the beginning a Nameless Wanderer was Man (or Being), all perfect, all sufficient, because IT had all the tools working perfectly turned into the All wisdom of power.

Of a poise so balanced that it excluded all else because it was all. And none but its own SELF could comprehend ALL that IT was in its personal universe, IT was all and it was ALL.

For it was unknown and unknowable. It was in poise and balance, therefore there was no resistance, no seeking, its comprehension was infinite.

IT had and was of a Great Splendor, Majesty, Magnificence and all Power and if still, once we find the SELF this is the Master Being.

To understand SELF is more than the MIND of Man can ever understand but we may understand our divine obligation and relationship to all functioning, moving form and forces.

For in the beginning was God and then God spoke the word and the Word was with God and the Word was God.

In all the splendor and Majesty and power this is more than the Mind of Man can understand. Only SELF can conceive this.

Then the Word took flesh and became the Man, the Christ-being, the God Man in all perfection, Magnificence and Power. Then He understood himself and the Word was God, and at this realization he was extremely humble.

Thus the Word was God, God in Great Humility and Power. For when He conceived of Himself, it evolved through Law into a fleshly body of a little child. The child knew of his Father but could not understand the Father, but this was not necessary. All He needed to know was Himself, or **SELF**.

For the Word was given to the Son and the Son JESUS CHRIST gave it to Man again. Man had the Word, but was not conscious of it.

Thus the involution of Man began and thus the mystery of Genesis is unfolded.

Then we gradually forgot that aspect of our nature, the Word, through working on aspects of physical life which were made prominent in our consciousness. This was due to the influence of the Electromagnetic fields of other planets in relation to the place in this solar system in which that particular birth took place.

Then also we forgot the Father, the Original Creator of all Creators.

Slowly, but surely, as He formed Creation including Beings and the Suns the memory of the original Creator became more and more vague.

Because of the change of consciousness from the original Creator this caused a breakdown of oneness with it and the created forms became less and less infused with the effluent LIFE. Certain parts of the Beings became less active and, therefore, internal formations became apparent.

Also alone-formness began to build because crystallization of the spirit became denser matter. There was a longing to draw closer to the source of life, a change of potential, and electrical potential, and from this developed prayer, eventually.

With the difference of density came the action of what we call knowledge and sensation. As this Creation sensed a difference in reaction of the spirit in its own universe It realized a revelation of knowledge.

This He transferred to his New Son. At this time the transfer was before the expulsion of the New Son into the space around it.

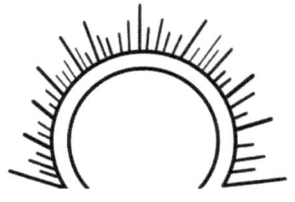

LESSON 6
RETURN ONE

All the great teachings of the earth have taught the way of man, the controlling of his mind and his desires that he may cut away the outer to reach the inner reaching into his true being. That is the eternal part of man which is free of all negation and which knows the whole creation as the Creator created it.

The return is the return of man to his real being, his original state of being in all the power and the glory of the great One.

Cutting away the dross gets rid of the desires which hold man to the binds and confines of the earth. When one breaks free of these limitations, he then becomes a free being, a son who has returned.

In the New Testament it talks about the son that was lost who returned. He became a slave to the world and to worldly desires and travelled far away. He then spent all of his inheritance. Then he saw the servants of his father and their good life. He decided it was better to be his father's servant than in his current condition of muck and mire. He turned his face from his poverty and started walking back to his father's house. When he was almost home his father saw him and brought him the rest of the way, giving him all the treasure of his kingdom.

Jesus, the first of many who have returned, showed man this inner road and how to rid themselves of their own blocks.

Many of the religions have taught of the outward appearances but have failed to teach the great path within, the eternal path of man raising himself through his service to his Creator.

This return isn't an abnormal state of being, for once the son has returned to the Father, he is then living a normal life, that which has been since the beginning and is now and ever shall be.

When man looks away from this world and from his own opinions, from his likes and dislikes, from his beliefs and disbeliefs, and begins to accept things just the way they are, then he is without dogma, creeds or interpretations. He is returning to the realness of himself and of his Creator.

The teachings of Jesus Christ are within man in their totality. Jesus uses the phrase "the return." The process of returning is remembering that which you already are, one with God. Using the term "return" points out man was there to begin with, for you cannot return to a place you have never been.

The return has no labels or that is to say, no "isms." The return isn't a religion but is a return of man to his original greatness.

Many people on this return have hung themselves up with beautiful words and catchy phrases, calling themselves Yogis, Buddhists, Christians, and what not. But when a great Nameless Being created you in His own image what could your name be but just a nameless wanderer. You are moving from one existence to another seeking to find a place where you fit, but when you have returned you find that place is within you, being the Self, being just what you are.

As man travels through this world he clings to it and to all the shiny things of the world trying to grab for himself something to call his own. He winds up losing it all when its time to leave. The only thing he leaves with is himself, that which he has tried to run away from for so long.

The return is a great reality. For Jesus didn't come to the earth spouting theology but he told man just what is. He had been there, he knew and experienced it, and he lived in it every day of his life. He was no freak. He was just like you and me except he let go of everything including himself.

When man takes God seriously and not as beautiful idealism or a beautiful concept but really seeks to find the truth, then he shall return. But until man accepts the reality of what Jesus taught, he'll roll in the muck and mire of his own making and the avoidance of himself.

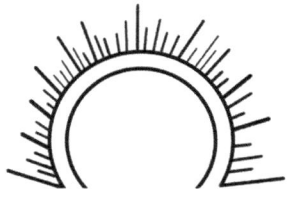

LESSON 6

RETURN TWO

THE PRODIGAL SON

Ever since our entrance into life we have been preparing to return to the Father.

St. Paul says in Romans that all have sinned and fallen short of the glory of God. Since the fall of Adam and Eve man has lost his control over the universe given to him by the Father at the beginning of His Creation. It is this power and authority, this Sonship, that we are returning to.

In St. Luke's gospel this is referred to as "the inheritance." St. Luke 15:12 begins our story.

We are told in this particular Bible reference that a man had two sons. The younger one said to his father that he wanted a share of all his property, and the father complied with his request. It was not long before the child went off to a foreign land and squandered all he had. And when he had run through all his inheritance a famine broke out in the land and the son began to feel it.

He hired himself out to a citizen of that land who put him in charge of feeding the pigs. He began to feed himself upon the things that were fit for pigs alone. He came to a great awakening and found out that his father's servants had a better existence than this.

In deep humility he returned home and made a plea before his father to accept him back as a servant only. The father welcomed him back with open arms and restored unto him his sonship by placing upon his finger the ring of authority. His brother was extremely jealous and complained to his father about his younger brother. The father replied to the older brother that he had him with him always and for this he was grateful. He explained that the younger brother was like a dead man who had come to life. The father thought he had lost him, but then the son returned. With great festivity and music the father accepted the wayward son.

One of the great lessons that we learn when we go through the great awakening is that we have been separated from our Creator through subjecting ourselves to the Father's Creation and wasting our Divine Inheritance as sons of the Creator. We lost our inheritance through misuse of the power and lack of understanding of the Law, and through stubbornness towards our Father's will. This is the way man has sinned.

Man has been made to be an heir of God and a joint heir with Christ, to have dominion over the things of this world. The things of the world are to be fully under man's control. Today we are living in an age which is divided into two, symbolized by the two sons of the father: an old order and a new order. The old order has been with the Father from the beginning. The new order is coming alive and into fulfillment.

The old order refuses to die out and make way for that which is coming into full manifestation. The old order is controlled completely by a mass mind which is the composite mind of the people of the earth who believe "all you see is all there is". It speaks in its own self-righteousness, thus keeping the former laws and regulations established by the Creator for a time and a season.

Mass mind refuses to allow the old order to realize the time is at hand for a transition to a complete change. Therefore, the mass mind is compelling the old order to transgress the law of God. The Son of God symbolized by the prodigal son has come through this new order and is defying the old order. At one time He had defied the very will of

His Father. Now He is returning to His Father's house in order to fulfill His mission as lord of this earth under Christ the Lord.

The purpose of this School through verses of the Bible, the sciences, and the tools provided is to place the Father's ring upon the restored Son's finger. We are returning to the Father in a humbler state than when we left but all shall be restored to us in greater measure than when we left. There shall be much rejoicing by God and his angels over one sinner that repents. Repentance is turning away and going forward.

Illumination and Realization bring us to this point, and we remember through these two sources.

When we come to the Great Return from dabbling in the lower nature to achieving the higher nature, we shall have no fear and have the ability to exercise our authority as Sons of God.

FIRST BORN SON

Through many lands I have wandered
Over trackless sand and trackless moons.
I've climbed mountains, vast and rugged,
To see the setting Sun.

In other worlds I searched for Gold,
And found it here and there—
Felt the arms of loved ones around me,
Knew of the presence of others everywhere.

Felt the Great Force flowing through me,
Known its ecstasy sublime.
But of these none has so much moved me,
As the little arms of my First Born Son.

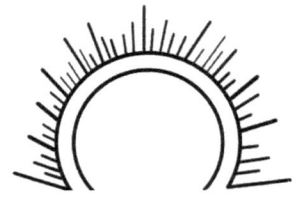

LESSON 6

FEAST ONE

All those who would enter the kingdom of God have been universally invited to a great Feast. The universal call has gone out to all, whosoever will may come. We are working toward this goal for all of us are here to prepare for this great Feast.

We will be using 3 basic Bible stories, the book of Matthew, chapter 22:2; the book of Luke, chapter 14:16; and the book of Revelation, chapter 19, verses 7–9.

In Matthew we read of a rich man who prepared a great wedding feast for his son. He sent forth his servants to tell the guests to come for everything was prepared. The wedding guests made light of this and treated his servants disrespectfully, abusing them greatly. In the New Age we are entering in we find a great desire for revelation and truth. Yet when the preachers of the Word go into the world as the servants of God they are abused and mistreated.

This angers our heavenly Father, the King of this Universe.

It is a privilege for all the sons and daughters of God and for the world in general to be invited to the great wedding feast. Yet how many are heeding the call? But the judgment recorded in the 22nd Chapter of Matthew is promised to this world if they do not heed the call to the great wedding feast.

Jesus tells us that the king sent his armies and destroyed those unworthy, whom Jesus called murderers, and burned their cities.

The king pronounced the wedding guests who didn't show up unworthy and went seeking those in the highways and byways. And he gathered both the good and the bad, and allowed them to participate in the great event.

The past generation in the old Age is likened to those who mistreated the servants of God. The Judgment of Fire will destroy the old Creation and those abiding under the old order will be destroyed by the Fire of God's Judgment. And those pronounced unholy and unrighteous by the old Age shall find themselves seated at the Master's table.

For we are living in the day when the Word of God is being physically manifested. There will be no more allegories, no more stories, and a definite end to fiction. All will be reality. Even in the New Age there are going to be found those who will try to enter without the wedding garment. And as in the Bible story of old they will be cast out and there will be weeping and wailing and gnashing of teeth.

The modern-day wedding garment for the New Age is nothing more than the glorious light of Christ, the physical manifestation of energy and force in both spiritual and physical action. Without this, regardless of the age we are living in, we are doomed.

This light of Christ comes to us through epigenesis, or as it is commonly called the grace of God.

The New Age is an age of physically spiritual enlightenment and one must abide in this Light. For in the true God Creation all is light and in It there is no darkness at all.

In the story found in Luke we are told that after the expulsion of the old guests and the entrance of the new guests there was still room at the table and the master bid his servants to go out and find some more guests. In Luke he also pronounces the old guests truly unworthy.

In the New Age, millions upon millions will enter through the light of Christ. It will be surprising to many whom they will find sitting at the master's table.

In order to find this light of Christ and be accepted at this great wedding feast, he must deny himself, take up his cross, and follow Him, as stated in Luke 14:27.

In the 19th chapter of Revelation, verses 7–9, the story is repeated.

This time it is called the Marriage of the Lamb. This is a New Age wedding. We are told in this School that in the New Age the Lamb of God is the Mind. This is a joining of the Mind to the Spirit and the physical so that they may perform one function, the glorification of God in unison.

This marriage feast of the Lamb must take place in every believer's being before it can be taken in a universal literal sense.

Revelation 19:7 says, "Let us be glad and rejoice and give honor to him, for the marriage of the Lamb has come and his wife has made herself ready." The Spirit has made itself ready for the proper function of use in this New Age and all have been invited to participate. But only those with the light of Christ will be accepted.

In the 8th and 9th verses of Revelation 19 we find an excellent description of the light of Christ and its functions. We find out through this scriptural verse that this light of Christ is the righteousness of the Saints.

In verse 9, it is stated, "and he said unto me, right blessed are they which are called unto the marriage supper of the Lamb. And he said unto me, these are the true sayings of God."

John the Revelator is hereby testifying to the verity of the truth of the marriage feast of the Lamb. In Matthew 25:10, the following story is recorded. The bridegroom came, and that the door was shut, and afterward came the five foolish virgins saying, "Lord, Lord, open unto us" and the answer came, "Verily I say unto you, I know you not."

Matthew cautions us by saying, "Watch therefore, for you know not, neither the day nor the hour, wherein the Son of God is coming."

The Son of God is the center of the marriage, the master of the Feast. He through the great light of Christ has created the possibility of our participation in this great turn of events.

The Lamb of God must be wedded to the Spirit. After the wedding takes place through the light of Christ and the force and energy of the Father, the mind of man and the mind of the Father become one as they were in the beginning.

Duality ceases to exist at this point, for man arises out of the state of physical concept, his mind becomes spiritually perfect, and he assumes his responsibility as the Son of God. After this has taken place in all of God's Creation of true Sons the world will come completely under the dominion of the New Order. And God's plan will have come to pass.

At this great feast there will be no spot nor blemish, no defilement nor any such thing. The day of the Lord will be accomplished. All will eventually turn toward him. Every knee shall bow and every tongue shall confess that he is Christ. Those who have been faithful over a few things will be rulers over much.

Since we are living in a day of active reality we cannot waste time nor suppose anything. Things actually are or they are not. Our God is a living vital force causing all things to be in existence. His feast is a feast of action and reality, a vital feast and one that all mankind must attend.

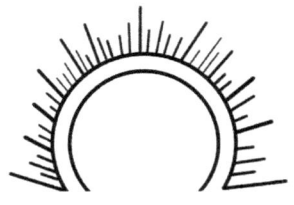

FEAST TWO

Lord be with the ministers of Thy table who serve to Thy children the Feast of the flesh and blood of Christ Jesus, that all may become not merely like unto him but actually part of his living body, here and now!

Let us not fatten up Thy congregation unto complacency with the misguided fare of self-indulgence or pseudo-spiritual food. Let us give them of Thy true nourishment which worketh unto wholeness and perfection of function that they may better perform Thy mission in vigor and strength.

Jesus said to Peter, "Feed my sheep." He did not mean feed their self-satisfaction as churchgoers with the spiritual candy of flattery. Neither did he mean to get them so bogged down with their own fatness of self-importance that they would become valueless as Christ's servants.

Let us rather give them the real nourishment of Truth and feed their hunger with "wholiness" and the Seed of Health, curing their indifference with the vitality of **involvement** in Christ. Let them be nourished with his Love, his Grace, and his Word.

Let not our spiritual service become a "habit" of schedule and form, to make an appearance for appearance's sake, always there on time. Neither should we just greedily gulp down any religious fare in sight just because it's there and we enjoy it.

266

True, new students are as little children and "have to" come to the table every time and partake, under discipline. But let their servant at that table, their teacher or priest, make sure the food served is not mere warmed-over scraps nor all sizzling with spice. Let them serve that healthful food which will bring forth their perfectness, giving them balance as their part in Christ.

Do you ministers stuff your congregation with the pastries of platitudes and the *hors d'oeuvres* of intellectuality? These are all right for embellishing the meal. But God's Truth is the real meat and His instructions the vegetables which are always for your benefit.

If you follow after these things, the fruits of attainment cannot be far off, for all sustained and faithful effort must be rewarded.

He who endures to the end shall inherit a crown.

Do you admonish them because it's expected of a minister with great flourishes of dramatic speech, while secretly chuckling with delight at the great show you are putting on for their benefit playing the "heavy"? After the sermon is over, they'll shake your hand and compliment you on a bang-up speech, but **do they change**? Or have they witnessed a good show? Broken up the weekly routine?

Or do you, worse still, hurl fire and brimstone upon them, threaded with fear and damnation, to the point of driving them forth from what should have been God's house (not yours) into the street. Now they are hopeless at the fate in store with no place left to turn, with not even the assurance of a loving God?

The only alternative to hell offered in cases like this is to align themselves with the hell-and-damnation shouters, a fate which hardly seems the lesser of two evils. They'd rather take their chances on living now and gamble that the day of accounting at the end of the road is far enough distant that by the time they arrive there, they'll have thought out an answer or way out.

There is a way out without the gamble, which is up to you to teach. They don't have to condemn everyone to death or join those who do. They can live and follow the Christ, become one with him, and live as he lived, loving, giving, doing. His joy was full in God. He knew God loved him, and he loved in return. Loving God, he also loved his fellow man and acted thereupon.

His sharp speech was to those who taunted and tried to trap him, who would not listen to the Truth. He did not go about indiscriminately threatening people.

Let us, as true ministers, invite them to the True Feast, the Lamb of God which was slain for us, and the Marriage Feast even now being prepared.

IT ALL BELONGS TO HIM

As each event or person comes along—
Unbidden—see it not as bleak or wrong,
Or fraught with weed or thorn.
Let not the burn of critic, nor the blast
Of cold, hard doubt to wither Good Unborn,
Hid like a Seed therein, by God's own Hand.
But seize each happening, and make it blessings yield!
Proclaim potential Good, and dedicate the field.
Acknowledge but the Best, and cultivate its Root,
Hovering over it with love, lest others blight.
Give full Attention to the unseen Light.
That God may reap His Spirit's fruit
In this which He designed. This is your chance.
Less evidence brings greater exercise of faith.
Rejoice and welcome oppor-tunes to "dance,"
To co-create with Him, through care
In thought and work—Divine Results to share.

LESSON 7:
BASIC RELIGIONS, PART 1

Lesson 7, Part 1: Confucianism • Hinduism
Jainism • Zen Buddhism • Buddhism

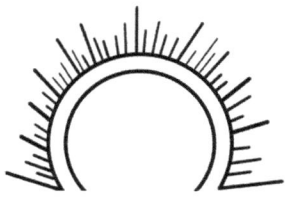

LESSON 7: BASIC RELIGIONS, PART 1
CONFUCIANISM

More than a millennium before Christ, a people known as the Shang or Yin lived along the Yellow River in China. We know very little about these people. What we do know tells us they were developed in writing, technical skills, and their civilization was very old.

About 1100 B.C. they were conquered by a neighboring people known as the Chou. The Chou Dynasty became the longest dynasty in the history of China. The fame of this dynasty rests on the fact that they developed an extensive written literature and new insights into philosophy.

In the sixth century B.C., significant intellectual developments occurred in China, providing material for their thought for over two and a half millenniums. This began with Confucius, 551–479 B.C.

Confucius came after five centuries of Chou kings who started strong, but deteriorated in character and ability as they became more prosperous.

The fierce conflicts and war between the many feudal states in China led to the establishment of the first absolute monarch, the Emperor of China. Many of those who had favored positions in the old feudal system were jobless and discontented. Confucius was one of these.

Before we can study Confucius and his teachings, we must look at the period that preceded him. Our knowledge of this period comes from the *Book of Odes*. These are poems. Some are from the Shang period, some are love poems and poems of feeling, and others comment on the Chou government, both complimenting and criticizing it. Confucius is said to have edited the *Book of Odes*. It is certain he learned much from it.

The *Book of Odes* came from an oral tradition. By the time it was written, it left no emotion untouched. Confucius quoted from the *Odes* often. He once quoted to his students:

> "My little ones, why don't you study the *Odes*? Poetry will exalt you, make you observant, enable you to mix with others, provide an outlet for your vexations. You learn from it immediately to serve your parents and ultimately to serve your prince. It also provides wide acquaintance with the names of birds, beasts, and plants."

The Odes follow the deterioration of the kings. There were too many political jobs, tyranny developed, and disorder became common. To add to this, natural calamities came to the people.

Before the Shang Dynasty, the gods were animistic and known from myth. The spirits were divided between the good (*shen*) and bad (*kwei*) spirits. Animism led to a concern with the dead.

Veneration of one's ancestors became of prime importance in the lives of the people and took on a religious significance that is still followed to this day.

By the time of the Shang Dynasty (1700–1100 B.C.), there arose a belief in an exalted being known as *Shang-Ti*. The lesser gods and spirits were still worshipped, however.

With the advent of the Chou Dynasty, an "impersonal" deity emerges, known as *Tien*, or *Heaven*. Later, only the Emperors were able to sacrifice to Heaven at the Summer and Winter Solstice festivals. And it followed that the importance of the gods you worshipped corresponded to your social position.

People revolted against the gods about mid-point in the Chou Dynasty. The common people were aware of the evils that had come their way and could see no other reason than the gods had failed.

Their rites and prayers were not heard. Some people became so disgusted that they went off to isolated places to brood. Many of these poems are the product of this brooding.

By the time of Confucius the *Odes* stated the nature of the evil that was affecting the people. Two schools of physicians arose to heal the sickness. One was the mysticism out of which the TAO TE CHING took form. The other was Confucius, who proposed the moral cure for an evil society.

Confucius was born during this time about 551 B.C., in the province of Shantung. From the ages of seventeen to twenty-two, he had worked out his philosophy and had become well-known as a teacher of the ancient writings. Confucius had not the intention of starting a new religion, but of bringing people into the full realization of the old, its utility, beauty, and truth. In 517 B.C. he went to the capital and visited with Lao-tse, the founder of Taoism. After fifteen years of teachings, between revolutions and political intrigues of those who were envious of him, he rose to a leading position in the kingdom with two of his disciples. But the intrigues caught him and he was removed from office in 496 B.C.

For the next thirteen years, he wandered through China. He then returned to the province of Lu where, after the death of his two disciples, he continued teaching with even greater followings.

> "All his teaching was devoted to practical morality and to the duties of man in this world in relation to his fellow man. In it was summed up the wisdom acquired by his own insight and experience, and that derived from the teaching of the sages of antiquity. He sought to attain a happy tranquility throughout the Chinese Empire which could, he believed, be attained by the observance of the five obligations of human society: (1) those between sovereign and minister; (2) father and son; (3) husband and wife; (4) elder and younger brother; and (5) between friends. It was, according to his teaching, incumbent upon all to perform the reciprocal duties arising from each relationship."

"In his teachings, there is a strong feudal leaning which advocates almost unlimited authority for the sovereign over the minister, for the father over the son, the husband over the wife, the elder brother over his younger. Subordination to superiors he looked upon as one of the greatest of all essentials for the existence and proper conduct of the state. To these must be added virtuous conduct among all and upright dealing among friends. The education of the young he declared to be the foundation of the welfare of the state. Confucius' ideal of government was a paternal disposition wisely and honestly directed and administered. This position he modified by the assertion that a ruler's maintenance of power should depend upon his just and upright conduct and his honest endeavor to make his government good." (*The Encyclopedia Americana*).

Confucius did most of his teachings in the towns and cities of China. Mysticism developed in the mountains and more isolated regions. Confucius spoke to the masses that were crowded together. Confucius felt himself divinely appointed to speak of moral virtue, and no more.

The concept of God was not stressed, for it was being worked out in other teachings of the time, namely Buddhism and Taoism.

From Chinese mysticism had come the idea of the Way— represented by the word **Tao**. To them this was an old sign with new meanings. They said nothing could exist without the **Way**:

Something there is, whose veiled creation was
Before the earth or sky began to be.
So silent, so aloof and so alone,
It changes not, nor fails, but touches all:
Conceive it as the mother of the world.

I do not know its name.
A name for it is "Way".
Pressed for designation,
I call it Great.
Great means outgoing,
Out-going, far-reaching,
Far-reaching, return.

The Way is great,
The sky is great,
The earth is great,
The king also is great.
Within the realm
These four are great:
The king but stands
For one of them.

Man conforms to earth.
The earth conforms to sky.
The sky conforms to the Way
The Way conforms to its own nature.

The Way of Life: Lao Tzu, No. 25

Confucius could not use the Way. He saw that people understood it wrong. To them it was keeping the gods happy with rites and rituals here on earth. But the evils which had happened led many to look for a new conception of the Way. Confucius said that one should be very strict about observing rites and sacrifices, but he said that his life was also a prayer. This was revolutionary for China. It meant that unless ones' life was moral, in other words a prayer, all the rites and sacrifices would not amount to anything.

Confucius laid down a Golden Rule of reciprocity:

"What you do not want done to yourself, do not do to others."

As mentioned before, this Rule was to guide the five obligations of human society.

Ritual was used by Confucius as intercourse between God and man, and, therefore, between man and man. It was an etiquette which controlled man's relations with his fellows. Ritual was an outward or visible sign of the inner goodness.

A man must be pragmatic. Even in ritual Confucius said, "Absorption in the study of the supernatural is most harmful." The proper attitude was "to devote oneself earnestly to one's duty to humanity, and, while respecting the spirits, to keep aloof from them, may be called wisdom." And it was pragmatic to carry out all of one's religious duties.

But to the ring of his inner disciples were taught the truths of Creation, the illumination and advancement of that illumination, the mystic teachings of the ages, and the reality of God. One of his later disciples remarked that it is hard, nearly impossible, to hear the truths as told by the Master.

Eventually elaboration led to set codes of conduct. A master had to know 3,300 rules of conduct. This often took so much energy that little time was left for developing moral character.

To Confucius, Li, or "propriety" meant conformity to the five obligations. This must begin with the family. Confucius explained its significance when he said:

> "The principles of *li* and righteousness serve as the principles of social discipline. By means of these principles people try to maintain the official status of rulers and subjects, to teach the parents and children and elder brothers and younger brothers and husbands and wives to live in harmony, to establish social institutions.... Through this principle of rational social order (*li*) everything becomes right in the family, the state, and world."

He later said,

"It is not possible for a man to teach others who cannot teach his own family, for from loving examples of one's family, the whole of society becomes loving; while from the ambition and perverseness of one man, the whole state may be led to rebellion and disorders. Such is the nature of influence."

Confucius saw the flaw in this when he said that "there well may be men who are superior but not good." It was hoped that by using the Way, honest and just men would run the government. But it often happened that they were gentlemen, and scholarly, but little else!

Confucius did not systematize his thought. He did not define the source of the moral force which gives man character (*te*). He stressed piety, but did not speak of God except in the sense of heaven, and even here he did not elaborate. This was not his way.

In preparation for the teachings and Teachers to come Confucius gave his disciples knowledge of God through the use of color, sound, and the forces of Nature. Only the most evolved students were taught this! To the people he taught, he said, "Let us leave the heaven to the angels and the sparrows," and, "while you do not understand life, how can you know about death."

Confucius' greatness was that he gave China a lasting discovery into the moral nature of man. Through service all desires were channeled into an understanding of right actions, which was man's role while on earth. Out of this came a massive humanism which served as a code of conduct for China. He was, so to speak, the Moses of China. He showed men how to be better and do better where they were. Peace and order in society were developed into an elaborate pattern of civilization. It was able to withstand numerous invasions by foreign races.

Confucius' teachings were common sense. For the deeper excitements of the spirit, the Chinese people found Buddhism and Taoism. Confucius, then, provided a code of moral conduct which enabled man to serve—this unending bending of oneself toward the pleasing and serving of another in a way as to allow that person being served to obtain his freedom.

Confucius collected, edited, and rewrote the classics of the Chou period. By doing this, he set the standard for Confucian orthodoxy and built the classics of Chinese literature.

The five classics of Confucius are:

1. *Yi-Ching* or *Book of Changes*: This is a book of divination. Confucius commented on it and rearranged it. It also contains the theory of Yang and Yin in words and symbols. Circumstances are always changing. One must know this and change accordingly as Yin and Yang achieve balance. There must be a tie between attitude and circumstance. One's balance must be maintained, for error is working against circumstance. If error succeeds, imbalance results.

2. *Shu-Ching* or *Book of History*: This is the history of the "Sage Kings" of the golden age.

3. *Shi-Ching* or *Book of Odes*

4. *Ch'un Ch'in*: This is a record of the events in the reigns of the kings in the province of Lu where Confucius lived.

5. *LiChi* or *Book of Rites*: This is a collection of writings on ceremonies and rites.

We also have the *Four Books*, which are:

1. *The Analects*: A collection of the Master's sayings

2. *The Great Learning*

3. *The Doctrine of the Mean*: Collected by his disciples

4. *Mencius*: The great disciple and successor of Confucius.

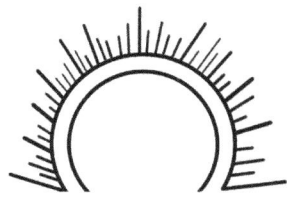

HINDUISM

One of the first things a student of Hinduism grasps is its unlimited diversity. From the Hindus, themselves, there are two definitions—one "broad" and the other "narrow." The broader definition means "the whole complex of beliefs and institutions which have appeared from the time when their ancient (and most sacred) scriptures, the Vedas, were composed until now." This meaning is preferred by many Hindus.

The narrow definition sees the Vedic and Brahmaninistic periods as preparatory stages to Hinduism, which is seen as "the vast social and religious system which has grown up among the peoples of India since about the 3rd century B.C.

Hindus may believe almost anything. The only common belief is in the caste system and the "trust" that they will be born into a higher caste in their next lifetime.

Hinduism is divided into three periods. The first period is called the Vedic and Brahman period. This is the period of growth from an optimistic polytheism to a monism. Second is the reform period in which Jainism (see Lesson on Jainism) and Buddhism (see Lesson on Buddhism) appeared. The final period is when orthodox Hinduism absorbed many of the beliefs from these reform movements and emerged victorious.

Before 2000 B.C., India was filled with the dark-skinned people called Dravidians who lived in southern India. These people produced a highly developed Bronze Age civilization. They planted the seeds for much of India's religious growth.

About the middle of the 2nd millennium B.C. a light-skinned people invaded India. These Indo-Europeans were part of the great movement of these people at this time. They found a home in northern India and called themselves Aryans. Once settled along the Indus River, they began to settle in small villages. There were many wars with the darker-skinned Dravidians, which were later written down in the *Ramayana* and *Mahabharata*.

Soon, the Indo-Aryans began to organize society into distinct classes. The move was necessitated by the growing need to master the many different types of peoples as more and more Aryans poured over the Kush mountains. Soon the divisions began to follow the lines of what labor each group could do.

The language these people spoke, Sanskrit, is the base of not only Latin but all of the modern European languages. It gave the Indo-Aryans a vehicle by which to transmit poems and prayers. It also allowed them to give distinct names to the emerging social structure.

These people were not yet content or stable. They began to express their wanderings in an oral tradition which contained folk tales, hymns, prayers, and epic stories. These became the first sacred writings of India, the *Vedas*.

Veda means "knowledge" (the same root as the English words "knowing" and "wisdom"). The most famous, the *Rig-Veda*, is "an anthology of religious poetry in ten books containing over a thousand hymns and representing the creative efforts of many generations." This was written down about the 8th century B.C.

The deities mentioned are the four elements and the many faces of nature a primitive people would have to deal with on a daily basis. Some sources say that the *Rig-Veda* is an account of creation wherein the god Indra is supreme. He is the god of monsoons and storms. He released the primal waters which were held by Vritra, thus releasing the hidden or unborn sun. From this emerged the four elements of creation and the pattern was then set.

There is much beautiful poetry in the *Rig-Veda* upon the nature gods. Dawn is the "young maid in white robes" shining afar in her chariot drawn by red-spotted horses. She is accompanied by a number of different sun gods (for the different manifestations of light).

At the pinnacle of this cosmology is Varuna. He is called the god "of the high-arched sky." His job is to keep order in the stars and to direct the forces so that orderly patterns of creation are maintained. He also keeps men obedient to the law for it is through him that man knows his sins.

All in all, the Aryans approached worship with confidence and joy. Their worship took place in the open air (there were no temples, yet) with offerings of such produce of nature as goats milk, grain or animals. All sacrifices were accompanied by elaborate ceremonies in the middle of which was the sacred petition, or "brahma" (the prayer).

Whenever worship took place, Agni, the god of fire had to be present. Although he was the god of celestial as well as terrestrial fire, his prime function was the altar fire. It is quite interesting to note the similarities between this god and the Zoroastrian conception of fire (these people passed through Persia in-route to India).

On a whole, this period was one of optimism. The priests were growing in number and in power. During the close of this period, the supreme deities emerged and gathered around "That One Thing," the great unnamed Cosmic Reality.

The Indo-Aryans moved down the Ganges Valley, finally settling down, when an interesting thing happened. The change they started overtook them! About the end of the 7th century, the caste system became the social order. With the Aryans at the top, four distinct classes emerged. First, there were the Kshatriyas (nobles), then the Brahmins (priests), then Vaisyas (Aryan common people) and finally the non-Aryan blacks, or Shudras. The first three classes held themselves off from the Shudras more and more.

The Brahmins were gaining much power for only they could utter the sacred prayer. They began to state that they were the pivot between the earth and higher planes. All who sought favor from a god had to come to them. They could even alter cosmic events if the sacrifice was correct.

From the development of the priestly order, there emerged a set of "textbooks of the different schools or classes of Brahmins, with a hint here and there of a philosophy of worship." These are called the *Brahmanas*.

In the *Brahmanas*, there is a growing sense of unity with the entire cosmos. At the apex is Brahma Svayanibhu (or Brahma Self-existing) who is Lord of all Creation. This was leading the priests to consider whether Brahman was the ultimate power in the universe.

About 300 B.C., one of the greatest periods of writing in the history of India began. What emerged was a set of treatises which were additions to all early writings, especially the *Brahmanas*. These are called the "Upanishads." Upanishads means "sitting near a teacher" in a close and intimate sense. The many different speculations and writings all agreed upon one thing: "The ground of all being, whether material or spiritual, whether in the form of men, beasts, or gods, heaven, earth, or hell, is an all-inclusive, unitary reality, beyond sense-perception, ultimate in substance, infinite in essence, and self-sufficient; it is the only really existent entity." This reality was called Brahman!

Brahman was no longer just the holy power of prayer, but all that was objective—the Limitless One, "He who awakens the world"—and all creation is a phase of "That One." Brahman is also all that is subjective (inward). Brahman is **atman**, the Self within. Thus, the philosophy became mystically oriented so that the being could enter Nirvana through the knowing of the Self.

The writers of the Upanishads rejected the three levels of consciousness and stated that there was a fourth: "…that which is conscious of the subjective, nor that which is conscious of the objective, nor that which is conscious of both, nor that which is simple consciousness, nor that which is an all-sentient mass, nor that which is all darkness. It is unseen, transcendent, the sole essence of the consciousness of self, the completion of the world."

Another doctrine which emerged from this period states that the world will dissolve away at the end of every period of created being, existing in a void until the next creative cycle begins. Simply, this is history repeating itself. With this doctrine, Indian religious speculations launched into the deeps.

Two more doctrines, which need little explanation, appeared at this time. The first of these is reincarnation (*samsara*), and the second is the Law of Karma, which determines one's birth in the next lifetime. Thus, one's every action determines whether his next lifetime will be higher or lower, for one "can find re-embodiment only a form into which that shape can squeeze." In this way, the Brahmans had grasped the true nature of the Father: impersonal, yet love incarnating in all His creation.

The caste system also took its final form during this period. At the top were the Brahmins, then the Kshatriyas, then the Vaisyas, and finally the Shudras (servants).

Outside of the caste system altogether were the "untouchables" or outcasts. One might be ousted from his caste for some infraction, but one could not enter another caste. One's social standing was the result of the Law of Karma and could not be questioned. One got what he deserved!

Men saw that "normal" consciousness was not all. The only way to achieve salvation was through the union with Brahman. Thus, many interpreted this as meaning the need to deny the world—a total renunciation.

Birth and death became an endless cycle, or Wheel, of despair. The Law of Karma worked and man could not control it except through good actions. A cry arose in the heart of all India:

"Oh, would that I could be delivered from
the power of my karma over me! What that
I could find my way into a state of being
where misery would be at an end and only
joy remain!"

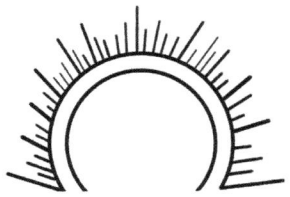

LESSON 7: BASIC RELIGIONS, PART 1

JAINISM

The answer to the questions raised by Hinduism found two "heretical" answers—Buddhism and Jainism. Of the two, only Jainism was able to survive the repeated assaults on it by the orthodox Hindu religion. One explanation given for the rise and growth of these two religions is their clarity against the multiplicity of Hinduism and their ethical strength.

Jainism was caused by the Brahmins. During the 6th century B.C., the caste system was yet in a state of flux with the priestly caste making even bolder claims. Naturally, the nobility was going to resist this, for the Brahmins put forth the claim that no one who was not a Brahmin could enter Nirvana.

Offsetting this was the great creative period of the noble class (the Kshatriyas), which produced the Upanishads. Minds began to turn towards a monastic idea, which openly declared that the physical world was not all there was (against the Brahmin idea of holding to it). All things were seen as having life and given the ability to experience reality.

Mahavira is the name accepted for the founder of Jainism. He came from the noble class and was born in 599 B.C. He was not the oldest son, which, perhaps, made his later renunciation of the physical world all the easier, for he would not inherit his father's wealth.

After his parents died, he gave up all his wealth and joined the Order of Parshva. He took an oath that said:

"I shall neglect my body and abandon the care of it.
I shall with equanimity bear, undergo, and suffer all
calamities arising from divine powers, men, and animals."

He soon left the order to strike out on his own. He wandered around southern India naked, seeking release from the "Wheel."

He had two convictions: (1) release of the soul by removal of all negation can only be done through the strictest asceticism, and (2) keeping the soul pure means that one must respect all living things. This is called *ahimsa*, non-injury.

Mahavira practiced this to the degree that he carried a soft broom to sweep his path so that he wouldn't step on ants or insects. He only ate food prepared for someone else and never raw meat. Once he received the food, he would look through it for anything which might have life such as sprouts, eggs, or worms.

Through all this, he sought to gain absolute control of his body and mind. Cold, heat, hunger, and pain were all accepted as chances to gain more control. He never spoke to anyone in order to avoid building any personal attachments.

For twelve years he followed this path, always seeking *moksha* (deliverance). It is recorded that as he was sitting "in a squatting position, with knees high and head low, in deep meditation, in the midst of abstract meditation, he reached Nirvana, the complete, the full...called Kevala."

He thus became the *Jina* (Conqueror), for he had achieved complete "victory" over his body and had left the world. He thereupon entered a period of teaching and gathering disciples for thirty years. Finally, at the age of seventy-two, he cut all ties with the earth plane and entered into Nirvana where he is now in a state beyond the Wheel of Karma and rebirth.

Jainism developed a doctrine that became distinct from both Buddhism and Hinduism. They accept the Law of Karma and believe the successive layers on the soul can only be worked off by going back to the ascetic Parshva. This will throw off as many as five layers of incrustations, which can cover the soul.

The Jainist knows of two states of vibration: gross matter and light. Matter is eternal and is seen as the atoms moving together in infinite patterns. Karma matter is understood as the least dense matter. As the being travels from lifetime to lifetime, this karma matter sticks to the soul. At transition, when the soul is released, the amount of matter on the soul determines whether it will rise or fall into the next lifetime.

All things were classified according to the sense they possessed. Those being with five senses (man, gods, animals, etc.) are the highest and so on.

Without matter, man is seen as perfect. When perfection is reached and one enters *Isatpragbhara*, there is no loss of consciousness as in Nirvana. Rather, all else is dropped so that the consciousness can be all there is.

Mahavira held that there was no Supreme Deity. There were a number of higher beings, but no help could be expected from them. There was, therefore, no Self. Even the higher beings were in need of redeeming. All salvation, both for the higher beings and those in dense manifestation was self-attained. Praying was of no use.

The fastest and surest way to liberation (*moksha*) is the practice of asceticism. Fasting and mind control were used to induce a trance-like state where one could in meditation transcend his own being. Severe control is needed of mind and body, for lack of purity will block the way and lack of control will lead one off the path.

Mahavira's monks took "Five Great Vows." These were: (1) renunciation of all killing, (2) speak only truth, (3) renunciation of all greed, (4) avoid all sexual contact, and (5) complete detachment from all things on this plane of existence.

Later, the Jainists wrote a watered-down set for lay disciples. These twelve vows were all centered around the first vow, which was against killing. As a result, many Jainists became bankers and professional tradesmen because these professions did not deal in any way with harming living creatures.

Even while he was alive, there were many stories growing around Mahavira, and many divisions were occurring within the faith. Later, he was obscured by the teachers who walked the path after him.

Temple worship consists of "a memorial service in honor of the teachers of the way of salvation." The major division occurred between those in southern India and who did not believe clothes were necessary and those in northern India (where it is colder) which said one garment was needed. These two divisions in the Order have spread even further apart, the one even admitting women and stating that they had a chance to enter Nirvana.

The effect of Jainism on India has been much, both in architectural design and in their disdain of knowledge. The one has given India an architectural form that carried over much from the past and gave it new expression. The other curbed tendencies of overstating things.

Although numbering only two million today, their philosophy has helped many people, including Mahatma Gandhi.

Lesson 7: Basic Religions, Part 1
Zen Buddhism

"The Great Path has no gates.
Thousands of roads enter it.
When one passes through this gateless gate
He walks freely between heaven and earth."

The way of Zen is that of self-searching to realize one's own true nature through meditation and self-discipline. Zen is a meditation for the becoming of Self!

The meaning of the word "Zen," according to the Master himself, is understood by no one, not even those who have attained its wisdom. For if it were definable, it would not be Zen. It implies a mystery revealed only to him who achieves it. The true secrets of life can never be communicated outwardly or verbally from one to another.

In description, it relates to the discovery of Self, and the contemplation of reality. "Zen" is actually a Japanese word, which in Chinese is called "ch'an" and in Sanskrit "Dhyana." The nearest to a literal translation of the word would be "meditation."

Zen cannot be studied nor taught in the usual sense. It must be achieved through the actual process of becoming it and is communicated as a state from those who have it to those capable of receiving it.

Zen is both within and without. Its writings are called its "flesh and bones," but the marrow of it comes not in words, only in being.

One of the old teachers explains Zen through a story:

A fish went to the Queen fish and asked her, "I have always heard of the sea, but what is this sea? Where is it?"

The Queen fish answered in this way, "You live, move, and have your being in the sea. The sea is within you, and without you, and you are made of sea and you will end in sea. The sea surrounds you as your being."

Gautama Buddha, the original founder of Buddhism in India, lived 500 years before Jesus. One day, he was preaching to his many followers, when some presented him with a golden lotus bloom. He sat enthralled with its beauty until one asked him to share what it was teaching him. But he remained silent and watched his disciples instead, until he discerned that one of them, without words, had grasped exactly what he had received concerning the "eye of the Right Law."

To this one disciple, he immediately transmitted the whole "treasury of Dharma" and caused him to become enlightened. Thus was born the Order of Silent Instruction. This enlightened monk became the first Patriarch of the Buddhist sect of Dhyana, which has sought ever since to preserve the true spirit of the Great Instruction— not permitting it to be confused by word or symbol.

From the first Patriarch of Dhyana, the Law was communicated to each successor without words, in an unbroken line of "meditating masters," until we come to the twenty-eighth Patriarch, who lived in the sixth century A.D. This 28th Patriarch of Buddhism, called Bodhidharma, became its greatest exponent and the First Patriarch of Zen.

He was in every way extraordinary, huge and ungainly in size, haughty and commanding in bearing. A blue-eyed Brahman of princely birth, like most other Patriarchs, he cared nothing for personal appearance, having renounced the world. He usually wore a tattered robe of red, or saffron, color, though the robe of the Zen patriarch is traditionally green.

A shabby exterior was sometimes cultivated by the old Zen priests to discourage applicants who did not have the perception, nor the worthiness, to pierce external appearances and discover the underlying reality.

Never before had one like this been seen crossing the mountains from India to China, where he went to bring the Dharma. He first presented himself before the pious Buddhist Emperor Wu, who wished to see him. But Bodhidharma, with aggressive and uncivil manner, seemed determined to humiliate the personification of worldly power, and left after a brief encounter. He never attempted to make himself agreeable to anyone and was sometimes a controversial figure.

From there, he went to the Chinese monastery at Shao Lin where he sat nine years facing a blank wall in meditation and awaiting the perfect outworking of the Law. He knew the Dhyana was the royal road to Selfhood and that those seeking its Great Truth would inevitably be drawn to him.

Finally, one came. But Bodhidharma knew that the Way was only for the strong and he ordered the man to leave. The seeker, according to the story, would not be discouraged and stood for several days in the snow, refusing to leave until an interview should be granted. When no invitation came, he finally cut off his right arm and sent it to the Patriarch. He was then received and the discipline bestowed upon him.

When the time came for Bodhidharma to leave his earthly mission after a long life and many disciples, this fierce, mysterious old man spoke to his followers. Again, like Buddha, he placed his great green cloak over the one who was silent with true perception and poured into him the everlasting waters of the Law. Then he went to his final resting place.

The peculiar vitality of their teachings emphasizes the achievement of tranquility in strength, rather than in weakness. Most of the Patriarchs have enjoyed extraordinary health and lived to great age.

Three years after his burial, strange stories began to circulate among the Chinese peasants concerning this fierce old philosopher. Some of them saw him resolutely treading the path over China's western mountains towards India barefoot, but carrying one shoe in his hand.

Finally, the Chinese Emperor heard the story and caused his tomb to be opened. Nothing remained in the grave but one shoe, supposedly the mate to the one he carried on the path.

There are other tales circulated concerning a visit to Japan, but not clearly authenticated. He was said to have walked across the water of the Strait of Korea, or to have been carried across while standing on a leaf, to reach Japan. Many stories, games, and pictures depict these various traditions.

The chief efforts of the Zen sect are directed toward the attainment of spiritual enlightenment through personal experience in contemplation. This is in addition to the living prayer of daily activity which brings full appreciation of life's simple beauties. As a result of this practice, there is manifested a strong individuality and a feeling for the tranquil beauty of nature, which in turn, produces a sort of serene "air-rhythm" of transcendence over the incidents of human life.

There is a method of Zen meditation called "Zazen." As quoted from a Zen authority, the instructions are:

Arrange a seat of matting at a suitable place and lay a cushion upon it. Then sit down cross-legged, placing the right foot upon the left thigh, and the left foot upon the right thigh. Put on robes and a girdle not too tight, and preserve their symmetry.

Then put the right hand (palm upward) on the calf of the left leg, lay the back of the left hand upon the palm of the right hand, and let the tips of the two thumbs touch each other.

Sit thus, keeping the body erect, inclining neither to the right nor to the left, bending neither forward nor backward. Let the ears be just above the shoulders and the nose be directed toward the abdomen. Lay the tongue against the roof of the mouth and keep the lips and teeth closed. The eyes should be kept open; the breath should flow gently through the nostrils.

When the bodily position is thus established, exhale a deep breath; then remain seated, after having examined the posture by swinging the body slightly to the right and left. Thereafter, proceed to the contemplation of what is beyond thought.

A famous Zen monk was once questioned by a temple official concerning the existence of a heaven or a hell, whether they really existed. The priest scornfully answered by calling him a fool, who lived off the temple, and was ignorant of its teachings. Then, he explained to the angered man, "You ask where is hell? Your mind is hell. I see hell in your face." When the temple official became immediately remorseful and set about to restore harmony, the priest remarked, "You ask where is heaven? Your mind is heaven now. I see heaven in your face."

THE ESSENCE OF ZEN

1. Its practices are as old as Buddhism and probably extend much further back into the dim past of the most ancient recluses of India.
2. Being of practical application rather than an abstract philosophy, it is equally as popular in present day usage at any level of society.

3. Zen rejects the importance of scriptural authority, saying that Truth can only be realized internally, and never communicated by outward means. They also reject prayer and fasting and monastic rules as representing worship of only the phantom of truth.
4. They reject the Buddha as a personality, saying, true Buddha is a state of consciousness. The contemplation of the Absolute into which all personalities are absorbed is conducive to the greatest good.
5. Zen is not idolatrous but preserves an exalted concept of Deity. An early Zen teacher, when cold, actually warmed himself by making fires out of statues from a nearby temple, insisting men are merely confused when encouraged to accept a symbol for the real.
6. A curious Zen method is to express profoundest realization by some simple or otherwise meaningless gesture. They have been known to box the ears of Emperors. Perhaps this is where the Zen stick comes in.

ZEN ANTIDOTES

Here are several examples of Zen stories of self-discovery. Let them be unto you a living experience. If they are not, the Zen student would say you have not Zen, and you would be sent to your meditation chamber until you knew from the story that reality within yourself.

"MUDDY ROAD"

Tanzan and Ekido were once travelling together down a muddy road. A heavy rain was falling.

Coming around the bend, they met a lovely girl in a silk kimono and sash, unable to cross the intersection.

"Come on, girl" said Tanzan at once. Lifting her in his arms, he carried her across the mud.

Ekido did not speak again until that night when they reached a lodging temple. Then he could no longer restrain himself. "We monks don't go near females," he told Tanzan, "especially the young and lovely ones. It is dangerous. Why did you do that?"

"I left the girl there," said Tanzan. "Are you still carrying her?"

"A Parable"

A man travelling across a field encountered a tiger. He fled, the tiger after him.

Coming to a precipice, he caught hold of the root of a wild vine and swung himself down over the edge. The tiger sniffed at him from above.

Trembling, the man looked down where far below another tiger was waiting to eat him. Only the vine sustained him.

Two mice—one white and one black—little by little started to gnaw away the vine.

The man saw a luscious strawberry near him. Grasping the vine with one hand, he plucked the strawberry with the other. How sweet it tasted!

"Black-Nosed Buddha"

A nun, who was searching for enlightenment, made a statue of Buddha and covered it with gold leaf. Wherever she went she carried this golden Buddha with her.

Years passed, and still carrying her Buddha, the nun came to live in a small temple in a country where there were many Buddhas, each one with its own particular shrine.

The nun wished to burn incense to her golden Buddha. Not liking the idea of the perfume straying to the others, she devised a funnel through which the smoke would ascend only to her statue. This blackened the nose of the golden Buddha, making it especially ugly.

KOAN

The Zen masters devised mental problems to stop their students' word-drunkenness and mind wandering. These were called Koan and were meditated upon by the students. Through these, the teacher said to his students, "Don't waste your life merely sensing, channel thought and feeling to one purpose and then let it happen."

To a Koan, there are many right answers and there are also none. The Koan itself is the answer. None of the stories make any pretense at logic. The intent was to help the student break the shell of the limited mind and attain enlightenment.

"JOSHU WASHES THE BOWL"

A monk told Joshu, "I have just entered the monastery. Please teach me."

Joshu asked, "Have you eaten your rice porridge?"

The monk replied, "I have eaten."

Joshu said, "Then you had better wash your bowl."

At that moment, the monk was enlightened.

"THE ENLIGHTENED MAN"

Shogen asked, "Why does the enlightened man not stand on his feet and explain himself?"

And he also said, "It is not necessary for speech to come from the tongue."

"Basho's Staff"

Basho said to his disciple, "When you have a staff, I will give it to you. If you have no staff, I will take it away from you."

THE TEN BULLS OF ZEN

The ten "Bulls" of Zen were adapted in the 12th century from earlier Tao works, their version being changed to pure Zen, and going deeper than before.

The bull represents the eternal principle of life and truth in action. The ten bulls represent a sequence of experiences concerning the realization of one's own true nature. They show understanding of the creative principle and a revelation of spiritual unfoldment with the progressive steps of awareness which lead closer to the instant of enlightenment.

1. The search for the bull.

"In the pasture of this world, I endlessly push aside
tall grasses in search of the bull."

The bull has never been lost, but because of separation
from my own true nature, I fail to find him.

2. Discovering the footprints.

"Along the riverbank, under the trees, I discover foot prints."

Not yet having entered the gate, nevertheless,
I have discerned the path.

3. Perceiving the bull.

"What artist can draw that massive head, those majestic horns?

When one hears the voice, one can sense its source.
The slightest thing is not apart from its source.

4. Catching the bull.

"I seize him with a terrific struggle."

If I wish him to submit, I must raise my whip,
for his mind still is stubborn and unbridled.

5. Taming the bull.

"The whip and rope are necessary."

When one thought arises, another thought follows.
Hold the nose ring tight. Do not let in one single doubt.

6. Riding the bull home.

"Mounting the bull, the voice of my flute
intones a rhythmic melody."

This struggle is over. Onward I go, no matter who may
wish to call me back. Those who "hear" will follow.

7. The bull transcended.

"Astride the bull, I reach home. The bull too can rest."

I have abandoned the whip and rope. All is one Law, not two.
One path of clear light travels on throughout endless time.

8. Both bull and self transcended.

"Whip, rope, person, and bull all merge in No-Thing."

Mind is clear of limitation. I seek no state of enlightenment,
neither do I remain where no enlightenment exists.

9. Reaching the source.

"Too many steps have been taken returning
to the root and the source."

Poised in silence, I observe the forms of integration
and disintegration. Everything "is." One who is not
attached to "form" need not be "reformed."

10. In the world.

"I am every blissful, though clothed in rags. I use no magic to
extend my life. Now, before me, the dead trees become alive."

Why should one search for the footprints of the patriarchs?
I go to the marketplace of the people of the world,
and everyone I look upon becomes enlightened.

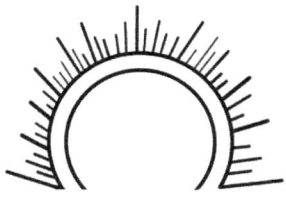

LESSON 7: BASIC RELIGIONS, PART 1
BUDDHISM

Buddhism is more of an ethereal and psychological approach to God than a religion. But because it has a systematic approach to devotion, it is classified as a religion. There are over 350 million followers of the enlightened one.

The doctrine and teachings of Buddha were handed down by oral tradition for several centuries after his transition. After this time, they were written and took the form of a canon. Some of the earliest writings we have are from the Ceylonese (now called Sri Lankan) monks. This is called the *Pali* version, which is the best authority for early Buddhism.

Another version of the canon is found among the monks of northern India. There are few basic differences between the two canons. After the advent of the Christian Church, these writings take on a remarkably different development. At this time, there was a scholastic expansion and elaboration of Gautama's teachings. During this period, the classification of the basic teachings was also started.

There are two major schools of Buddhism. The "Mahayana" School follows the path of "glory realization," meaning they see Buddha as one who gave up the world so all man might find the Truth. The sutras, which are distinctively Mahayana, are explained by stating that each branch of Buddhism was given teachings by Buddha according to their spiritual development. These sutras hold the key to realization so one may become either Buddha Amitabha (those who have gained Buddhahood and continue evolving after transition) or Bodhisattva (those who have gained purification and emancipation but refuse to enter Nirvana out of love of mankind and return to help them find salvation).

The other school of Buddhism is called Theravada Buddhism. It holds closely to the original ideal set by the first followers of Gautama. The ideal monk is called the "arahat," one who has renounced all so he has obtained "tanha," thus going beyond the life cycle into Nirvana. Yet there is joy and hopefulness here not displayed even among Buddha's disciples.

In a cosmic sense, the Theravadas hold the whole cosmos in "momentariness." Yet this lack of stability within a form does not hamper one's spiritual development or the growth of the cosmos. The real line of continuity is in the "causal laws," which no follower of Buddha denies. All being is thus causally interrelated to the total beingness of the cosmos.

Buddhism is then an extension of Hinduism, cleaned and strengthened with an esoteric-scientific knowing. Buddha gave his followers four "Noble Truths" as guidelines; they are:

1. "The Noble Truth Concerning Suffering"

All sentient existence is suffering continued through an endless succession of lives under the inexorable law of retribution.

2. "The Second Noble Truth"

The origin of suffering is the craving and desire, either on a physical level or a spiritual level. This is caused by ignorance.

3. "The Third Noble Truth"

If one wishes to end the suffering, this can be done by letting go of desire.

Buddha said, "Whatsoever is subject to origination is subject to cessation."

4. "The Fourth Noble Truth"

This is the "Middle Path" which leads to the cessation of suffering.

It is above the sensual plane and keeps away from self-torture.

It is the "Noble Eight-fold Path": Right View, Intention, Speech, Action, Livelihood, Effort, Mindfulness, and Right Concentration.

The goal of the path is Nirvana. This is not defined in Gautama's teachings, though all disciples seek this goal.

The canon which contains these laws is called the <u>Dharma</u>. The Dharma consists of "Three Baskets"
Monasticism
Discourse (sutra)
Abstract Doctrine

We must not assume that all the teachings were written. Buddha said that the "Noble Truths" must be learned from the Supreme Buddha. Only after countless reincarnations on this plane with the sole aim of each lifetime of becoming a Buddha can one achieve the full Light. He then descends from Heaven in a dense body, gaining the supreme illumination, and preaches the Truth. When the Buddha goes through transition, he enters complete Nirvana and can neither hear nor answer prayers. His memory is honored by the brothers who meditate upon him and receive much from doing this.

The external "Order" of Brothers is on an equal basis with Buddha and the Law and Doctrine. It is one of the "Three Jewels" and, therefore, of supreme veneration.

For over two centuries, we have little or sketchy accounts of the growth of Buddha's teachings. Between the transition of Buddha and the time when the religion started gaining national attention, two Councils were held, which are of importance. The first Council is called "Rajagaha." It was held shortly after Gautama's transition and defined and fixed the canon of discipline and doctrine. The other Council, held a century after, is called the Council of "Vesali." This Council settled ten disputed points of discipline.

After 250 B.C. Buddhism began its conquest of India. Missionaries were sent into the Himalayan regions, south to Burma and west to the Greeks. Even though other dynasties were hostile to Buddhism, the missionary work bore fruit and areas like Ceylon (now Sri Lanka) became strongholds.

Soon after the spread of Christianity, two schools appeared. Mahayana, or "Great Vehicle," and Theravada "Little Vehicle" school.

Through the seventh century these two schools existed side by side although some of their teachings were radically different. Buddhism adjusted itself to its surroundings and merged comfortably with Hinduism, although the two faiths remained distinct. In the twelfth century, Islam dealt an all but fatal blow to Buddhism in northern India. Monasteries were destroyed or forced to close and many ancient writings were reduced to ashes. After the initial wave had passed, Buddhism was all but extinct in India proper.

Buddhism was brought into China about the first century C.E. By the fourth century, it had become part of the cultural heritage of China. From China, Buddhism was transmitted to Korea and Japan.

Buddhism as taught by Gautama is today found only in Ceylon and parts of Vietnam and Burma. In the last twenty years, the West has become increasingly aware of Buddha's teachings. Unfortunately, the teachings are often altered to fit the Western mind and end up a collection of moralistic sayings. Buddhists in some areas of Asia, especially Japan and Vietnam, have become increasingly militant. The message of Buddha, the Enlightened One, is the same as the message of Jesus Christ. His teachings are now coming to their culmination in this New Age.

"I pile no wood for fires or altars.
I kindle a flame within me…
My heart the hearth, the flame the redeemed self."

When Buddha began his work, it was a period of "radical social readjustment and deepening religious need." There were wars between the local rulers which gave added power to the formation of a rigid caste system. Life was becoming a fight just to have enough food and shelter.

The past was choking religion to death. The Vedas were taught as the final authority rather than living truths, which were to be viewed through each generation's eyes. Rite and ceremony became the norm of one's devotion rather than actions. Cosmologies abounded, some teachers holding more than one and each teacher claiming his was reality.

Yet Buddha saw at the core that religion was once again losing contact with the people. Dogma and ceremony were choking all practical fulfillment. Into this, Buddha infused light and love and swept it clean.

Buddha taught that the Self is Lord. Man should seek to walk with God always. Tibetan Buddhists look to the manifestation of God in every facet of human life. Out of this, an abstract system of thought emerges, a belief which remains stubbornly practical at its core.

Buddhist logic relies very much upon the Law of Cause and Effect. All things spring from a cause, and the First Cause is God. Man awakens (thus, Bodhisattva, "an awakened being"; Buddha, "awake" or "The Wake") through a chain of causes. The being striving to become awakened in many lifetimes, that is, possessing the "will to live," works with and through the wheel of karma to achieve further lifetimes until he is able to achieve Nirvana.

As stated previously, Buddha did not bother to define Nirvana or Heaven. He was much too concerned with the practical needs of the people. From the bits and pieces where he alludes to Nirvana it might be likened to "the flight of the Alone to the Alone, ascending into Heaven."

Buddha did not have much to say about Karma. He stated that the Law of Karma controls the universe as well as individuals. It is due to ignorance ("avidya") and involves many rebirths. A Doctrine of Ignorance resulted with twelve Nidanas, or steps on the causal chain. According to the *Abhedharmakosa*, "Being ignorant in our previous life as to the significance of our existence, we let loose our desires and act wantonly. Owing to this karma, we are destined in the present life to be endowed with consciousness, name-and-form, and six organs of sense, and sensation. We then cling to these illusive existences which have no ultimate reality whatever."

Much of this has to do with Knowledge. Each school defines different forms of Knowledge. These different views are taken from Buddha's teachings. **Illusion** is one form that appears in every school. It is stressed that many of life's troubles are illusions springing from ego, which is nourished by ignorance. **Relative** knowing accepts the fact that the absolutes cannot be gleaned from everyday life. To therefore deal with everyday situations, relative truth is sufficient.

Absolute Knowledge (Truth) is for the enlightened. It is perfect knowing and is the goal all Buddhists strive towards. Absolute Knowledge (*prajna*) leads to Nirvana.

Buddhists also stress the doctrine of Tathata or "suchness." This is taking things as they are. It is not, however, a separate entity in itself, but is the one-ness of all things. Suchness means, "being so."

Finally, Buddhists imply void when speaking of suchness. Void, or **Sunyata**, is the state of all objects which are experienced and which we incline ourselves to these are: Void, of Void, from Void, with Void, and in Void.

Buddhism can teach us much. In a fundamental sense, it is Logic and Reason spiritually applied in a practical way. Buddha knew that only after man can control his own universe, his own animal, can the Light become a part of his reality. Buddha once told his followers that "I live, yet not I, but the Law within me." St. Paul told the Galatians that he also lived, yet did not, for it was Christ within him.

LESSON 7:
BASIC RELIGIONS, PART 2

Lesson 7, Part 2: Amenhotep IV • Thales
Democritus • Heraclitus • Socrates

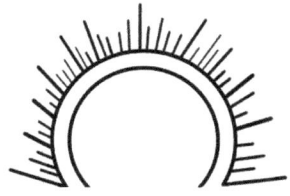

LESSON 7: BASIC RELIGIONS, PART 2
AMENHOTEP IV

Pharaoh Amenhotep IV of Egypt was a mortal truly illuminated by the Cosmic.

Today those of the scientific and literary world regard him as "the first individual in history."

His conduct and his conception were centuries beyond the level of human thought of his time. He advanced religions of mankind more than any other human before his period.

Biologists refer to him as an example of "saltation," a leaping ahead in the progressive order of the evolution of man's mentality.

Amenhotep IV reigned during the period of 1375–1358 B.C. (allowing for discrepancies in the various calendars).

His was the 18th dynasty. He was the son of Amenhotep III and Tia.

He despised the ignorance and superstitious practices of the priesthood.

He rose up and thrust aside the multitudinous deities of Egypt and the mythologies of Heliopolis.

He came to respect the sun as the visible source of life, creation, growth, and activity. It became to him the symbol of an everlasting God.

He declared that God was a vital intelligence existing as a single deity upon which all things in the universe depended.

The creative forces of this God, he explained, radiated through the sun.

Let us realize the courage and forethought it took to defy all existing convention and religious beliefs, for the first time in recorded history deny polytheism, or the existence of many gods, and declare that there was but one God and that He was Supreme.

Never had the mind of man dared to venture such a stupendous thought; that is, to entertain monotheistic views.

Remember, this was thirteen centuries before Christianity adopted the doctrine of a belief in a single God.

He established this new religious movement and was declared a heretic by the priesthood of Ammon.

His dislike for the priesthood was so great that he changed his name meaning "Ammon is Satisfied" to Akhenaten, "Pious to Aten."

Aten was the name he gave to this single God, which manifests through the sun. He was the world's first great pacifist.

He despised war and tried to discourage it, which resulted in Egypt losing a great deal of her temporal power, especially in Syria.

He left the traditional capital at Thebes and built a new and splendid city known as Tell el Amarna.

In this city he gathered together the most learned men and women of the time and organized them into a great brotherhood, the foundation of a vast mystery school, the teaching and ideals of which were to spread across the face of the earth.

All had to pay adoration to this one God and devote themselves to the study of science, religion, or art. It was the most revolutionary step ever taken to further the cultural interests of man.

Amenhotep IV married the great Nefertiti, meaning "beauty's arrival," and they had seven daughters who were always portrayed as participating in the sacred rites of the new religion.

We must hail the memory of this great individual who was neither swayed by public opinion nor bound by traditions hoary with age and disintegrating from their own stagnation.

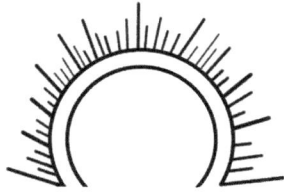

Lesson 7: Basic Religions, Part 2
Thales

The philosopher Thales lived and worked during the time between c. 625–640 BC and passed through transition c. 543 BC. He formed the earliest philosophies in Greece and founded the Ionian school.

Thales employed the first and greatest part of his time in travel. He went to Crete to inform himself of the mysteries of their religion. His last journey (being in years) was into Egypt to confer (as he acknowledged in his epistle to Pherecydes) "with priests and astronomers."

He was in Egypt during the reign of Amasis by whom he was much favored and admired for many things, especially for measuring the height of the pyramids by their shadows.

He is the father of abstract geometry and was the first person to demonstrate that a circle is bisected by its diameter, as shown below:

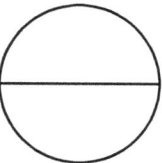

...and that the angles at the base of an isosceles triangle are equal:

∠ A   ∠ B

...that two straight lines intersecting produce opposite and equal angles:

∠ A = ∠ B
∠ C = ∠ D

...and that the angle of a semicircle is a right angle:

∠ A = 90°

When Molpagoras, an eminent person of Ionia, demanded what was the strangest sight Thales ever saw, he answered, "A tyrant old."

Thales, being demanded what **God** is, answered "That which hath neither beginning nor end."

Another asked if a man might do ill and conceal it from God: "How," answered he, "when a man that thinks cannot."

Thales said the most ancient of all things is God, for he is not begotten; the fairest is the world for it is his work. He said that the world is animated and that God is the soul diffused through each part, whose divine moving virtue penetrates through the element of water. He said that matter is fluid and variable, that **motion** is made by composition of the elements.

He affirmed that there is no difference between life and death; being thereupon asked why he did not die, he said, "Because there is no difference." To one who asked which was eldest, night or day, he answered, "Night by a day."

Being demanded what was difficult, he answered: "To know thyself." And, what is sweet: "To follow one's own will." And, what is divine: "That which has neither beginning nor end." He said, "It is hard, but good, to know ourselves, for that is to live according to nature."

The story is told that, when his mother tried to force him to marry, he replied that it was too soon, and, when she pressed him again later in life, he replied that it was too late.

Hieronymus of Rhodes, in the second book of his scattered notes, relates that, in order to show how easy it was to grow rich, Thales, foreseeing that it would be a good season for olives, rented all the oil mills and thus amassed a fortune.

Thales is considered one of the Seven Wise Men of the ancient world. He advised in political matters, and often his wise counsel saved the Ionic states from an invasion by Cyrus. Thales' doctrines were preserved only by oral traditions. Aristotle finally wrote of his wisdom hundreds of years after his death. Thales considered water the element of all things and the earth floated upon it like a ship.

His pupils included Anaximander, Anaximenes, and Pherecipdes.

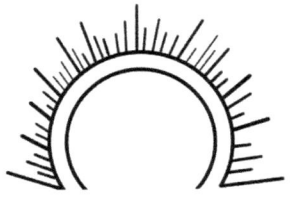

LESSON 7: BASIC RELIGIONS, PART 2

DEMOCRITUS

The Greek philosopher Democritus of the 4th Century before Christ was called the founder of the atomic theory. His teaching was a philosophy, most likely received from the Cosmic Mind. He had also spent much time studying in Egypt.

It was a Rosicrucian, John Dalton, who published the laws and conclusions of this same theory in 1805 A.D., and whom scientists accredit with bringing it to a scientific basis.

Democritus was considered crazy, and Hippocrates was sent to cure him. Yet, he was also known as the "laughing philosopher."

In his system, he developed still further the mechanical or atomical theory of his master Leucippus. Thus, he explained the origin of the world by the eternal motion of an infinite number of invisible and indivisible bodies, atoms, which differ from one another in form, position and arrangement, and are alternately separated and combined by their motions in infinite space. In this way, the universe was formed, fortuitously, without the interposition of a First Cause.

Although denying the presence of design in nature, he admitted that of **law**. He called the common notion of chance a cover of human ignorance, the refuge of those who are too idle to think.

The eternal existence of atoms (of matter in general) he inferred from the consideration that time could be conceived only as eternal and without beginning. In the atoms he distinguished figure, size, gravity, and impenetrability.

According to him, **fire** consists of active globules and spreads like a light envelope round the earth. The **soul** consists, insofar as it is a moving power, of the finest fire-atoms. Since it is acquainted with the other elements, and anything can be known only by its equal, the **soul** must also be composed in part of the other elements.

Knowledge by sense is due to contact with atoms emanating from the sensed objects through the mediation of the organs of sense. Direct contact and mediated by the organs of sense gives rise to "trueborn" knowledge.

The continuation of the soul after death was denied by Democritus, who divided it into two parts: the rational part which has its seat in the breast, and the sensual part, which is diffused through the whole body. Both constitute only one substance.

He also applied his atomic theory to natural philosophy and astronomy. Even the gods he considered to have risen from atoms and to be perishable like the rest of things existing.

In his ethical philosophy, Democritus considered the acquisition of peace of mind as the highest aim of existence. The purest joy and the truest happiness are only the fruit of the higher mental activity exerted in the endeavor to understand the nature of things; the peace of mind arising from good actions and a clear conscience.

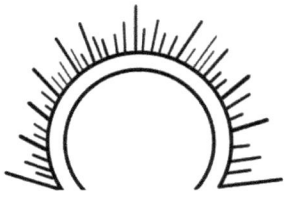

Lesson 7: Basic Religions, Part 2

Heraclitus

536–476 B.C.

L ittle is known about this famous philosopher of the Ionic school. We have only a few fragments from his writings and what is written about him by other writers and philosophers.

We do know that he traveled many years before settling down. Most of these travels were in North Africa. He most likely became acquainted with the Mysteries while in Egypt. Upon his return to Ephesus, he was offered, and turned down, the office of chief magistrate.

Heraclitus differed in many ways from the majority of Ionic philosophers. He said **Fire** was the first principle of all. Fire was an ethereal substance, "self-kindled and self-extinguished." The world is not made from this Fire, but it has **evolved** by a "natural operation." Fire is the symbol of reality in flux.

He said it is also the source of the **human soul** or rational principle.

Phenomena are always existing in a state of constant flux. They assume many and varied forms but always return to their original source. What his contemporaries called the **cosmos,** he said was but the dynamics of existence.

Heraclitus changed the pattern of thinking from that which is known to the knowing of the object.

He called this knowing **Logos.** "It is wise to harken, not to me, but to the Logos and to confess that all things are one. This wisdom is to know the thought by which all things are one." This wisdom is to know the thought by which all things are stirred through all things. Thus, the cosmos is intelligible since **thought** stirs all things.

There are no opposites, only the cosmos in tension. "Men do not know here what is at variance agrees with itself. It is an attunement of opposite tensions, like that of the bow and the lyre." *The attunement of the opposites is the essence of existence.*

Heraclitus states there is no origin (as in the manner of myth). "This world, which is the same for all, no one of the gods or men have made, but it was ever, is now, and ever shall be everlasting fire, which measures of its kindling, and measures going out."

Therefore, "the way up and the way down is one and the same." "For the sun will not overstep his measures; if he does, the Erinyes, the handmaids of justice, will find him out." Thus, to Heraclitus, there is a governing force behind all things.

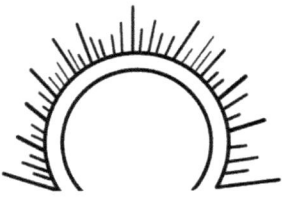

Lesson 7: Basic Religions, Part 2
Socrates

Some twenty-three and a half centuries have gone by since Socrates, sentenced to a felon's death by his fellow-citizens, drank hemlock in his prison at Athens.

Socrates was born in Athens in 470 or 469 BC, ten years after the victories that barred Greece to the Persian advances.

We must resign ourselves to ignorance about the childhood and youth of the son of Sophroniscus, the artisan-sculptor, and Phenarete, the midwife. As a modern author remarks, "You would think the master was born an old man, with no childhood."

In 399 BC, Athens' great age in politics, economics, and art had ended. But the great age of Greek philosophy was only just beginning. Plato, who was twenty-eight at the death of Socrates, had known only decadence. Aristotle, chosen as tutor for Alexander after despicable competition between the Greek intellectuals, decided for Macedonia and the vassalization of Hellas.

It is significant that in his seventy years of life, Socrates witnessed both the greatness and the decline of his country.

Socrates was an Everyman, and the sincerity of his irony is the reverse of condescension.

In this Athenian community, both egalitarian and profoundly aristocratic, he seems to have seen all men just as they were, with the same brotherly regard, the rich and the beggar, the talented and the simple, the refined and the rough, the Athenian and the foreigner.

But this brotherliness is innocent of all interested preference for the plebeian (a commoner), and we know that his political views did not incline him to demagogy (a focus on emotion over reason to persuade). His brotherly eye seemed rather to pierce straight through those outer rinds of human nature, which are the realm of idiosyncrasies, the external and the accidental, to that deeper region where a person has his roots.

Yet this Everyman was a man with a mission. He devoted his whole life to seeking and provoking, untiringly and obstinately, whatever the discussion with his interlocutor. He did so in obedience to a divine command so imperative that he preferred death to silence. He was a man with a mission, not a teacher. There was something profoundly humble in the way he harassed a man who shunned his presence. He had nothing to teach them; he only wanted to make them see themselves, nakedly revealed.

This man wrote nothing. He had no care for his succession, as if, in virtue of some profound necessity, this questioner had nothing to leave to future ages but uncertainty and questionings about himself.

Cicero related that when someone asked Socrates what country he belonged to, he replied, "The whole earth," meaning that he was a citizen of the world.

Yet, he was an Athenian to the fingertips.

Socrates was not the first in Athens, or elsewhere, to quarrel with a proud and rigid State ideology. This same ideology had persecuted Anaxagoras before him, indicted Diagoras of Melos for impiety and betrayal of the mysteries, condemned Protagoras as an atheist and burned his books in the marketplace.

The city lived spiritually on its heritage: it had a patrimony of the soul to maintain, of which the State religion formed a part.

Socrates aimed to shatter the massive certitudes of unawakened men; like those before him, he was a stimulator of doubt.

Diogenes Lacretes once said: "Socrates met the young Xenophon, whom he did not know, and was struck with the beauty of his face which radiated goodness. Barring his way with his staff (the famous staff which marked the pilgrim), he asked him where the necessities of life could be bought. "In the market," answered the youth, not understanding the double sense of the question. "And to become a good man, where must you go?" Xenophon stood puzzled. "Follow me, then," said Socrates, "and you shall know."

The innocence of Socrates lay in wishing the interlocutor to have the same freedom he had given himself.

He believed that man without thought was not a man, but a thing, that "the unexamined life was no life for a human being."

If there was one thing Socrates wanted to teach his fellow citizens, it was to be hungry for a certain hunger.

"I practice the same profession," said Socrates, "as my mother; my task is to be the midwife to men's souls, not to bear them; that is the work of God."

This spiritual midwife contributes nothing, transmits nothing to the soul whom he awakens. He leaves it naked in its own sight.

He put an end to his peace of mind. He who, like every sage, held up happiness to men as the supreme good. He began by depriving them of the happiness which was nearest and most accessible—unawareness, without conflicts or problems. He would not let the Athenians sleep.

It is always the pupil who seeks out the Sage and the favor of his teaching. But this man comes to you, rather like a petitioner, he begs you for something obstinately.

Wherever men gathered for their ordinary business, in the market or the public square or a courtesan's apartments, there came Socrates bringing his talk.

In the particular juncture of his own time and place, this brotherliness was historically premature, a fact that earned him the contempt of some distinguished Athenians: some notorious ill-wishers would use it to give him a reputation for vulgarity. Even Christians would be surprised to see it in a sort of vague anticipation of St. Paul's words: "There is no respect of persons with God." (Romans 2:11)

There is a power in man which can take place in the imperfect world of things so as to create the kingdom of man, a freedom which can safely take over from the old, tottering certainties. This power is precisely self-awareness.

"For know that this is the command of God, and I believe that no greater good has ever happened to the state than my service to God."

Socrates' whole intellectualism consisted in this, that the condition of becoming self-aware was speech, the ordered and fruitful speech of the man who seeks to know himself. Logos: discourse and reason.

"When I trust in my daemon, I report to my friends the will of the gods; it always comes to pass and never once has daemon deceived me."

Euthyphro, Socrates' accuser, was a "Doctor of Divinity." He was, therefore, a "theologian" with complete mastery of those mythological stories which here took the place of dogmas. He was an expert to be consulted in cases of doubt on all questions of ritual, a professional soothsayer competent to assume the essential function of interpreter (the "augur" of the Latins). The gods speak in a cipher language, the code to which is learned not by an effort of the mind, but by information obtained from without.

Euthyphro looked for piety in the realm of deeds. It was for that reason that he began by defining piety in terms of pious actions, not because he was "a rebel against abstractions," as was said. Socrates, on the contrary, with a restrained anguish which gave the dialogue a touch of poignancy, looked for piety in the realm of the soul's inner relations to the deity.

By refusing an easy flight and letting the city commit a crime, he was being obedient to the end to the Delphic command. His post was here, not elsewhere.

According to Athenian law, when the accused man was called on to name a sentence in place of the capital sentence demanded by the prosecutor, he proposed that he be supported at State expense in the Prytaneum (the Town Hall of a Greek city-state). Can this unexpected detail be an author's investigation? The irony was fatal: at a stroke, he put eighty more judges on the side that condemned him.

"Knowing my unknowing; all my knowing lies in that, and it is just because I believe that virtue lies in this knowing that I proclaim to others the spiritual pilgrimage I have followed for my own benefit." This precious poverty, which strips one of all illusory possessions, was that very self-knowing, hungry, and never satisfied. (The Socratic sage seeks his true being in this renunciation of all kinds of having.) Socrates was poor, that he wrote nothing, that he left nothing of himself that could be possessed, not even some definite certainties about himself, not even disciples to hand on his teachings.

Intelligence is not something to be dispensed with; it is the only instrument through which the soul can come to see clearly.

It was by detaching himself from things, not by losing himself in the object, that the subject attained his emancipation. He lived by objective observation.

Socrates said before he died:

"When my sons are grown up, I would ask you, O my friends, to punish them: I would have you trouble them as I have troubled you, if they seem to care about riches or anything, more than about virtue: or if they pretend to be something when they are really nothing—then reprove them, as I have reproved you, for not caring about that for which they ought to care, and thinking that they are something when they are really nothing. And if you do this, I shall have received justice at your hands, and so will my sons."

He said: "I search."

Didn't this man keep on repeating that he Knew nothing?

The last words of Socrates were, "Crito: I owe a cock to Thesculopius. Will you remember to pay the debt?" Thus, the wise Socrates made his final initiation sacrifice while on this plane.

www.ingramcontent.com/pod-product-compliance
Lightning Source LLC
Chambersburg PA
CBHW051506120626
46551CB00012B/803